# NOTES

ON

# THE STORY OF SINUHE

BY

Alan H. GARDINER, D. Litt.

WIPF & STOCK • Eugene, Oregon

Wipf and Stock Publishers
199 W 8th Ave, Suite 3
Eugene, OR 97401

Notes on the Story of Sinuhe
By Gardiner, Alan H.
Softcover ISBN-13: 978-1-6667-4979-3
Hardcover ISBN-13: 978-1-6667-4980-9
eBook ISBN-13: 978-1-6667-4981-6
Publication date 6/7/2022
Previously published by Librairie Honore Champion, 1916

This edition is a scanned facsimile of the original edition published in 1916.

TO

Bernard Pyne GRENFELL

*in friendship.*

# PREFACE

The present work, save for the new English translation and the indices now appended, is reprinted from the *Recueil de Travaux relatifs à la Philologie et à l'Archéologie égyptiennes et assyriennes*, vol. 32-34, 36. The considerations that led to the inception of the task, and the debt I owe to Sir Gaston Maspero in connection therewith, are recorded in the opening pages; and it has been my pleasant duty to note, in their appropriate places, many valuable observations and corrections communicated by friends and colleagues who have kindly lent me their help. I have now to express my gratitude to Mr. Battiscombe Gunn for assistance in the revision of the translation, and to Mr. T. Eric Peet for undertaking the extensive indices and carrying them out in so admirable a fashion. To my publishers I am deeply indebted, not only for their patient tolerance of my repeated delays, but also for their extreme courage and obligingness in producing the book in times of unparalleled difficulty. The long intervals at which the different sections were written are responsible for many inconsistencies in the spelling of transliterated words and the like; for these I crave the reader's indulgence.

# CONTENTS

# NOTES

ON

# THE STORY OF SINUHE

The plan of the series to which my recent volume on the Story of Sinuhe[1] belongs did not admit of a full commentary on the text. There are several excellent reasons, which need not here be specified, why Museums should restrict their publications to the bare communication of new material, leaving the elaboration thereof to private initiative; and this general principle was certainly rightly applied in the case of my book. The inclusion of a translation already passed beyond the strictly legitimate scope of such a work, but seemed justifiable on grounds of general utility and because of the small space it would occupy. I must confess it was this part of my task which cost me most labour and interested me most keenly, for not only did I spare no pains to investigate the sense of all the rarer words in the tale — here the materials of the Berlin Dictionary[2] stood me in good stead — but I also tried to reconstitute the text of the archetype, and not to adhere slavishly either to one or to the other of the manuscripts. By this means my translation came to differ considerably from the renderings of other scholars. I feel that I should be risking the charge of having made far too many and too daring innovations if I did not publish some defence of my views; and I hope it will become plain from the series of articles of which this is the first that I have not been guilty of ignoring the labours of my predecessors. I have found with some embarassment that the work from which I have most often to dissent is one which a delicate attention on the part of its author

1. *Hieratische Papyrus aus den Kgl. Museen zu Berlin. 5 Bd. Literarische Texte des mittleren Reiches. Herausg.* von A. Erman, II, *Die Erzählung des Sinuhe und die Hirtengeschichte. Bearbeitet von* Alan H. Gardiner, *Leipzig, 1909.*

2. This essay was compiled away from Berlin. I am indebted to Herrn Grapow for verifying some references in respect of which my notes proved deficient.

had closely connected with my own name. Still, the occasions are very few on which free and open discussion is not both in place and of positive benefit; nor is so eminent a scholar as M. Maspero the one to discourage it. So far from that being the case, he has most readily consented to extend the hospitality of the *Recueil* to my remarks; an additional courtesy, for which I herewith sincerely thank him.

I shall begin with a discussion of the *primâ facie* view to be taken in the examination of particular critical details[1], and shall thence pass to the analysis of all the more difficult passages in the tale. This done, we shall be in a position to formulate a final judgement as to the respective value of the various manuscripts. The remainder of my essay will be devoted to the consideration of the literary and historical aspects of the tale.

## I

### PRELIMINARIES ON THE COMPARATIVE CRITICAL VALUE OF THE MSS.

It will be impossible to form an entirely correct estimate of the relative value of the two chief manuscripts B (the Berlin papyrus 3022) and R (the Ramesseum papyrus) until the individual readings of those manuscripts have been compared and tested one by one. This however is a task which itself requires for its proper carrying out an *a priori* judgement as to whether the authorities ought to be compared as equal with equal, or whether one should start with a decided preference, based on general considerations, for one source of testimony as against the other.

In this section therefore the ground will be cleared by the discussion of such matters as the date of the various manuscripts, and the relationship of the three later sources of the text to the two older ones. First with regard to the age of the papyri. That B is the oldest of them will hardly be disputed; in agreement with Möller I assign it to the very end of the 12th. or to the beginning of the 13th. Dynasty[2]. As for R, I was at first tempted to claim for it the same antiquity as B, but subsequent study has convinced me that it occupies a position intermediate between B and the group of papyri which Möller, in his admirable book on hieratic palæography, regards as typical of the Hyksos period[3]. On the one hand a number of signs in R seem to attach that papyrus to the Hyksos group; such are (15), (38), with dash at side (84), (43) and (55). On the other hand certain signs appear to link R no less decidedly with the papyri of the 12th. Dynasty; examples are (25) and (39), both of which have the dash at the side higher than is later usual; so too (7) without a dot over it, and (19) with legs

1. Even if I could accept the general position adopted by M. Maspero towards the critical problems of the tale, a new treatment of the matter would be necessary for two reasons : (1) because new portions of R have been found since M. Maspero wrote his book; and (2) because I have greatly improved upon my first transcription of R, as could hardly fail to be the case with closer study.

2. M. Maspero (*Les Mémoires de Sinouhit*, p. II) admits the possibility that B may even belong to the 14th. Dynasty.

3. *Hierat. Palæogr.*, I, p. 17, foll.

not clearly distinguished but represented by one stroke, [hieroglyph] *(passim)* that has a form analogous to that found in the *Prisse* and the Illahun papyri. In the spelling of the verb *ḥw* "to strike" [hieroglyph] is indeed no longer written as in the 12th. Dynasty, but has not yet become disintegrated, as in the *Ebers*, into two distinct signs[1]. More important than such details is the fact that R shows no leaning whatsoever towards the elaboration of form affected by certain signs during the Hyksos period; in R [hieroglyph] (161), [hieroglyph] (86) and [hieroglyph] (42) have simple hieratic equivalents, free from all superfluous strokes. Nor again does R display any taste for the rounded contours and flourishes which Möller holds to be the most prominent characteristic of the *Westcar* and its congeners[2]. Möller's verdict on R, which deserves much respect, is that it is "etwas jünger" than B. For my part I am ready to concede a considerable latitude for error, and therefore content myself with maintaining, as I did before, that the latest possible date for R is some time before the writing of the *Rhind Mathematical*. M. Maspero seems to me to err when he compares R with the manuscripts of the early 18th. Dynasty[3]. It was hardly to be expected that he should accept without question my statement that all the other papyri emanating from the same find display an early type of writing; but that statement, for which the evidence is yet unpublished, cannot be disposed of by the brief comment that : "les bibliothèques renfermaient souvent des livres d'époques très différentes". It is surely significant that the objects found together in the same box with the Ramesseum papyri have been pronounced, on excellent and unbiassed archæological authority, to belong to the 12th. Dynasty. M. Maspero writes : "Si Gardiner adopte la chronologie réduite de Borchardt et d'Édouard Meyer, la distance est, somme toute, assez faible entre la date qu'il admet et celle que je propose." But unless I am mistaken, the reduced chronology is not accepted by M. Maspero. For him therefore the interval assumed between B and R may be a matter of considerable importance, and I believe that it has influenced him greatly in his hypothesis of two recensions, an early Theban (M. K.) and an Ahmesside (18th. Dynasty) recension. My conclusion as to the date of R, to put it briefly, is that that manuscript may be a hundred years or so later than B. But B was doubtless separated from the archetype by one hundred and fifty years, at the very lowest estimate. Judging from the criterion of age alone one might expect B to be a somewhat better authority for the text than R; but that criterion is, as textual critics are well aware, a very precarious guide to the value of manuscripts, and the relative value of B and R may be exactly the opposite. With regard to the date of the later texts M. Maspero's opinion is probably correct, or approximately so : G (the Golénischeff papyrus) he assigns to the middle of the 19th. Dynasty, C (the Cairo ostracon) to the 20th., or at latest to the 21st., Dynasty, and L (the ostracon in the British Museum) to about the same date as C.

The relationship of C and G is at once clear; C is the corrupt descendant of a

1. See *Ä. Z.*, 44 (1908), 127.
2. *Op. cit.*, p. 17.
3. *Op. cit.*, p. v.

manuscript quite or almost identical with G. Wherever C and G differ from one another C is invariably wrong[1], a conclusion that may often be confirmed by comparing G with R or B[2]. The value of C is therefore confined to such passages as are missing in G.

The common ancestor of C and G, which may here be named GC, was, as M. Maspero has also recognized[3], more nearly related to R than to B. This is proved by the following evidence[4] :

(a) R20 and GC, ; B (Amherst frag.), .
(b) R25 and GC, *iw-f mdw-f;* B2, *iw-f ḥr mdt.*
(c) R25, supported by G ; B2, .
(d) R33-34 and GC, *wrš-ni im m ;* B9 omits *im.*
(e) R43 and C, *r ptpt nmiw-šꜥ;* B17 omits these words.
(f) R44 and C (the latter with some transparent corruptions), *wršy tp inbw imy hrw-f;* B19, *wršyw tp ḥꜣ-t im-t hrw-s.*
(g) R45, , also indicated by of C; B19, only .
(h) R46, *ḫn-kwi ḥr,* with C; B21 gives *r* for *ḥr.*
(i) R84-85, *hꜣ-f iꜣbtiw; hꜣ-f* is indicated by *hꜣb* in G; B60, *mꜣ-f ꜣb-t.*
(k) R87 and G, *bhꜣ Pdtiw ḥr ḥꜣt-f;* B63, *bhꜣ Pdtiw ꜥwy-f.*
(l) R90 and G, *iṯ-nf m mrwt;* B66, without *m.*

Of these deviations (a), (c), (d), (f), (g), (i), (k), and (l) point clearly in favour of RGC as against B; in (b) the rival variants have about equal claims, and the other two cases (e) and (h) are doubtful.

In the few instances where GC agrees with B against R, it is usually in order to correct obvious and unimportant errors in R : thus in R27 or is wrong against of B4 and GC; in R48 the verb *sꜣk*, attested by B24 and C, is omitted; in R49 *ḫrw* " sound " is left out, though present in B24 and C[5]; *ikm* and *titi* in R86 are somewhat inferior to *ikm-f* and *titi-f* in B61 and G; and similarly R88 seems to have only *ꜥḥꜣ* where B64 and G have *ꜥḥꜣ-f.* These insignificant differences hardly militate against the near relationship of GC and R that has been asserted above. The

---

1. Instances are given by M. Maspero, *op. cit.*, p. XXVIII, and a long list might be made. It will suffice to quote one or two examples : *mry* (C 1) for *mry-f* (G 2); *sꜥrw-f pt* (C 2) for *sḥry-f r pt* (G 5); *bs* (C 2) for *sb* (G 7); *n nis-ntw* (C 4) where G 13 omits the negative; *pnsrḫ, sdꜣw-f* and *nfft* in C 4 for *psḫ, sdꜣw* (without suffix) and *nftft* in G 14. — A single case where C corrects G is in the passage corresponding to R32; G 17 reads *nmi-ni r mꜣꜥwti;* C rightly omits the preposition but wrongly forgets *-ni* in *nmi-ni.*

2. Thus for example in G10 is confirmed by R18, while in C, though in itself just defensible, is disproved by the agreement of G and R. — Similarly where G is lost : in B18 = R44 we find *m snd mꜣꜣ wršy* "for fear lest the watcher...... should see (me)"; C has here the easier reading , but the consensus of B and R makes it almost certain that this improvement is due to the scribe of C or to one of his immediate predecessors.

3. *Op. cit.*, p. XXVI, foll.

4. Obvious corruptions on the part of C are here ignored; for further details the notes on the passages quoted must be consulted.

5. In the facsimile of C clear traces of are visible; is represented by the stroke at the side.

two remaining cases where CG supports B against R are more troublesome to account for. In R13-14 occur the words [hieroglyphs]; they are absent not only from GC but also from the Amherst fragments of B. This sentence in R fits admirably into the context where it occurs, and both M. Maspero[1] and myself[2] have attempted to vindicate its authenticity. However if the affiliation of manuscripts here maintained be correct, we can escape the view of these words being an interpolation only by supposing that B and GC have independently fallen into the like error of omitting the sentence owing to the homoioarchon *tisw*. Another difficulty occurs in R47 [hieroglyphs] (*sic*) [hieroglyphs] "thirst fell and overtook me". B21 gives [hieroglyphs] which, as *ꜣs-nf* cannot refer to the feminine *ib-t*, can only be rendered "the falling of thirst overtook me"; this curious phrase seems to be supported by C [hieroglyphs] and must therefore be original. I am unable to account for the reading of R except as due to emendation.

Occasionally GC differs from both B and R; it may then generally be shown to be wrong. GC has *šmw-sn* or *šmt-sn* where B5 and R29 have *šmw-s;* no clear sense can be made of the former reading. The learning of the scribe of GC did not extend to the knowledge of the obsolete verb *ḫmt* "to think" in R30 = B7; he therefore substituted for it [hieroglyphs], understanding this as *n ḫm-ni* "I was not ignorant". In R 44 = B 18 we find the obviously correct reading *m bꜣt;* GC replaces the preposition *m* by the gentive exponent *ni(niw)*. G43 gives *sḫm ḥr* or *sḫm ib* instead of *wd ḥr* of B60 = R84; the latter seems the more forcible and preferable phrase. In B7 we find the phrase "I did not expect to live [hieroglyphs] after him", i. e. after the death of Amenemmes I. The pronoun here is rather obscure, and the reading of R31 [hieroglyphs] "after these things" may be an attempt to remove the obscurity. A more clumsy expedient is adopted by GC, where the words are expanded into "after that good god", *nṯr mnḫ* being borrowed from a later passage B44 = R68[3]. In B17 = R42 *inbw ḥkꜣ* is obviously the correct reading, and whether or not *itf-i* in the variant *inbw itf-i* in GC be due merely to the misreading of the hieratic *ḥkꜣ*, there can be no doubt of the inferiority of GC here. In the very difficult sentence B5 = R28 all the texts are at fault; B has [hieroglyphs], R [hieroglyphs] and GC [hieroglyphs]. I shall try to show that R is nearest to the original reading *iwd*, while the others are guessing. In R1 we do not find the titles "chancellor of the king of Lower Egypt, unique friend", which occur in GC; M. Maspero may be right in regarding these words as part of the original text[4], yet such an expansion of titles is no unlikely trait of later manuscripts[5]. R6 gives [hieroglyphs] where GC has [hieroglyphs], B being lost;

1. *Op. cit.*, p. xxx.
2. *Sitzb. d. kön. preuss. Ak. d. Wiss.*, 1907, 145.
3. C reads *sꜣ pfi nṯr pn* (sic!) *mnḫ;* G has first a lacuna, then *nṯr pn mnḫ*. M. Maspero takes a somewhat different view of these variants (*op. cit.*, p. xxix); his view does not seem to account for the genesis of the reading of GC.
4. *Op. cit.*, p. xxviii.
5. So too C has extended the word "harim" in the titles of R3. Moreover the newly-discovered text

here *ʿr* is to be preferred, on the ground of its being the choicer word of the two.

The passages in which we have been able to consult more than two manuscripts with regard to the reading are so few, that it would be rash to base any very positive conclusions on a genealogical view of the various sources of testimony. However so far as the evidence goes, it is all in favour of the common source of R and GC, namely RGC. By checking R with GC and B several of the most careless blunders of R have been seen to have been absent from RGC, and conversely several mistakes shared by C and G have been disposed of by R. Where it has been possible to contrast RGC with B I have usually had to affirm — the proof remains to be given later in the notes — the superiority of RGC. But apart from these conclusions, based, I repeat, on too little evidence to be really cogent, the mere fact of the consensus of three manuscripts against one raises a distinct presumption in favour of the majority; the suspicion is at once suggested that the isolated witness contains an eccentric or faulty text. If GC, which is separated from R by a very considerable space of time, nevertheless shares most of the readings of the latter, it is probably because both were, in their common origin, not distantly related to the archetype. Thus to my mind the support given to R by GC may be reckoned as at least compensating for the later date of R as compared with B.

Though M. Maspero takes much the same view of the interdependence of the Mss. as that above outlined, the conclusions which he draws thence are very different from mine. From the agreement of GC with R as against B he immediately infers the existence of two "versions" or "redactions" of the text[1]. The older of these, represented by B alone (*plus* the Amherst fragments of course) was, according to M. Maspero, the version current towards the middle of the first Theban period. The second version, known to us through R and the three posterior manuscripts G, C and L, is termed by him the Ahmesside edition. The flaw which I think I detect in this manner of presenting the case lies in the employment and implications of the words "version", "redaction" and "edition". All that can be fairly concluded from the mere agreement of GC with R as against B, without a subjective valuation of the readings involved, is that there are two "families" of text; nor does it of itself follow that the elder branch resembles the common ancestor more closely than the younger line of manuscripts; on the contrary I have pointed out that the inclusion of three members at least in the younger line gives *a priori* some support to the tradition of that line, sufficient to counterbalance the fact that B is of somewhat earlier date than R. This argumentation proceeds of course on the usual assumption of textual criticism that the bulk of the differences found in the Mss. is due not to any deliberate tampering with the text[2], but to the natural deterioration of the readings

parallel to the beginning of Prisse gives a good illustration of this; there the titles of Ptahhotp are much more elaborate than in the earlier manuscript; see *Rec. de Trav.*, 31, 146.

1. *Op. cit.*, p. VII.

2. Of course a very considerable number of variants is due to some conscious reasoning on the part of the scribes. But since they are as a rule due to a misunderstanding of the original they may be classed together with the automatic errors. As an example may be quoted *rnti pʿt* (C 1) for *rpʿtt*.

owing to the carelessness and ignorance of the scribes through whose hands the text passed. M. Maspero's theory of two successive " redactions " or " editions " implies, or at least seems to imply, that a *wholesale revision* of the text was undertaken at some date posterior to the writing of B, so that the direct tradition of the archetype (B) was abruptly changed and replaced by a new and artificial version (RGC). Now if such a revision were due to a conscientious modern editor, who spared no pains to ascertain the original readings, it might well turn out to be superior to the debased descendant of the archetype which it was designed to replace; but M. Maspero certainly does not intend as to think that R (or rather RGC, the common source of R and GC) was the work of so scrupulous a scholar, but seems rather to wish us to believe that certain apparent improvements of R are really the arbitrary and groundless emendations of a scribe. The conclusion hinted at by this " redaction "-theory is that the later redaction is necessarily less faithful to the archetype than the earlier one, and thus the agreement of the latest manuscripts with R and not with B is used, not as a point in favour of R, but rather as one against it.

Now though M. Maspero's hypothesis of two successive versions is no legitimate deduction from the premisses on which it is based, it is nevertheless a possible hypothesis. The probabilities are however against any editorial revision of the text on a large scale. We may perhaps concede that the Egyptians were in the habit of " editing " their religious texts[1]; but the extreme corruption of most of the literary classics, such as the Instructions of Amenemmes I or the ironical letter of the Papyrus Anastasi I, makes it exceedingly unlikely that those compositions passed through several redactional stages. Nor is there, so far as I can see, any indication that RCG contained such artificial improvements as the theory seems to postulate. Such suspicious deviations from the text of B as R contains should probably be put down to the account of R alone and not to RGC; I have above mentioned the addition in R13-14 and the writing *ꜣs-ns* for *ꜣs-nf* in R47, where GC agrees with B against R. However these instances are to be explained they tell heavily against the "redaction"-theory. We may possibly have to admit that R was somewhat too free in transposing or interpolating sentences; but it must be remembered that this is only one of the two possible ways of regarding the complete divergence of B and R in certain passages (R65-66; R156; R190-193, etc.). At all events we must not be overhasty in assuming that the editor of R has improved his text, when R seems to give a smoother and more readily intelligible text than B. The principle of the *difficilis lectio* can very easily be misapplied, and where this is done textual criticism becomes impossible. I fancy M. Maspero falls into this error when, for example, he prefers his subtler and less obvious interpretation of the readings of B35-37 to the simple meaning that results from the text of R58-61.

I am not sure that I have not construed M. Maspero's remarks on the two versions more literally than he intended, for when we turn to his diagram of the genealogical

1. The Saitic recension of the Book of the Dead appears to be a real "recension"; but is this true of the *Todtenbuch* of the 18th. Dynasty ?

relations of the Mss.[1] we find no discontinuity of the tradition of the archetype marked above R[2]. Nevertheless I have felt that a protest was needed, as the very phrase "Ahmesside edition" seemed to prejudice the authority of R from the outset. As I have said above, I do not myself believe that any very satisfactory result is to be gained from the genealogical arrangement of the Mss. of Sinuhe, the evidence being too slender to warrant any certain conclusions. I hope to have made it plain however that one should start with the hypothesis that R is probably as good a text as B; when we have compared both manuscripts, passage for passage, we shall be able to sum up our results and possibly to express a more decided opinion as to which is superior[3].

## II

### COMMENTS ON THE TEXT

Besides the abreviations B. R. C. G and L above employed for the various Mss. I shall use the following : Masp., *M. S.* = Maspero, *Les Mémoires de Sinouhit;* Masp., *C. P.* = Maspero, *Les Contes populaires*, 3rd edition ; Gr. = Griffith, *The story of Sanehat* in *Specimen pages of a library of the World's best Literature*, pp. 5237-5249 ; Erm. = Erman, *Das Leben des Sinuhe* in *Aus den Papyrus der königlichen Museen*, pp. 14-29 ; Gard., *Sitzb.* = Gardiner, *Eine neue Handschrift des Sinuhegedichts* in *Sitzungsberichte der kön. preuss. Akad. d. Wiss.*, 1907, pp. 142-150.

*R1-2.* — The story opens with the titles supposed to have been attained by Sinuhe at the end of his career, followed by his name and the words "he says". The analogy of this beginning with that of the autobiographical inscriptions found in the tombs is very striking[4], and is shown by other details of the text not to be fortuitous. Above all this is clear from ll. 309-310, where the correct translation is : "I enjoyed the favours of the king until the day of death came". Again the introduction, by means of a new heading, of a royal decree granting Sinuhe permission to return to Egypt (l. 178) may be paralleled in the tombs of the Old Kingdom, cf. *Urkunden,* I, 60. 62. 128.

*R1.* — After *rpꜥti ḥꜣti-ꜥ* G and C give the late Egyptian equivalent of . It is doubtful whether the archetype contained these titles, see above § 1.

*R2.* — R should be completed

1. *Op. cit.*, p. xxxii.

2. That I have *not* misinterpreted M. Maspero's meaning seems now clear from his latest utterance (*Rec. de Trav.*, 31, 153) : "J'ai déjà montré, en éditant les *Mémoires de Sinouhit*, que, dans l'ensemble, les manuscrits du second âge thébain, tels que celui de Gardiner, ne s'éloignent pas trop des manuscrits du premier : les changements qu'on y remarque portent presque toujours sur des détails de grammaire, de vocabulaire ou d'histoire devenus peu compréhensibles, et pour lesquels on remplace la leçon première par une leçon plus conforme à la langue ou aux conditions politiques du moment."

3. I have hitherto omitted all reference to the London ostracon (L); later on I hope to show that even from its corrupt text some readings superior to those of B may be obtained.

4. It might possibly be objected that the *Proverbs of Ptahhotep* (*Prisse*, 4, 2) have a somewhat similar beginning. But there *ḏdf* "he says" is shown by the preceding title to mean "he spoke to king Issi", which the Carnavon writingboard actually has, whereas here *ḏdf* is quite vague, as in the tomb-inscriptions.

[hieroglyphs]. The fish as determinative of *ʿ(n)ḏ* is made probable by the traces and by the corrupt sign (like hieratic [sign]) in C; G replaces the fish by [sign], Both C and G spell out *ity*. On the title *sꜣb ʿnḏ mr* followed by a geographical designation, see Sethe, in GARSTANG, *Mahasna and Bet Khallaf*, p. 21, and for the meaning of these words as applied to Sinuhe see Maspero's interesting note *C. P.*, p. 60, footnote 2.

The name [hieroglyphs] occurs again in the M. K. *Pap. Kahun*, 9, 11; *Turin*, 10; *Turin*, 94 = *Rec. de Trav.*, 3, 122. Maspero is therefore not justified in using the name as evidence that the tale is wholly fictitious (*M. S.*, p. xxxv).

*R2-3.* — R and G rightly *šmsw šmsi nb-f;* C first omitted *šmsi* by haplography, but afterwards added it in red above the line.

*R3.* — The reading of R is [hieroglyphs] (*sic*) [hieroglyphs], etc. There can be little doubt about the reading of [sign], though the hieratic sign is not elsewhere known, unless it be in B204; and as we shall see, it is indirectly confirmed by C. The word *rpʿtt* (the reading of R is unhappily incomplete) seems to be a genitive after *ipꜣ-t stn*, so that the whole title would be "servant of the royal *harîm* of the princess, great of favours", etc. The beginning of these words is unfortunately lost in G. C has [hieroglyphs] with two indeterminate hieratic groups: [hieratic].

The reading of C is clearly a corruption of [hieroglyphs], cf. such titles as [hieroglyphs], *Rec. de Trav.*, 21, 73; the reading *pr ḫnti* is made certain (1) by the stroke after the first [sign], (2) by the shape of the corrupt sign, which closely resembles [sign], and (3) by the termination *ti* [1]. On the word *ipꜣ-t* see my note *Ä. Z.*, 45 (1909), 127, and on the writing of *pr ḫnti* see *Admonitions*, p. 47.

*R4.* — For the curious form of the titles of the princess Nofru see the parallels quoted by Sethe and Maspero, namely L., *D.*, II, 116a; MARIETTE, *Abydos*, I, 2; MARIETTE, *Mastabas*, p. 360. — I had overlooked the fact that the name of the pyramid [2] of Sesostris I occurs actually at Lisht itself in the formula [hieroglyphs] (*sic*) [hieroglyphs], GAUTIER-JÉQUIER, *Fouilles de Licht*, p. 60, fig. 69; and now a new instance of the name (*Ḫnm-iswt- Ḫpr-kꜣ-rʿ*) has been published from a 12th. Dynasty decree in PETRIE, *Memphis*, I, 5.

*R5.* — Read probably "month 3" with G; so R, though not quite certainly. C wrongly "month 2".

*R6.* — R [hieroglyphs], GC [hieroglyphs]; here the reading of R is, as being the rarer word of the two, preferable to that of GC. Note that *ʿr* here means "to enter" not to "mount" "ascend"; see the remarks on *m ʿrw* below B2.

1. Possibly the Ms. from which C copied had simply [hieroglyphs] instead of [hieroglyphs]. — Note too C's absurd interpretation of *rpʿtt* as *rnti pʿt*.

2. *Ḫnm-iswt* not *ḫnmt-iswt* as Maspero reads (*M. S.*, p. xxxvii); the word to be supplied is the name of the king, which is of course masculine.

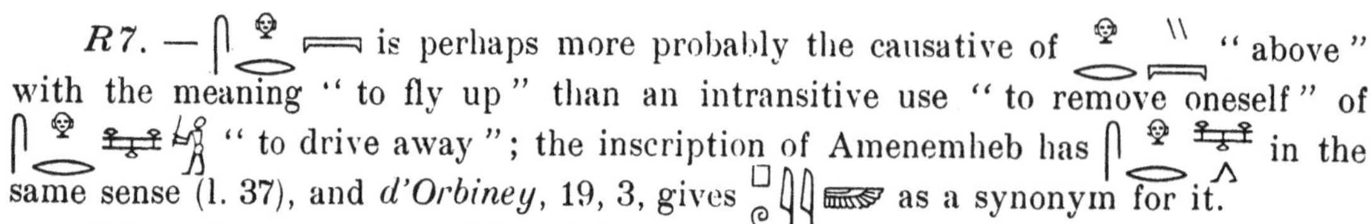

*R7.* — … is perhaps more probably the causative of … "above" with the meaning "to fly up" than an intransitive use "to remove oneself" of … "to drive away"; the inscription of Amenemheb has … in the same sense (l. 37), and *d'Orbiney*, 19, 3, gives … as a synonym for it.

*R8.* — On *sgr* see my *Admonitions*, p. 103.

*R9.* — The word … has in G and C the determinatives …, which connect it with … *Kahun veterinary papyrus*, 19; cf. too … *Totb., ed.* Nav., 7, 3; … "I am in mourning", *Famine Stele of Sehel*, 1-2. — At the end of the line R had possibly …, not merely …; so C. Masp., *M. S.*, p. 1, gives *ḫtm-ti*, but one must read the 3rd. masc. sing. pseudop., agreeing with a feminine dual substantive, see Sethe, *Verbum*, II, § 42.

*R10.* — Restore in R […] …, lit.: "the courtiers (sat) with head on lap", i. e. in mourning; cf. … *Westcar*, 12, 20. The reading of *Amh.* agrees, so far as it goes, with R, but C omits …, an omission which is paralleled by the late passage … *Festival songs of Isis and Nephthys*, 4, 17, and also to some extent by … *Sall. IV*, 16, 5.

*R10-11.* — In R we should probably read …[1]; C has …[2]. On *im* "grief" see my note *Admonitions*, p. 35. — …, which follows these words in C, may have arisen from … "moreover", a gloss on, or variant of, *ist rf* at the beginning of the next sentence.

*R12.* — C reads *mš' 'š3*; G is lost at the critical point, but as R and *Amh.* agree in omitting *'š3* there can be little doubt but that it was a later addition.

*R13.* — It is very tempting to regard *tisw ḥ3b(w)* etc. as part of the original text; for not only does this sentence give the necessary explanation of the purpose of the expedition, but it also provides a reason for the adversative particle *ḥm* in *tisw ḥm* R13. However GC omits the words, and that *Amh.* did so too is shown by the size of the lacuna; in face of this agreement it is difficult to deny that the sentence may be an interpolation. See above § 1.

*R14.* — The damaged word can only be […] …, but the expression *imiw Tḥnw* as a paraphrase for *Tḥnw* (R16) is strange. Note that the determinatives … do not necessarily apply to the land, but to the people living there, cf. … R12. 62; […] … C1; … *Admonitions*, 3, 1.

*R16.* — For *Tḥnw* of R we have … in C, apparently a cor-

1. In my transcription I gave …, in deference to Möller's opinion, but myself believe the sign to be simply an ill-formed ….

2. Here I unintentionally misled M. Maspero with regard to the reading of R.

ruption of *Tmḥi,* though that ethnic is correctly spelt in C a few words previously; or possibly a mixture of *Tmḥi* and *Tḥnw* (?). In G and *Amh.* there are lacunæ.

*R18.* — C has *śtn* for *s: stn* (R, G), of course wrongly; see above § 1. — C gives [hieroglyphs] for [hieroglyphs] of R; G has not room for *-sn*, which is meaningless and obviously faulty. — [hieroglyphs] both here and in B174 is masculine singular.

*R20-22.* — All texts, so far as they are preserved, are in substantial agreement with R, which reads [hieroglyphs]. — The variant [hieroglyphs] of *Amh.* is instructive for the pronunciation *en* of [hieroglyph] at this date; conversely *Peasant* B1, 2 has [hieroglyphs] for [hieroglyphs] in R[1]. — The first sentence is very difficult. Maspero, *C.R.*, renders: "n'est-ce pas le cas qu'il fasse une hâte extrême", and Griffith "it was a time for him to hasten greatly", but it would not be easy to justify these translations grammatically. Retaining [hieroglyph] of *Amh.*, one might possibly render: "the occasion pressed greatly"; but one would then expect *sin* (participle) instead of *sinn-f* (SETHE, *Verbum*, II, § 752); nor does *sin* mean "to press", but "to hasten", and G and C[2] both confirm the reading [hieroglyphs] of R. In my translation I have proposed: "never had he hastened (so) much" *scil.*, as he now did; but the sense is not very satisfactory, anticipating as it does the next clause, and the curious gemination *sinn,* which is supported by C [hieroglyphs] and by G [hieroglyphs], is not accounted for. I now believe that the determinative [hieroglyph], characteristic of verbs of stopping or restraining *(grḥ, ḥd, win),* gives the real clue to the sentence. *Sinn-f* has nothing to do with *sin* "to hasten", but is the causative of *in* "to delay" of which I have elsewhere[3] quoted an instance (LACAU, *Textes religieux*, ch. II = *Rec. de Trav.*, 26, 68-69). The sense would then be "he made no halt", a rendering which has a good deal of point when we recollect that the last words have related that "the messengers reached him at night-time[4]. For the somewhat unusual sense of *n sp* "not a moment", "not at all" (reinforced by the adverb *rsy*, which here plays much the same part as the later *in* [demotic], *cf.* for example *Urkunden*, IV, 1074), cf. [hieroglyphs] *Hirtengeschichte*, 6.

The next sentence "the hawk flew away[5] with his followers, without letting his army know it" belongs to a type not uncommon in this tale, *e. g. smrw nw stp-s: ḥ:b-sn*, R17; *wpwti ḫdd ḫnt r ḫnw :b-f ḥr-i*, B94; *sḫr pn innf ib-k*, B185; it is only excep-

1. Vogelsang translates "tritt nicht auf meine Kleider!" Surely this is impossible (*n* instead of *tm-k*); we must render: "Be so kind, thou peasant! dost thou tread on my garments?"

2. C has [hieroglyphs].

3. Cf. *Ä. Z.*, 45 (1909), 60-61.

4. Not "at eventide", as Erm. and Gr. wrongly give. The point is that the king sped homewards away from the main body of his troops under cover of night.

5. For *'ḥ* of R we have *'ḫ* in *Amh.*, G and C. — Maspero is wrong in reading [hieroglyphs] in C (see *M. S.*, p. 2, note 6); the reading of C is [hieroglyphs], in which [hieroglyph] is borrowed from *'ḫ* "to hang up".

tional insofar as *bik* is a descriptive epithet of the subject of the preceding sentence, so that here there is only a grammatical, but not a logical, change of subject. In English we may perhaps render : " a hawk, he flew away with his followers ". — I was formerly inclined to reject the idea that Sesostris fled away with a few followers so as to return as quickly as possible to Egypt (GARD., *Sitzb.*, p. 6, note 3); but M. Maspero's excellent remarks (*M. S.*, p. XXXVII-XXXVIII) have convinced me that I was here in error.

*R22.* — is of course the *sdmw-f* form impersonally used (cf. SETHE, *Verbum*, II, § 469); C and G have the *scriptio plena* .

*R23.* — C wrongly *mḫt mšʿ pn* instead of *mḫt-f m mšʿ pn* (R, G); and it falsely inserts before *nis-ntw* against *Amh.*, R and G.

*B1*[1]. — C has expanded *wʿ im* (B, R and G) into *wʿ im-sn*.

*2.* — B has , while R, supported by G and C, has [2]. From a grammatical point of view there is nothing to choose between the two readings; see ERMAN, *Gramm.*[3], § 243, where the following sentences are compared with one another : " a man on whose neck are swellings " *Ebers*, 51, 20; " if thou seest " ..... *Ebers*, 25, 4.

, the reading of R, is supported by G ; B has . The usual translation " et je m'enfuis au loin " (MASP., *C. P.*), " I fled far away " is open to serious objections. On the philological side it may be argued (1) that *ʿr* cannot bear the meaning here assigned to it, (2) that the well-supported *ʿrw* must then be wrong (an infinitive would be needful, and indeed, for that matter, *ḥr* and not *m*), (3) that can only introduce, in a M. K. tale, a descriptive clause, not a principal sentence[3]. Besides this, the psychological progression of the passage is spoilt by the old translation : the order of events clearly is first, that a secret is overheard by Sinuhe; second, that he is filled with dismay (*psḫ ib-i* etc.); and third, that he flees away (*nfʿ-ni-wi*). My own proposal is : "as I was nigh at hand a little way off". *M ʿrw* seems to mean "in the proximity " " near " or the like : cf. " words which this god speaks to them in nearing the gods of the netherworld ", JÉQUIER, *Le Livre de ce qu'il y a dans l'Hades*, p. 54; , *Libro dei Funerali*, 56;

---

1. From here onwards the numbers of the lines of B are used at the head of the notes.

2. The writing of G shows that the scribe was no longer familiar with the obsolete construction *iwf sdm-f*. C has attempted to emend and has written ; *iwi* is due to *sdm-ni* preceding and *iwi m ʿrw* following, and is an excellent example of that type of corruption which I have called "assimilation of pronouns", *Ä. Z.*, 45 (1909), 64.

3. The narrative tenses employed by *Sinuhe* are : (1) *ʿḥʿn sdm-nf;* (2) *sdm-nf;* (3) *sdmtf* (see below note on B4-5); and (4) *sdm-f* with emphatic subject preceding (see above note on R20-22).

[hieroglyphs], *ibid.* Here *'rw* is clearly a substantive meaning "nearness"; for its form cf. [hieroglyphs] "the opposite quarter" in the common phrase *m ḫsfw* "opposite" and in *irt ḫsfw* "to go to meet" (below B250). In connection with this substantive it is necessary to observe that "to ascend" is neither the sole nor even the most common sense of *'r* (what is the relation of *'r* to [hieroglyphs]?); that verb often means "to approach", cf. above R6 and [hieroglyphs] (sic) [hieroglyphs] "he found that the water had drawn nigh to the walls", *Piankhi*, 89; so too late *'r m*, "to approach" (*'r* being here construed like [hieroglyphs]), cf. [hieroglyphs] *Louvre*, C 65; [hieroglyphs] *Mission*, V, 625 (tomb of *'Ibi*).

At this point we may pause to resume the difficult context of which the philological details have now been fully discussed. The messengers bringing the news of the old king's death found Senwosret, his younger partner on the throne, returning from the Libyan campaign. They came upon him at dead of night; but in view of the gravity of the situation, no delay was granted and Senwosret fled away towards Egypt with a handful of followers, leaving the army in ignorance of what had happened (R19-22). Thus far all is clear; but what follows is so obscurely expressed that it is difficult to escape the impression that the obscurity is intentional. The lively particle [hieroglyphs] in R22 seems to imply some contrast with the preceding words: "but lo a message had been sent to the royal children who were with him in this army"; and, the text continues, "a summons was made to one of them" (*nis-ntw n w' im*, R24). It is hardly possible to regard *nis-ntw* as a mere synonym of *smi-ntw*, and the temporal nuance "it *was being* reported to one of them", which that supposition would demand, is not quite a legitimate interpretation of the simple narrative form *nis-ntw*[1]. The most straightforward way of understanding these words is to suppose that one of the princes was incited to put himself forward as a claimant of the throne; this supposition has the advantage of giving *nis* its due and proper meaning "to call". The alternative is to conjecture that Sinuhe merely overheard the news of Amenemmes' death, which was communicated to the royal princes but not to the rank and file of the army. M. Maspero thinks it possible that such an offence, even though involuntary, may in Egyptian law have been punishable with death (*C. P.*, p. 62, footnote 1); elsewhere he suggests that Amenemmes may have perished in a harem conspiracy, and that this was the ground why secrecy was so imperative (*M. S.*, p. XXXIII-XXXIV). The objection to these hypotheses is first, the peculiar wording of the sentence *nis-ntw n w' im* and second, that Sinuhe is said to have overheard, not the voice of a messenger, but the voice of the prince himself[2]; the natural deduction is that the dismay of Sinuhe was caused less by the message brought from Egypt, than by the attitude adopted by the prince on hearing it. But as has been said before, the obscurity of the context was probably designed, and we

1. One would then expect *iw nis-tw*, or *iwtw nis-tw* or *iwtw ḥr nis*.
2. There can be no doubt about this; else there is no possible antecedent to the suffix of *ḫrw-f* in B1.

are therefore reduced to guessing. It is not the least attractive point about this fascinating tale that its very mainspring is so elusive.

*2.* — The descriptive sentences that follow are marked off from the progressive narrative tenses *sdm-nf* by the use of the *sdmf-* form. — [hieroglyphs]; R. G *psh* [hieroglyph], C quite corruptly [hieroglyphs]. The verb is rare : it is used of the disarray of a person's hair [hieroglyphs] *Totb., ed.* NAV., 17, 101 (cf. *ibid.*, 107), parallel with [hieroglyphs]; as a corrupt variant *ibid.*, 64, 28; 151 d (*Ani*, 34). Elsewhere only DÜM., *Geogr. Inschr.*, IV, 124 (Dendera) [hieroglyphs] "scattered with all kind of sacred plant".

*3.* — B suppresses, in accordance with its wont, the suffix of *m 't-i nbt* "in my every limb" (R); the singular of R and B seems more literary than the plural "all my limbs" of G and (in corrupt form) C.

*3-4.* — R27 gives [hieroglyphs], lit. : "I removed myself in leaping", i. e. "I leapt away", with a rare word *nf'* known elsewhere only from [hieroglyphs] *Pyr.*, 500 (variant from the tomb of *H' mh3t* = *Miss.*, I, 125 [hieroglyphs]); B has wrongly [hieroglyphs]. The readings of C and G are derived from a slightly corrupted form of [hieroglyphs] (R), in which [hieroglyph] had been changed into [hieroglyph] (an easy hieratic confusion when the sign is small) possibly under the influence of *nftft* : G omits the determinative [hieroglyph] and the first [hieroglyph], thus obtaining [hieroglyphs]; C gives [hieroglyphs], which is obtained by the transposition of *t* and *f*, making [hieroglyph] of the latter, and by misinterpreting the first [hieroglyph] as determinative of *iw* "to come"[1]. — As Maspero has rightly seen, *nftft* is a formative in *n* of [hieroglyphs] "to spring" (BR., *Wörterb.*, 556; *Suppl.*, 498); cf. C [hieroglyphs] (N. B. ×!) and G [hieroglyphs].

*4.* — [hieroglyphs] of R is a mistake for [hieroglyphs] B; see above § 1.

*4-5.* — B [hieroglyphs]; R [hieroglyphs]. B, which frequently omits the suffix of the first person singular, shows a special tendency to do so before the absolute pronoun *wi*, cf. below *di-n(i)-wi* 200; *hm-n(i)-wi* 253; in this point it resembles the *Schiffsbrüchiger*, cf. ERMAN, *Ä. Z.*, 43 (1906), 2. — The *sdmtf* form (properly, according to Sethe, feminine infinitives absolutely used; cf. *Verbum*, II, § 357) is fairly often used in the tale of Sinuhe as a substitute for the narrative tense *sdm-ni*; cf. below 5 [hieroglyphs] (so to be read too in 19); [hieroglyphs] 15; [hieroglyphs] 23; possibly [hieroglyphs] 24; [hieroglyphs] 86. 107.

The second half of the sentence is difficult : "I placed myself between two bushes" [hieroglyphs]; R28-29 [hieroglyphs]; G [hieroglyphs]; C [hieroglyphs]. The disagreement of B, R and GC here seems to show that difficulties were early felt as

1. The first [hieroglyph] has the curious additional stroke which initial [hieroglyph] nearly always shows in N. K. hieratic.

to the sense of this phrase; each version has a different infinitive beginning with the letter *ỉ*. With regard to the last two words, we may at once exclude *-sn* in GC owing to the agreement of B and R; and , as it is simply the isolated reading of the worst text C.  can only be the masc. sing. of the imperfect active participle; forms from the 3æ. infirmæ with *-w* written out are quoted by SETHE, *Verbum,* II, § 882. But in this case *šmw-s*, litt. "its goer", i. e. "him who was travelling upon it" must be[1] the second object (*wꜣt* being the first) of the preceding infinitive. Verbs taking two objects are in Egyptian by no means common, and one can hardly fail to emend [2] of R into  "to separate", on the construction of which see the note *Admonitions*, p. 41. The meaning would then be: "in order to separate the road from him who was going upon it" (i. e. myself), or, in other words: "in order that I might avoid the road". The extreme artificiality of this sentence is undeniable, but when one compares such expressions as "I gave a way to my feet" (16), "I gave the sand to those who are in it" (294), this objection vanishes; moreover Sinuhe is fond of referring to himself by an *epitheton ornans*, e. g. "a lingerer lingered through hunger", 151; "him whom he had chastened", 161; "him who works for himself", 216. I am unable to explain the meaning attached to their variants by the scribes of B and GC[3]; for the writing of  in B, cf. 117. 282.

*6.* —  of B is of course to be explained as equivalent to  [] R30 "I did not intend to come to the Residence"; for the construction see SETHE, *Verbum*, II, § 553.

7. — For the variants of *ḥmt-ni* see above in § 1.

B has ; R31 ; GC <*r*> *sꜣ pfi nṯr pn mnḫ*. See above § 1; I believe the original reading to be that of B "after him", i. e. after the death of Amenemmes, a reading which GC has attempted to make clearer, and R to emend. In my German translation I have preferred the version of R and have rendered: "ich meinte ich würde danach nicht leben"; but perhaps one should understand: "I did not care ("hope", "consent", see the note *Admonitions*, p. 20) to live after him".

*8.* — B ; R31-2 [4] [5]; G ; C . Gr. alone of the translators has had an inkling of the sense; he renders: "I wan-

1. Grammatically it might also be a genitive; but "the way of him who went on it" can hardly be right!

2. My former suggestion for *iwt* "vermeiden" was a pure guess.

3. GC may have been intended to convey the meaning: "to linger behind (*isk*) the way which they were going". For an instance of  being construed as a masculine Prof. Sethe quotes me  *Ebers*, 52, 3 = 25, 4.

4. In my edition of the text I have read  here and in R43. 49, as is generally done. However there is no early hieroglyphic authority for this determinative, and its appearance in our transcriptions is due solely to the fact that  and  have an identical form in hieratic. The ancient scribes have been guilty of the same mistake when, for example, they write  for  *Admonitions*, 6, 7.

5. The final determinatives are probable, but not quite certain.

dered across my estate (?)". [hieroglyphs] means "to cross", "traverse" water; good examples *Pyr.*, 543. 544. 1224; MAR., *Mast.*, D10. Hence in early times often determined by [hieroglyph], cf. too the [hieroglyphs] -boats *Weni*, 30. Metaphorically the verb is used of traversing (1) the heavens, and (2) the desert; the latter employment occurs only in the phrase [hieroglyphs], which therefore contains the same image as our "ship of the desert" for the camel. *Nmi* is never used of crossing land; the earliest instance of the determinative [hieroglyph] in this word is *Brit. Mus.*, 614 = *Piers-Breasted stele* (dyn. XI). It must be carefully noted that *nmi* is quite distinct from [hieroglyphs] *nmti* "to traverse" (e. g. *Pyr.*, 325. 854. 889); cf. too [hieroglyphs] *Zauberspr. für M. u. K.*, Rs. 6, 3. — *Mꜣwti* must thus be the name of a lake or water-way; its location will be considered further on. The sign [hieroglyph] in B is superfluous. The entire sentence may now be translated : "I crossed over the water Mewoti in the neighbourhood of the sycomore". For the variant [hieroglyphs] in B, not in R and C, one may compare "Hathor lady of [hieroglyphs]" MAR., *Mast.*, D 61. 65; perhaps there was a well-known or sacred sycomore in the region referred to.

*9.* — RGC *wrš-ni im;* B omits *im*. The reading of RGC is clearly superior, as it must be meant that Sinuhe avoided the inhabited part of the "Island of Snofru", and spent the day in some pasture-lands there. — B [hieroglyphs]; G [hieroglyphs]; C [hieroglyphs] (*sic*); R34 [hieroglyphs].

*10.* — B [hieroglyphs]; R34 [hieroglyphs] (wrong GARD., *Sitzb.*); GC [hieroglyphs]. Here by common consent of the two oldest manuscripts, *ḥd* must be taken as a verb of motion, "I went forth at dawn, and it became day"; but such a derivative from *ḥd* "to be bright", which only means "to dawn" in conjunction with [hieroglyphs] (*ḥd-tꜣ* "the land became light"), is extremely curious.

*10-11.* — The words [hieroglyphs] are susceptible of several different renderings. Note first of all that on the showing of R *ri-wꜣt-i* [hieroglyph] is to be read, "in my way" or more vaguely "in meiner Nähe"[1]; and that [hieroglyphs] (R35 [hieroglyphs][2]) means, not "to ask mercy of" nor "suppliant" nor yet "grüssen", but "to stand in awe of" "respect", the old form being [hieroglyphs] (SETHE, *Verbum*, I, p. 144), and cf. [hieroglyphs] MAR., *Abyd.*, I, 20c, 2; other good instances *Totb., ed.* NAV., 38a, 7; *Millingen*, 2, 12; *Munich, Bekenkhons statue, back*. *Ḥp-ni* might be translated : (1) "I went on", (2) "there came to me", or (3) "I met". (1) So MASP., *C. P.* : "..... je voyageai : un homme qui se tenait à l'orée du chemin me demanda merci, car il avait peur"; the construction of the last clause (emphasized subject followed by *sḏm-nf*) might be supported by B142-3, but the brief "je voyageai" without further qualification, is not possible, (2) Erm. "es begegnete mir ein Mann, der am (?) Wege stand; er grüsste (?) mich

1. The translation "in meiner Nähe" is that of Sethe, who regards *ri-wꜣt* as the equivalent of the Coptic ⲣⲁⲧⲛ. In this case [hieroglyphs] *Peasant* R49 can, I suppose, only be translated "the neighbouring bank". But is not *ri-wꜣt* often merely an equivalent of *wꜣt*?

2. C *r tri* "at the time of"! — Other examples of the word are quoted by MAX MÜLLER, *Rec. de Trav.*, 31, 197.

und fürchtete sich"; an ungainly translation, which I have tried, with dubious success, to soften down into "ein Mann begegnete mir, und stand in meinem Weg; er scheute sich vor mir und fürchtete sich". (3) Better than these renderings is Gr.'s: "I came to a man standing" etc.; I doubted the transitive use of *ḥp*, but it seems clearly proved by *Hirtengeschichte*, 23.

The entire context should therefore be rendered: "I set out in the dawn, and it became day; I met a man standing in my path, and he was in awe of me and was afraid". Sinuhe's wild appearance strikes terror into the only man that he encounters.

*12-13.* — R, *dmi* ; C, *dmi* . It is not possible to decide with certainty whether B had or *dmi* : the writing with ꜣ speaks perhaps somewhat in favour of *Ngꜣw*, since this spelling of (L., *D.*, II, 3) is found elsewhere in the M. K. (below B120 but not R144; Lacau, *Textes Religieux*, I (A. C.) = *Rec. de Trav.*, 26, 64)[1]. On the other hand in R and C we must translate: "the town of Gu"; for (never early written *gꜣw*, so far as our evidence goes), cf. *Pap. Kahun*, 16, 14; 17, 2; *Ebers*, 22, 7.

*13.* — In my transcription of B I have an unfortunate *lapsus calami*, being written with instead of with .

*14.* — in R39 is confirmed by B, as now correctly mounted (see Möller, *Lesestücke*, plate 7); B has . *Swt* is a ἅπαξ λεγόμενον; *ni* (not *nt*) shows it to be a masculine word.

(so too R; GC ) is not a proper name, as it has hitherto been taken to be, but a word for "stone-quarry", cf. *Pap. Kahun*, 31, 25.

*14-15.* — C (supported for the first two words by G) shows that R40-41 should be restored , which can only be translated: "in (the locality named) Lady of Heaven, mistress of the Red Mountain". Both the geographical name and the construction are well illustrated by *Rec. de Trav.*, 30, 214 (*temp.* Rameses II); and the indications of the same inscription afford definite proof that the Gebel Aḥmar in the neighbourhood of Cairo is meant.

*16.* — *Dmi-ni*, lit. "I touched", i. e. "I reached" or "passed beside".

*17.* — "The walls of the Prince" (*inbw ḥkꜣ*) are mentioned again in *Pap. Petersburg I*; see my remarks *Admonitions*, p. 112, footnote 2. I shall revert later, on B72-3, to the variant of GC.

The additional words in R43 are also found in C [and G]; they are open, as Sethe points out, to the objection that walls, though they may be "made to hold back the Asiatics",

1. The word seems to be derived from *ngꜣ* "to be long" (cf. *Pyr.*, 504); the *ngꜣw* or *ngw* is a long-horned species of bull, cf. L., *D.*, II, 22.

cannot be said with equal propriety : " to crush the desert-farers ". But perhaps this is pressing the literal meaning too far; and I am inclined to think that B72-3 must be interpreted in such a way as to dispose of Sethe's contention (see the note on that passage). Nevertheless it is not clear whether *r ptpt nmiw-š*ʿ is here an interpolation of RGC from the later passage or whether it is original. — R has for of B; not so good a reading, since is elsewhere reserved for the intransitive sense " to sail against the stream ", " to go upstream ". — *Nmiw-š*ʿ, see above the note on B8.

*17-18.* — (var. R44 ) must be literally " my crouching posture ", cf. for example " in obeisance ", *Hatnub*, 8, 3. " I took my crouching posture " (so too Masp., *M. S.*, p. 170) is an artificial periphrasis for " I crouched down ". — B and R give *m bꜣt;* GC incorrectly replaces the preposition *m* by the genitive exponent (G , C ).

*18-19.* — R44-5 has " from fear lest the watchman of the day upon the wall should see (me) ". The singular " watcher " is a spelling that otherwise occurs only late, cf. (*sic*) in the Theban tomb of *Ns-pꜣ-nfr-ḥr* (copied by Sethe); however one may compare such forms as " loiterer ", B151; " robber ", *Eloquent Peasant*, B1, 302. C gives with substantially the same text as R, but for one or two easily explicable corruptions[1]. On the other hand B deviates considerably, having . The plural *wršyw* (Sethe, *Verbum*, II, § 867) for the rare singular *wršy* (R) was the first faulty step taken by B; and C seems to have made the same blunder, though independently, unless the determinative of is to be explained on the analogy of Sethe, *Verbum*, I, § 207. Next, [2] in B is due to the similarity of and in hieratic; some predecessor of B had the abbreviated writing for *tp inb* of the archetype (cf. B17), which was subsequently read and regularised into . These errors entailed another : *wršy* having been modified into a plural *wršyw* and *inb* into a feminine *ḥꜣ-t*, there no longer remained any masculine singular substantive for *imy hrw-f* to agree with; this was therefore changed in B to *imt-hrw-s* so as to suit the nearest substantive *ḥꜣ-t*, though it is doubtful whether the scribe can have made any sense of the alterations for which he was responsible.

*19.* — B has , but the *sḏm-f* form is not thus used in the tale

1. The pronoun in *mꜣꜣ-wi* is doubtless secondary, see above § 1. On *wršy(w?)*, see below. for has arisen from just such a hieratic form of as is found in R45. *ʾIn* for *inb* is a mere blunder : [Masp., *M. S.*, p. 5, footnote 5, is entirely wrong, and due to a confusion with the *inb* of B17. Here G. is lost].

2. Elsewhere *tp-ḥꜣt* is a compound word for " roof ". Max Müller (*Asien und Europa*, 39) rendered " auf der Zinne ", but rightly remarked that *ḥꜣ-t* is here a very ill-chosen word.

as a narrative tense, see on B2, footnote. Read therefore with R45 (C ), cf. above B5; for the *sḏmtf* form, see the note on B4-5.

*21.* — R46 and C have for of B; there is little to choose between the two readings. — B and C agree in giving *n Km-wr* "the island of *Km-wr*", not "the lake ( ) of *Km-wr*" as most translations have; cf. "the island of Snofru", B9 = C5. G is missing here, and of the reading of R there is only a trace. Max Müller (*Asien u. Europa,* 39, footnote 2) proposes to emend "island", which he recognizes to be the reading of B, into "lake" ( ); in view of the consensus of B and C I doubt whether we should be justified in adopting this course. — For *Km-wr,* see Ed. Meyer, *Gesch. d. Altertums*[2], § 227, note.

*21-22.* — B ; C ; R47-48 [ ] . The *crux* of B is that *ꜣs-nf wi* "overtook me" (*ꜣs* transitively "ereilen", cf. B169) cannot refer to *ibt* "thirst"[1], that noun being feminine (cf. *Pyr.,* 552). The difficulty is removed by R, the text of which may be rendered : "thirst fell and overtook me". But the agreement of B and C makes it probable that *ꜣs-nf* is the more correct reading : if so, the antecedent of the suffix can only be *ḫr,* and this must be an infinitive substantivally used. B should therefore be rendered : "the fall of thirst overtook me"; an artificial expression, but one not wholly out of harmony with the style of the tale. C seems to have understood : "falling into thirst overtook me", which is of course impossibly harsh. R's text seems due to emendation.

*22.* — B with an unknown word *ntb;* this may easily have been, and doubtless is, a palæographic corruption of *nḏꜣ,* which is found in R47 (C [*sic*]). For this word, cf. (read [3]) L., *D.*, III, 140 b, 3; *Theban tomb of Ṯꜣy.* — At the end of R47 read [ ]; B and C agree in giving as the determinative of *ḫmw* here, obviously a more appropriate determinative than in reference to the human throat.

*23.* — C has *dpt ni mt nn ḥrs,* an apparently meaningless expansion of *dpt mt nn.*

*23-24.* — B ; R omits *sꜣk* and reads *ḥꜥ-i* for *ḥꜥw-i,* but wrongly, as these words are correctly given by C[4]. On the *sḏm-tf* form *ṯs-ti* see on B4-5; but *sꜣk-ti* is a difficulty. (1) Möller doubts the reading , and refers me to his *Hieratische Paläographie,* I, 243, where he explains the hieratic form here as due to a confusion with No. 241 . I cannot agree : as noted in my palæographic comment, the crocodile would then stand too much towards the

1. In my transcription of R has been wrongly omitted.

2. Maspero (*M. S.*, xiii) assumes that *ibt* has changed gender : but (1) this is an unproven hypothesis in the case of this particular word, and (2) such a change is common in Coptic, and not rare in late Egyptian, but no example has yet been quoted from Middle Kingdom texts.

3. in the original is due to a confusion between hieratic and .

4. C gives however *ṯs-ni* for *ṯsti* and *sꜣk-i* for *sꜣkti.*

left. In answer to Möller's further objection, that my assumed [hieroglyph] has a wrong shape, I would refer him to the *t* in [hieroglyphs] B101; it is true, one might expect a rather different form, but it seems to me hypercritical to argue from so small and variously-made a sign. (2) Sethe has the grammatical objection to *sꜢḳti*, that the *sḏmtf* form is found only with verbs that have a feminine infinitive, or with such verbs as may be suspected of having formerly belonged to a verbal class with feminine infinitives. The objection is certainly strong, and one might feel inclined to emend *sꜢḳ-i*. But against this must be set the excellent parallelism of *sꜢḳti* with *tsti*, and it may be questioned whether the amount of our evidence for the *sḏm-tf* form warrants the generalization that this form cannot be found with a triliteral such as *sꜢḳ*. The same doubt occurs in the case of [hieroglyphs] *Urkunden*, IV, 1090, which Sethe similarly rejects (*Die Einsetzung des Veziers*, note 91).

*24.* — [hieroglyphs] BC; cf. *Zaubersp r. f. Mutter u. Kind*, 1, 6; *Amduat* (Sethos I), IV, 48; R omits *ḫrw*, an unimportant alteration, since the sense remains the same.

*25.* — Maspero (*M. S.*, IX and 7) reads [hieroglyphs] with C[1] against [hieroglyphs] of R49 and B, but I can see no reason for the preference thus given to the worst authority. The reading of C is surely another case of "the assimilation of pronouns" (see above on B2, footnote) due to following [hieroglyphs] (R50 = B25; note the strange writing *sꜢi* for *siꜢ* in B).

*26.* — *Mtn*, cf. B276 and Borchardt's note *Ä. Z.*, 29 (1891), 63; and for *pꜢ wnn* "who had formerly been", see my remarks *Ä. Z.*, 45 (1908), 76.

*27.* — [hieroglyphs] is quite meaningless as it stands[2]. Since the scribe of B writes [hieroglyphs] in 88, we should doubtless here emend [hieroglyphs] (following C [hieroglyphs]; R51 [hieroglyphs]); the error of B is due to some confusion of the radical *f* and the suffix *f*.

*28.* — The variations in the spelling of the collective noun [hieroglyphs] (so B94. 113; [hieroglyphs] 240) seem to be groundless; R52 has characteristically the normal spelling [hieroglyphs], but in B we find [hieroglyphs] 28, [hieroglyphs] (*sic*) [hieroglyphs] 200, [hieroglyphs] 130 and [hieroglyphs] 86. On the word, see LACAU, *Rec. de Trav.*, 31, 86.

*29.* — B has [hieroglyphs]; R53 [hieroglyphs]. *Fḫ* as verb of motion again in [hieroglyphs] "I departed in the first month of summer" (WEILL, *Recueil de... Sinai*, 63, 16), where [hieroglyph] prohibits the reading *ʿrḳ*; the sense in this passage is clear, *Ḥrwr-rʿ* having reached Sinai in the third winter-month and having started homewards in the first month of summer. In the Sinuhe context

1. In C itself [hieroglyph] in [hieroglyphs] was an afterthought, as is shown by its position and by the greater blackness of the ink.

2. MASPERO (*M. S.*, 6, note 3) writes : "Le [hieroglyph] final du verbe [hieroglyphs] aura trompé le scribe et entrainé la chute fautive du pronom [hieroglyph] ". But the verb "to cook" is not to be read *psf*, but *ps* or *fs*, see SETHE, *Verbum*, I, § 216. Cf. too the correct writings of the verb, B83. 92.

the preposition *r* might mean "in the direction of" or "from" (cf. *wꜣ r* "far from"); the latter alternative gives a better meaning, but philologically is less easy to defend.

The reading "Byblos" in R53 was accepted without question in my preliminary paper on the Ramesseum papyrus, and von Bissing, Ed. Meyer and Sethe have expressed or implied adhesion to my view; Maspero and Weill refuse to admit that Sinuhe touched Byblos in the course of his wanderings, though they differ in the reasons which they give for their refusal. Three considerations seemed to me to militate strongly in favour of and against the reading of B : (1) the general superiority of R over B both in text and in orthography; (2) the fact that R names a well-known place, as is obviously required, while the reading of B neither corresponds to any known locality nor yet is in harmony with the usual mode of spelling foreign names; and (3) that the signs in B may more readily be explained as corrupted from R's reading than *vice versa*. I will deal with these points in turn. (1) The first is denied by Maspero, who favours B as representing the oldest recension of the text. But as I have tried to show, M. Maspero's unfavourable estimate of R is due in some measure to his unfortunate use of the term "recension", and I have argued that B and R are entitled, on a cursory view, to about equal credence, so that the value of individual readings must be determined on the merits of each case, not in accordance with any theory prejudicial to one or other of the manuscripts. This seems to be the position on which we ought at present to take our stand; though later a general inference from our judgments in particular passages will enable us to assert the superiority of R and to use this verdict as corroborative evidence in a retrospective survey of the details. (2) Palæographically the reading of B might be interpreted as or as , see note *h* on B29 in my volume on the text, plate 5a. But apart from the fact that no such place-names are known, the spelling of the name of a foreign locality without any of the usual phonetic signs would be quite contrary to custom; the sound of outlandish foreign names had obviously to find clear expression in the writing, and it is this necessity to which is later due the so-called syllabic writing. The only possible exception to this rule is when a foreign place happened to be exceedingly familiar to the Egyptians, as was "Byblos", the spelling of which contains a somewhat uncommon sign. The very fact that the reading of B contains an unusual sign proves that it must conceal the name of some well-known place, not an unheard-of *swn* or an unauthenticated *ẖkr*. Moreover the context in the tale shows that some famous locality was meant. Here a contrast may be drawn between the story of Sinuhe and the ironical letter contained in the first Anastasi papyrus. The last-named text was composed in an age where every scribe with any pretence to erudition made it a point of honour to be familiar with hundreds of uncouth Syrian words, and these are enumerated with prolixity and relish whenever occasion arises. Not so in the twelfth Dynasty : Sinuhe is content to summarize weeks and months of travel with the laconic words "land handed me on to land"; what need to trouble his readers with a host of tiresome barbarian names? The corollary of this argument is that the places that Sinuhe does name must have possessed some meaning and interest for Egyptian ears; this is certainly true of Retenu, and is probably true of Kedme, a word of which the literal meaning could not fail to be known to anyone with the least smattering of a Semitic tongue; as a third name of equal celebrity none could be more appropriate than that of Byblos. (3) M. Maspero writes (*M. S.*, p. XLII-XLIII) : "Je concéderais, à la rigueur, que le copiste de PB eût passé la syllabe *néî, nî*, mais je comprends mal comment il aurait été entrainé à commettre cette faute, énorme pour un homme habile en son métier, de tourner la griffe [1] dans un sens contraire à celui qu'elle avait dans l'écriture hiératique. Ce que Gardiner dit de la direction du signe (I had pointed out [*Sitzb.*, 8, footnote 1] that the direction of the hieroglyph *kp* was variable), vrai pour les inscriptions hiéroglyphiques, ne vaut pas pour l'hiératique : dans cette forme de cursive la direction ne varie jamais et les caractères sont toujours tracés de droite à gauche. La faute de transcription est donc de celles qui ne pouvaient même pas venir à l'esprit d'un scribe." The principle to which M. Maspero here appeals is undoubtedly sound, and for a moment his objection caused me, I admit, a certain unease. However the rule quoted, though correct as a generalization, does not apply in this particular instance. In a letter from Kahun (Griffith, *Hieratic Papyri*, 28, 5) the name of Hathor, lady of Byblos, is written with an inverted [2] such as would require but little alteration to become identical with the form of or in B. This objection therefore is now categorically disposed of. But in any case M. Maspero's statement that the error is one such as could never have occurred to the mind of a scribe far overshoots the mark, as is proved by the fact that Prof. Spiegelberg [3] actually conjectured for the of B long before the Ramesseum text was discovered; it is hardly to be supposed that a modern Egyptologist could have seen a similarity between the two writings if an ancient scribe would have been unable to do so. Now we have good evidence for the fact that the scribe of B knew the sign , but it is less certain that he was acquainted with . There is no difficulty in the supposition that, having failed to recognize the name "Byblos", he corrupted the less-known sign into one familiar to him, and omitted the accompanying phonetic signs as unessential. The mistake is one not at all too grave for a man who was ignorant of the proper spelling of *Rtnw*, and who imagined that the king Kheperkere was an Amenemhet.

In the foregoing discussion I have tried to steer clear of all historical considerations, or at least of such as are open to dispute. Those who doubt whether the conditions of life described in the tale are applicable to the region of the Lebanon are free to maintain, if they choose, that the tale is worthless as evidence for *Kulturgeschichte*, but the reading may as little be called in question on this

1. The writing of the sign for *kȝp, kp* with a claw is, so far as I am aware, quite a late innovation (18th. Dynasty ?). One form of the sign, given by Möller in his *Hieratische Paläographie*, I, 516, seems to be a sack. But this is by no means the only ancient form : the hieroglyphs for *kp, kȝp* deserve careful study.

2. A reference to Möller's palæographical work will convince anyone that neither nor nor indeed any other sign than *kp* can here be read.

3. Prof. Spiegelberg informed me of his conjecture by letter on the appearance of my article in the *Sitzungsberichten*.

ground as the mention of Israel on the Merenptah stele. That the rejection of is due in reality to objections of a historical, not of a philological order, is indicated by a theory put forward by M. R. WEILL (*Sphinx*, XI, 201-205), where the reading is retained, but explained to mean, not Byblos, but some other *gebel* "de la région où l'on admettait jusqu'ici que l'écrivain avait placé son histoire". M. Weill quotes *Gebalene* and *Gobolitis* as proof of the frequency of the word *gebel* in Semitic geography. I will concede the proposed etymology of *Kbn, Kpny*, though I am told it is far from certain; but it will be a sufficient rejoinder to M. Weill that when I read of Boston, of Cambridge or of Frankfurt in an English newspaper I require some more conclusive evidence than the knowledge that these names belong to several towns apiece before I can believe that the places meant are not those in Massachusetts, in Cambridgeshire and on the Main respectively.

"I approached Kedme". *Ḥs* in its intransitive sense is a simple verb of motion, "to approach" or the like, cf. LEGRAIN, *Annales du Service*, IV, 130 (Karnak, stele Amenothes, II, l. 9); *Millingen*, II, 10; R., *I. H.*, 248, 88. The literal sense may be "sich nähern", as was proposed by MAX MÜLLER (*Asien und Europa*, p. 265, footnote 1); transitively "to approach" a person, cf. *Rekhmara*, 2, 6. — For of B23 we find [ ] R59, showing that B 182, 219, is to be read *Ḳdmi*, 'קדמי'. On this country, see ED. MEYER, *Gesch. d. Altertums*[2], I, § 358 Anm.

*30.* — is *in-n-wi*, the *sḏm-n.f* form, cf. B103 parallel to . B is here typically inconsistent, as the *sḏm-n.f* form is spelt with two in lines 39. 143. 185; R54 has the normal writing . — The spelling *'mwinši* in R54 (cf. R169) is interesting as evidence for the value of *ši* (not *š;*[1]); B30 *'mwyinši* as in B143.

*31.* — B ; R55 must have had [ ] , the spelling that is actually found in R135, since otherwise would not have been written above (see GARD., *Sitzb.*, 8). I see no reason for believing that *Tnw* in B is a legitimate variant of *Rtnw;* it is far more probably an error due to the scribe's ignorance.

"thou art happy with me"; see now for the construction my remarks *Admonitions*, p. 104, and for the sense of *nfr*, cf. below B75. 76. — "the language", a sense which I cannot quote from other texts; as Sethe points out, the use of ⲁⲥⲡⲉ in Coptic is somewhat similar. *Wenamon*, 77, has in this sense, cf. ⲙⲛⲧⲟⲩⲉⲓⲛⲓⲛ, ⲙⲛⲧⲣⲙⲛⲕⲏⲙⲉ; and the quotation well illustrates *sḏm* = "to understand".

1. A *nisbe*-form? Note that is here *-mi*, taken over from *(i)mi* ⲙⲟⲓ (SETHE, *Verbum*, II, § 538; another instance is the particle ; *mi*, on which, see *Admonitions*, p. 105). Maspero is therefore wrong in transcribing *Qâdoumâ* (*M. S.*, p. 171).

2. Had the word been *š;* it would doubtless always have been written . Similarly I have shown (*Admonitions*, 30, footnote) that is to be read *si*; likewise I prefer to read *ri*, not *r;*, the latter combination of letters not being known in any Egyptian word, though *;r* of course occurs.

*34-35.* — R58 seems much superior to (" wherefore art thou come hither? what is it?") in B, the end of which is very lame. A very close parallel occurs at Deir el Bahari, where the envoys of Queen Makere are greeted by the prince of Punt with the words (*Urkunden*, IV, 324); if, as is probable (*Sitzb.*, 3, footnote 3), this is a deliberate quotation from the well-known tale of Sinuhe, then it would have some slight textual value as a confirmation of R. Another example of the interrogative expression is found on the stele of Teti-sheri (*Urkunden*, IV, 27), in a text composed in choice and somewhat high-flown language[1]. The expression thus seems to be peculiar to the higher style of diction; and the more pedestrian in B may well be due to a gloss upon it.

*36.* — in B is less appropriately spelt than R59.

*36-44.* — Here B and R diverge widely. The most vital points of difference are two insertions in R which affect the order of the interlocutors and consequently the entire drift of the passage. (1) In B34-5 Amuienshi inquires of Sinuhe the reason of his flight, hinting by means of the words that for this there must have been some political cause. B then continues without a break (ll. 36-37). As the text stands these words must apparently be taken as the continuation of Amuienshi's question, and we must translate with Maspero (*M. S.*, p. XXII) : "Est-ce qu'il serait survenu quelque chose à la cour, et Amenemhaît serait-il allé au ciel sans qu'on sût ce qui s'est passé à ce propos?" R59 however inserts after *in iw wn ḫpr't m ḫnw*. By this means we obtain a straightforward answer to Amuienshi's query; Sinuhe replies that Amenemmes had died, but that further details were unknown. (2) Later on, in B43, the question had even previously to the discovery of R been conjectured to belong to Amuienshi[2]; the confirmation of this conjecture is to be found in R67, where the words are prefixed to the question. Here M. Maspero accepts the sense given by R's reading, but considers that the explicit mention of the change of speaker was unnecessary.

The earlier insertion in R59 is discussed at length by M. Maspero, who finally rejects it in favour of the text of B (*M. S.*, p. XIX-XXV). I find to my great regret that an error of my own has been responsible for no small part of his argument. As we have already seen, R59-61 puts the reference to the aged monarch's death into the mouth of Sinuhe. It seemed natural therefore, on a first reading of the manuscript, to construe the words next following as a comment on the part of Amuienshi; and I had no hesitation in reading (*Sitzb.*, 3), *ḏdf* ap-

---

1. Quoted by MASPERO, *M. S.*, p. XIV, where the example is used, with the two others, to prove that this expression was "plus usitée aux débuts de la XVIIIe dynastie"; with this I cannot agree, as all three texts are clearly composed in the literary language, not in the vulgar dialect of the 18th. Dynasty. Nor do I understand the grounds for the statement that "procède d'une forme hiératique de ".

2. See *M. S.*, p. XXI.

pearing to me as the correct interpretation of the hieratic traces. Since however the sentences that follow *m iw-ms* clearly represent Sinuhe's words, it now became needful to assume that , or a similar equivalent, had fallen out between the end of R61 and the beginning of R62. This difficulty, coupled with M. Maspero's objections, led me to re-examine the original here with minute care. The result of the re-examination was to show that is not a possible reading, but that should be read; in fact precisely the same reading as we have in B37. In order to clear up this important point I must here go into palæographical details. My earlier reading was due to the fact that above in (R62) there is a very tiny trace, which I took to be the oblique part of the tail of ; the head of that sign seemed to be represented by a thick black stroke after . However if one examines the hieratic sign for elsewhere in the papyrus, it will be seen that the head is always very thin (e. g. R70, 71, 72). Moreover the tail of everywhere ends in a long thick, almost vertical stroke; of this some vestige would assuredly have been visible in the well-preserved line R62, had been the true reading in R61. These are ample grounds for rejecting the reading *ḏdf'*. The only possible alternative, so far as I can see, is to read as in B37; the black trace visible after *ḏd* may well be part of the ligature for *ni* that is found in R148-149, though it is rather thicker than we might have expected.

To turn now to the sense of the sentence, M. Maspero's rendering : "Je lui dis : 'Il n'en est rien'" will not bear the test of criticism. Here again the original error was mine; for in my preliminary article (*Sitzb.*, 3) I translated : "Er sagte zu mir : das ist nicht möglich." The objection to these renderings is twofold. (1) Though M. Maspero may be right in connecting *swt* etymologically with the old absolute pronoun (*M. S.*, p. xx)[2], in the language of the Middle Kingdom it is never anything but an enclitic particle, usually with adversative meaning (see below)[3]. (2) *M iw-ms* does not mean "pas possible" "unmöglich", but, as I have shown *Admonitions*, p. 22, is an adverbial expression appended to verbs of speaking with the sense "incorrectly", "falsely". Thus the real meaning of both in B and in R can only be that assigned to it by Erman, namely : "Ich aber antwortete lügnerisch" (see *M. S.*, p. xx, footnote 2).

The *crux* of R59-61 consists in the appearance that we have there two consecutive speeches of Sinuhe. The solution of the difficulty is that *ḏdni swt m iw-ms* is a parenthetic addition, designed simply and solely for the purpose of marking the exact place at which Sinuhe's answer to Amuienshi's question begins to deviate from the strict truth. The parenthetic nature of these words may be proved by a nice grammatical point. *Swt,* as I have remarked above, is an enclitic particle. Now since *swt*

1. There remains the trace above to be accounted for. I will admit that I cannot explain this away otherwise than by supposing it to be fortuitous.

2. Cf. the similar development of the Coptic ⲛ̄ⲧⲟϥ "however".

3. Even if *swt* were still employed as a pronoun, it could not have the neuter sense "das" but could only mean "he".

is enclitic, the words *dd-ni* are included in the contrast which it expresses, not excluded from that contrast : we cannot translate : "I said, but falsely", but only : "But then I said falsely[1]". In other words what Sinuhe said falsely (R 62 foll.) must be contrasted with something that he has previously said truly (R 60-61), i. e. the words [hieroglyphs] in R 59 are no erroneous interpolation, but part of the original text.

This may be thought to be pushing logical analysis too far, and I shall probably make my case both clearer and more convincing by discussing the sense of the entire passage. I shall follow the text of B, except for the insertion of *'ḥ'n dd-ni nf* (R 59) in B 36, and of *'ḥ'n dd-nf ḥft-i* (R 67) in B 43. The dialogue between Amuienshi and Sinuhe is opened by a question put by Amuienshi : "Wherefore art thou come hither? Had aught happened in the Residence?" (B 34-35). To the latter part of the query Sinuhe gives a direct and accurate answer, in which he recalls the state of affairs at the moment when he left the Libyan army[2] : — "Thereupon I said to him : Shetepebre had departed to the horizon (i. e. had died), and it was not known what had happened in the matter" (B 36-37). The motives of Sinuhe's own flight however needed more delicate handling, and in relating to the visitors of his tomb, many years after the event, the way in which this awkward point was evaded by him he does not shrink from admitting that he then prevaricated. "But then I said falsely : I had returned from the expedition to the land of Temhi, and a report was made to me (*wḥm-tw ni*); my reason was perturbed, my heart was not in my body, it took me away on the road of the desert[3]" (B 37-40). Now as B 1-2 tells us, though in somewhat obscure language, it is not true that the news of Amenemmes' death had been reported to Sinuhe himself; that news he had learnt only accidentally, by overhearing certain words, probably treasonable words, let fall by one of the royal children. Thus Sinuhe here deliberately misrepresents the real reason which led to his flight, and it is this misrepresentation that is alluded to by the parenthesis *dd-ni swt m iw-ms*. In the next sentences Sinuhe seeks to clear himself from a suspicion that would very

1. Note than [hieroglyphs] means rather more than merely "but"; it very distinctly contains a notion of *addition* besides that of *contrast*. Thus it corresponds to the Greek δέ when this has been preceded by μέν in a previous clause : e. g. in such common phrases as [hieroglyphs] "*but again* he whe shall not...". A good instance that will bring out my point is [hieroglyphs] *Eloquent Peasant*, B 1, 81 : *op. cit.*, R 129, paraphrases this with [hieroglyphs], where *ḥn'* helps out the sense of addition already connoted by *swt*. Again, *op. cit.*, B 1, 123 : [hieroglyphs] "Moreover thou art sated", is instructive; there the sense of contrast is reduced to a minimum. In modern languages, the French particle "or" seems to me most nearly to correspond to the Egyptian *swt*. From these remarks it will be clear why I render : "But *then* I said falsely" — not merely : "But I said falsely".

2. When I wrote my German translation, I had not yet realized that *rḫ-ntw* referred to this moment; my rendering "man weiss nicht, was dabei vorgefallen ist" employs the wrong tense, to the serious detriment of the sense.

3. Or "of flight".

naturally arise in the mind of Amuienshi; he denies that his flight was due to any disgrace incurred by him whilst serving in the Egyptian army :—"I had not been talked of, none had spat [in] my [face], I had heard no word of reproach, nor had my name been heard in the mouth of the herald" (B 40-42). He then sums up : "I know not what brought me to this land, it was as the counsel of God" (B 42-43). Amuienshi does not appear to have troubled himself further as to Sinuhe's motives, but goes on to make enquiries about the more interesting question of political conditions in Egypt :—"Then he said to me : How fares that land without that excellent god, fear of whom pervaded the lands like (the fear of) Sekhmet in a year of pestilence" (B 43-45). This query gives Sinuhe an opportunity of eulogizing the young king Kheperkere, which he does in a passage occupying nearly thirty lines.

The explanation of the context above set forth is, so far as I can see, the only one which satisfies both the requirements of philology and those of the sense. It is not a little different from the interpretation which I originally proposed, so that some of M. Maspero's objections no longer require an answer. I shall now deal briefly with his own view of the passage and with those of his criticisms which still apply to my revised translation. M. Maspero translates B 34-39, ignoring the insertion in R 59, thus :—"Il me dit : 'Comment se fait-il que tu en sois arrivé là? Est-ce qu'il serait survenu quelque chose à la cour, et Amenemhaît serait-il allé au ciel sans qu'on sût ce qui s'est passé à ce propos?' Je lui dis : 'Il n'en est rien. Lorsque je vins dans cette armée du pays des Timahiou et que cela me fut annoncé, mon esprit s'échappa[1].'" I have already shown that the translation : "Je lui dis : 'Il n'en est rien'" is philologically indefensible. The minimum of alteration with which M. Maspero's rendering can be made at all defensible is to substitute for these words the sentence : "Or, j'ai parlé d'une façon mensongère." With this change the sense is no longer very satisfactory : Sinuhe would then have passed over the allusion to the king's death in complete silence, a very strange proceeding, seeing what a large portion of Amuienshi's question is, on M. Maspero's view, devoted to it. Moreover, to construe the nominal sentence *Sḥtp-ib-rʿ wḏꜣw r iḫwt, n rḫ-ntw ḫpr-t ḥr-s* as a question is, to my mind, a very dubious possibility from a grammatical point of view; one might certainly have expected 𓇋𓈖𓇋𓐍 by way of introduction to this sentence.

I repeat, I can see no loophole of escape from the conclusion that the words : "Shetepebre had gone to the horizon, and it was not known what had happened in the matter" belong to Sinuhe. That Sinuhe should give this information to the Syrian prince will not appear strange when it is noted that he later (B 46), in answer to a question, relates the accession of Kheperkere. Above all things let it be remembered that we are dealing with a tale, and that the same respect for probabilities cannot be demanded from an imperfect work of fiction as from a sober narrative of facts. Still I will admit that so long as *ḏdf ni swt m iw-ms* was translated : "He said to me : that is impossible!" we were dangerously near the boundaryline of what is legitimate

1. *M. S.*, p. XXII.

in this respect. The prince Amuienshi may have been, indeed seems to have been, rather ill-informed as to Egyptian affairs, but to make him deny or at least doubt Sinuhe's first-hand information is perhaps too crass an improbability even for a tale. With the change of the reading and the translation this objection, in which I consider M. Maspero to have been wholly justified (*M. S.*, p. XXII), is now happily disposed of.

Now how are the two omissions in B (our starting-point in this lengthy discussion) to be explained? With regard to the second, the omission of in B 43, I have no suggestion to offer; but since scholars are agreed that these words must be either inserted or else understood in that line, we need scarcely trouble ourselves further with the question. On the other hand a very plausible reason at once suggests itself for the omission of in B 36. The scribe of B was puzzled, as we have been ourselves, by the apparent anomaly of two successive speeches of Sinuhe, without an intervening question on the part of Amuienshi. He did not recognize, as I hope my readers now do, that *ḏd-ni swt m iw-ms,* is nothing but a parenthesis. So he thought to improve the text by omitting *ʿḥʿn ḏd-ni nf;* the next words thus became a part of the question put by Amuienshi. The sense of the passage was spoilt (that at least is my opinion), but a correct alternation of question and answer was gained.

M. Maspero explains the second omission, in B 43, as not really an error at all. He considers (*M. S.*, p. XXIII) that the formula intimating a change of speaker need not, in a poetical work like the tale of Sinuhe, be actually inserted. It is my own impression that Egyptian taste would have required some consistency in such a matter; I feel it to be probable that the scribe of B, if he had *intended* to dispense with the formula *ʿḥʿn ḏd-nf ḫft-i* in B 43, would have also omitted the phrases "he said to me" and "I said to him" in B 34 and B 45. But this is a matter of literary judgment, and in such questions we have the best of reasons for deferring to M. Maspero's opinion. I will only point out that if the change of speaker can be implicitly read into B 43 it can be so also in B 36, so that my attribution of B 36-37 to Sinuhe would, if we accept M. Maspero's decision on the point here under discussion, still be a possible theory even without the insertion of from R 59.

We must now turn our attention to the less crucial differences which B and R reveal in this passage. The version of B (with the necessary emendations) has already been given in translation; in place of it R has the following sentences :—"When [I was] in the army of the land of Temhi, a report was made to me; my reason was perturbed, it carried me away on the road of the desert (?). Yet had I not been [spat upon], men had not talked against my face *(sic)*, but [it was as a dream (?)], as though a man of the Delta marshes should see himself in Elephantine, or a man of the swamps in Nubian land." Which of the two versions is to be preferred is more a matter of taste than a subject for serious discussion; both yield substantially the same sense[1], and both contain phrases absent from the other in this part of the

1. M. Maspero attempts to distinguish between the sense of the two versions (*M. S.*, p. XXII-XXIII) but to my mind wholly without success.

tale, but re-appearing in subsequent passages. For my own part I incline to give the preference to B, since that manuscript gives a more flowing text than R. After this long discussion of the general drift of the passage I now pass to philological details.

*36.* — B ; R 60 . How the lacuna in R ought to be filled I do not know; hardly *mꜣʿ-ḫrw*.

*37.* — For the words *ḏd-ni swt m iw-ms*, see above.

*38.* — B has (read ) ; R 62 . The text of B must be translated : "I had returned from the expedition to (lit. "of") the land of Temhi." The word is quite correctly written, and means not "warship" but "expedition". The credit of having first recognized this meaning is due to Mr. Griffith (*Hieroglyphs*, p. 14), who points out to me that it affords the true explanation of *Weni*, 40-42 : "I brought them (i.e. the sarcophagus, doorposts, lintel, etc.) downstream to the Pyramid 'Merenre shines forth beautiful' in 6 *wsḫt*-boats, 3 *sꜣṯ*-boats and 3 .....-boats in one expedition; never had Ebhat and Elephantine been achieved in one expedition under any former kings." Erman's rendering "bei (?) (nur) einem einzigen Kriegsschiff" (*Ä. Z.*, 20 [1882], 23) not only is open to the objection that never occurs elsewhere in the sense of "warship", but also postulates an unknown use of the preposition [1]; here is clearly used in its temporal sense (cf. "in seven months", *Urkunden*, I, 124; similarly, *Shipwrecked Sailor*, 168) and the point of the sentence is that *two* quarries, that of Elephantine and that of Ebhat, had been worked in *one single* expedition; herein lay the singularity of Weni's feat[2]. Cf. too (? read ) "death is before me today like a trodden way (?)[3], as when men return to their houses from an expedition", *Lebensmüde*, 136-138. *Mšʿ* "expedition" may also be written without , cf. "ye tell of your travels to your wives", *Ä. Z.*, 39 (1901), 118 (stele in Stuttgart); "when the Sovereign is on an expedition", NEWBERRY, *The Life of Rekmara*, p. 26 (from the tomb of *'Imnmipt*); the later equivalents are (e.g. *Wenamon*), 2, 22, Coptic ⲙⲟⲟϣⲉ. The verb *mšʿ* (ⲙⲟⲟϣⲉ) from which the noun "expedition" is derived, is also found written with the soldier and the ship; I am indebted to Dr. Möller for the following instances from the quarries of Hat-nub :

1. The proportioning or distributive preposition "to", German "bei", "auf", is in Egyptian represented by .

2. With the usual translation the mention of Elephantine here would be absurdly tautologous, as Elephantine had always to be passed on the way to Ebhat. On the other hand the delay which was caused by the hewing of the red granite lintel and doorposts at Assuan would obviously greatly enhance the magnitude of Weni's enterprise.

3. The Ms. reading, which Erman takes as referring to the welcome rains that relieve the dryness of the desert wady, does not suit the second half of the verse. For *wꜣt ḥyt*, see my *Admonitions*, p. 38.

"its troops entered amongst the common folk, and sat in their houses, they made no expeditions in (my?) time through (? read for ) fear of the king's house", *Hatnub*, 24 = *Blackden-Frazer*, 8; "when I made an expedition they came (*spr-tw*) to praise me every year", *ibid.*, 38. — In R 62 [ ] barely fills the lacuna, but I have no other suggestion. , thus written, can hardly be "expedition", though the Stuttgart stele above quoted has in that sense. As a tentative translation I propose: "when I was in the army against (lit. "belonging to") the land of Temhi." B's text seems preferable.

*38-39.* — B ; the verb *ꜣd(w)* occurs elsewhere only in the phrase B 255, and is not to be identified with "to be enraged", "perturbed", the meaning of which suits *ib*, but does not suit *ḥʿw*. R gives the better reading , this being a rare verb used of the heart, *Ebers*, 102, 7, and of flesh in *Destruction of men (Sethos)*, 29; R., *I. H.*, 145, 56. Had R been preserved in the passage corresponding to B 255, it would doubtless have been found to give *ꜣhd(w)* in place of *ꜣd(w)* the reading of B.

*39.* — in B is obviously identical with , B 255; the meaningless determinatives are due to some wrong interpretation of *ntf* (so too Masp., *M. S.*, p. viii). For the phrase, cf. *Anast. IV*, 5, 3. — This clause in absent from R.

*40.* — B ; R 63 [ ] . *Wʿr-t* in both Mss. is probably not the word for "flight" that occurs often in the tale of Sinuhe (Erm. "auf den Wegen der Flucht" and similarly Gr., Masp.), but a geographical term. As such, *wʿr-t* is known (1) either in an administrative sense, e. g. , (see Griffith, *Kahun Papyri*, p. 21), or (2) as a designation for the desert-plateau where tombs were built, cf. *Siut*, III, 1; similarly, *op. cit.*, pl. 20; *Bersheh*, II, 21; *Sheikh Said*, 30; and the frequent expressions and on funerary stelæ (see Br., *Dict. Géogr.*, p. 1128-9); (3) here *wʿr-t* must have a wider signification "desert-plateau" or the like, and the same meaning seems required by the parallelism in B 257 "thou hast trodden the foreign lands, thou hast traversed the desert wastes"; whether the word , which seems to mean "desert" in *Salt 124*, 2, 7; L. *D.*, III, 140 b, 3 (Redesieh), should be read *wʿr-(t)*, is rather uncertain. — in R is obviously a superior reading to of B.

*40-41.* — B ; R 64 . The restoration of B is almost certain; the traces suit, and the reading *r ḥr-i* is suggested by R. — The rare word *wfꜣ* seems to mean "to talk about"; the clearest instance is *Rekhmere,* 8, 29, where my own collation of the original gives "I was the subject ("talk", a substantive) of all conversation". In *Piankhi,* 111, a somewhat obscure passage, the prince Peteese first appears to lay a curse upon whosoever should conceal his wealth from the king, and then goes on to say that he has done this in the consciousness that when his deeds have been examined and talked about, he will be found to have concealed nothing; "This have I devised (or "said")[1], in order that ye may discuss this your servant in all that ye know concerning me; then shall ye say whether I have concealed from his Majesty anything belonging to the house of my father". Further, *Prisse,* 5, 14, "do not keep silence, when he speaks evil; great will be the talk (of thee) on the part of the listeners, and thy name will be fair in the opinion of princes". Lastly, *Eloquent Peasant,* B 108, , is wholly obscure. From these examples it seems plain that *n wfꜣ-twi*[2] in B should be rendered : "I was not talked of", the context showing that depreciatory talk, gossip, is here meant. — means "to spit" (*Pyr.*, *pśg*), the later equivalent being *pgs* with metathesis, cf. ⲡⲁϭⲥⲉ "spittle"; and the text of B should therefore be translated : "no one spat in my face"[3]. — The first half of the version substituted by R *n* [*psg-*]*twi* "I was not spat at" is quite defensible, as the *Pyramidtexts* always give to *psg* the transitive sense "bespucken", cf. *Pyr.*, 142; other examples, 521, 2055, 2056. However *wfꜣ-tw r ḥr-i* yields no good sense.

*41-42.* — B ; R lacks these words, which are reiterated in B 227-228. — *Ts-ḥwrw* only here; the expression must mean "insult", "reproach", cf. the causative *sḥwr;* in *Eloquent Peasant,* B 1, 106, 168, 263 (= B 2, 18) means "ignominy", "disgrace", or the like. — The exact meaning of the title *wḥmw* here is not clear; there were local functionaries (apparently vested with judicial powers *Pap. Kahun,* 34, 38)

1. Breasted (*Ancient Records,* IV, 439) and Griffith (*Egyptian Literature,* p. 5291) translate : "So be it to me"; I doubt whether this rendering is justifiable.

2. In R the passive ending *-tw* is everywhere written in full. B on the contrary always writes it defectively before suffixes (so here, 40, 53, 72, 198, 200, 233, 234); before nominal subject or impersonally the ending is sometimes fully (e. g. 37, 38, 183, 184, 191, 192), sometimes defectively (e. g. 90, 91, 181, 205, 227, 260) written.

3. Surely M. Maspero is confounding *psg* with when he translates : "il ne me piqua point", *M. S.*, p. XXII, and in the index *sub voce.*

that bore this name, but it was also applied to the military officer who reported to the king deeds of prowess performed on the battle-field (e. g. *Urkunden,* IV, 3).

*42-43.* — "I know not what brought me to this land; it was as it were the disposition of God". These words form the conclusion of Sinuhe's speech in B; they are omitted in R, which substitutes for them some sentences that are found again in B 224-226 (see the note there). — For the indirect question : "I know not what brought me to this country" Egyptian idiom employs the masculine participle; in illustration of the gender, cf. *Shipwrecked Sailor,* 70-71, and on the participle, see SETHE, *Verbum,* II, § 751.

*43.* — Before the question *wnn ỉr̯f tꜣ pf mi mi,* R 67 rightly (see above) inserts . *Ḥft* here means little more than "to"; cf. below B 75 and SETHE, *Die Einsetzung des Veziers,* note 7. Similarly *Rekhmere,* 7, 10.

*43-44.* — B has , with an utterly false spelling of "without", and with a superfluous suffix. R 68 [ ] is rather better, though not quite correct.

*44-45.* — *Wnnw snd-f ḫt ḫꜣs-wt,* for the construction, see SETHE, *Verbum,* II, § 745. — B; R 69[1] "like Sekhmet in the year of pestilence"; cf. *Rec. de Trav.*, 15, p. 179 (Konosso, Thutmose IV); *rnp-t n idw,* L., *D.*, II, 150 a, 6. In the *Eloquent Peasant,* B 1, 120, a goddess is named , and in the tomb of the Vizier *Intf-iḳr* at Thebes (*temp.* Senwosret I) a hymn begins with the words : . On *idw* see further the note, *Admonitions,* p. 25.

*45.* — ; *ri* emphasizes the first person of the verb, just as and (later for all persons) often emphasize the second and third (see ERMAN, *Æg. Gram.*[2], § 372). Sethe tells me that can be illustrated from the *Pyramidtexts* (e. g. 1124, 1125); in later times it is rare, the only example that I have been able to find being "look at me, I have proved it in my own person", WEILL, *Sinai,* 63, 5.

*46.* — B ; R 70 more correctly , which moreover is the spelling below in B 118. On the particle *nḥmn,* see SPIEGELBERG, *Rec. de Trav.*, 24, p. 35, and my note, *Ä. Z.*, 43 [1906], p. 159-160.

*48.* — For the preponderative use of "before him", "superior to him", see SETHE, *Die Einsetzung des Veziers,* note 175.

, cf. the epithets (? read ) (? read ) *Siut,* I, 182; the context there and in the present passage

---

1. In my edition of the text I have wrongly transcribed the sign for with ; the former has here the same shape as in the *Ebers papyrus* (79, 13). R 14, 16, has a totally different sign for *tḥnw,* which of course in its older forms has nothing to do with the sky , see MÖLLER, *Hieratische Paläographie,* I, no. 417.

(the next words are *ỉḳr sḫrw, mnḫ wd-t mdw* "excellent of counsels, effective in commands") suggests that MASPERO's rendering : "un maître de sagesse[1]" is not far out (so too GR.). *Sꜣ-t* must be the infinitive of a verb 3æ infirmæ; (1) with this view agree the geminated forms (participles) found in the following instances *Mission,* XV, 10, 3 (Luxor, epithets of Amenophis III); Louvre C 167; *Hat-nub,* 8, 2; Louvre C 174 (= CAPART, *Recueil,* I, 22); further, cf. Louvre C 26, 13. Less comprehensible examples of the geminated from occur also *Prisse,* 12, 10; 15, 12; *Leiden,* V 4, 5. 6. From the frequency with which the double ꜣ occurs the doubt arises as to whether *sꜣꜣ* is not a verb 2æ gem.; in this case *sꜣ-t* in the *Sinuhe* and *Siut* passages could not well be connected with it. (2) The alternative is to translate, as ERMAN does, "der Sättiger", d. h. seines Volkes, deriving *sꜣ-t* here from *sꜣw,* ⲥⲉⲓ, saturare. This however does not give good sense.

*50-51.* — "He subdued the foreign lands, while his father was within his palace; and he reported what had been commanded to him to be done." So B; *šꜣ-t,* thus spelt, is probably passive participle (cf. B 126) and *ḫpr* is, as often, the passive of (cf. fieri). R 75 gives "and he (Sesostris) reported to him (Amenemmes) what he (A.) decreed should be done". The addition of *nf* certainly improves the text, but *šꜣt-nf* is urgently needed, whether this be construed as a passive participle ("what was decreed to him") or whether it be taken as the relative form ("what he had decreed").

*51-52.* — , cf. , epithets of Thutmose III, *Urkunden,* IV, 809 (Wady Halfa).

*52.* — , so too *Urkunden,* IV, 809, as continuation of the words quoted in the last note[2].

*52-53.* — B "when he is seen charging the Re-pedtiu, and approaching the mellay (?)". R 77 gives, as usual, the fuller writing . *Hꜣ* transitively, cf. R 84, B 61; for *Ri-pdtiw,* a derivative of *pdtiw* the meaning of which is not clear, cf. B 61 = R 85. — Instead of *ḫʿm-f ri-ḏꜣw* R 78 gives ; the obscurity of *ri-ḏꜣw* makes it impossible to decide which Ms. has the better reading. For or the following passages may be compared : (1) transitively, cf. R 164 = "he drew nigh me", B 137; "evil came not nigh them", *Harris I,* 77, 10; "nought hostile cometh nigh thee", *Anast. III,* 4, 6;

1. *Sꜣ-t* is of course to be connected neither with *sꜣ* nor with *sꜣr-t.*

2. The Wady Halfa inscription writes ; the last is derived from a misunderstood hieratic .

(2) with [hieroglyphs], cf. [hieroglyphs] "it shall be approached by no man", L., *D.*, III, 140 c, 17 (Redesieh); [hieroglyphs] "the evils that approach his heart", *Pap. Leiden* 345, recto, G 2, 3; (3) with [hieroglyphs] (like *tkn*, *ʿḳ*, *ʿr*, etc.), cf. [hieroglyphs] "their noses approaching the ground", *Inscr. dédic.*, 34. — [hieroglyphs], cf. [hieroglyphs] "captain of foreign troops, of good counsel in the encounter (?)", Mar., *Abyd.*, I, 53; [hieroglyphs] "a king by whom men boast, giving due meed to[1] his hands in encounter (?)", *Amada Stele*, 6; in the phrase [hieroglyphs] *Urkunden*, IV, 657, *ri-ḏꜣw* cannot be translated "mellay", "encounter" unless *m* be emended before it; otherwise, and if Sethe's restoration be correct, *ri-ḏꜣw* must here be an abstract word parallel to, and co-ordinated with, *pḥti Stḫ*. No other examples of the word occur.

*54-55.* — B [hieroglyphs]; for the last word R 79 has [hieroglyphs]. Both Mss. are at fault, but B is nearer to the archetype than R; we must clearly emend [hieroglyphs] "his enemies cannot order their ranks", for *ṯs skw* see my *Admonitions*, p. 20.

*55.* — [hieroglyphs], which is often found in the literal sense of "washing the face" (e. g. *Pyr.* 1443, 2067; *Ebers*, 87, 12), occurs nowhere except here in a metaphorical sense. Perhaps it has the same meaning as [hieroglyphs] "rejoicing", "exulting", on which see B 149, note.

[hieroglyphs] B; [hieroglyphs] R 80. The absence of ꜣ after *šꜣ* in B is contrary to rule; nevertheless the reading of B should be given the preference, as it is supported by later parallels, cf. [hieroglyphs] Piehl, *Inscr. hiér.*, II, 104, and twice similarly in Naville, *Mythe d'Horus*, 2. Spiegelberg quotes an instance of ⲧⲱϣ meaning "to smash", *Rec. de Trav.*, 23, p. 205; and *tš* is used of "grinding" corn to make beer *Destruction of Men* (Sethos), 18. — *Tšb* in R is an unknown word.

*55-56.* — [hieroglyphs] "none can stand in his presence", cf. *Urkunden*, IV, 187 (Thutmose III); *Piankhi*, 95; *Urkunden*, II, 14 (stele of the satrap); Rochemonteix, *Edfou*, I, 150.

*56.* — For [hieroglyphs] "wide of paces", cf. [hieroglyphs] L., *D.*, II, 138 d (Hammamat, collated), — [hieroglyphs] "he destroys the fugitive", B; R 81 has [hieroglyphs] "he shoots (pierces) the fugitive". [hieroglyphs] and [hieroglyphs] are extremely similar in hieratic, whence the variants of our Mss. *Sk*, the reading of B, should be preferred, as it is supported by the Hammamat text above quoted; moreover the omission of *t* in [hieroglyphs] is unusual.

*57.* — "There is no end for him who turns his back to him", i. e. perhaps, the fugitive whom he pursues never reaches his goal of safety. *Di sꜣ n* "to turn

1. Lit. "equivalent to".

the back to", cf. L., *D.*, II, 136 h (Semneh stele); *Piankhi*, 13; *Urkunden*, II, 13 (stele of the satrap).

*57-58.* — "he is persistent in the moment of driving back". only here. *Sꜣsꜣ* is a transitive verb[1] possibly derived from *sꜣ* "back", cf. "I travelled down stream in strength to drive back the Asiatics", *Carnarvon tablet*, 10 (Hyksos period); "I repulsed him, I destroyed his wall", *ibid.*, 14.

*58.* — For (so too G) I can find no good parallel[2]; the probable sense is "he is one who always returns (to the fray), he does not turn his back".

*58-59.* — , cf. Louvre C 123 (Ptolemaic); for *wmt ib* (or *wmt ḥꜣti*), cf. further *Brit. Mus.* 334; R., *I. H.*, 206; *op. cit.*, 239, 34 = *Sall. III*, 3, 7; *Urkunden*, II, 13 (stele of the satrap).

*59.* — "he does not allow lassitude to enter his heart". The analogy of the sentence (*Urkunden*, IV, 1077) shows that must here, in spite of the determinative , be an abstract "lassitude", "sloth". For similar abstracts, perhaps ending in *-w* and therefore sometimes written as plurals, cf. (see B 17-18, note), "misery", *Urkunden*, IV, 1076; "height"; "depth"; (see B 17-18, note); "proximity"; "loss"; "cold"; "heat" (cf. *Admonitions*, 11, 13); "beauty". — M. Maspero is hardly justified in regarding as simply synonymous with (*M. S.*, p. 128, 131).

*60.* — B has ; R 84-5 ; G . The reading *sḫm-ḥr* (or *ib*?) in G cannot be upheld against *wd ḥr*, the common reading of R and B. *Wd ḥr* occurs nowhere else; literally "thrusting forward the face", i. e. "eager" or "bold". In the following temporal clause the text of R should be accepted, and rendered : "when he attacks the Easterners"; for transitively, see B 52-53, note, and *hꜣb* in G is probably a corruption of it (see below B 73, note). The version of B is untranslatable, being an unknown word[3]; moreover for we require in the temporal clause , cf. B 52. 59, and see Sethe, *Verbum*, II, § 253, 2.

1. In one example (Golén, *Hammamat*, 10, 2) *sꜣsꜣ* might have an intransitive sense "to go forward (?)" "its (the gazelle's) eyes looked straight ahead (?)"; but it is also possible to retain the transitive sense here, and to render "its eyes seeing and driving back" (i. e. boldly confronting the people as it approached).

2. For , Möller, *Hier. Pal.*, 1, no. 89, reads (the eye-brow); but the original seems to me here to have but an exaggerated form of , cf. *op. cit.*, no. 121, the examples from the *Lebensmüde* and the *Eloquent Peasant*.

3. It can hardly be connected with "to delay", as is done by Griffith ("when he seeth hesitation"). I am ignorant of the grounds for the rendering "assaillir" (Maspero, *M. S.*, p. 51).

*60-61.* — B and R here differ considerably, and the text of R being incomplete, it is impossible to judge between them. B has "his joy is to attack the Re-pedtiu"; is an afterthought of the scribe and should in any case be omitted; for the construction, cf. *Eloquent Peasant,* B 1, 176. To this version of B it may be objected that the transitive use of occurred in the very last sentence, if we there accept, as we have done, the reading of R; the repetition of the word so soon afterwards would be very awkward[1]. — The version of R, so far as it is preserved, is "[He is ..... to] plunder the Re-pedtiu". I hold M. Maspero's suggestion to be impossible, as is never so spelt, nor does it seem to have acquired the meaning "to rejoice" in the time of the M. K. (see my note on the word, *Ä. Z.*, 45 [1909], 129).

*61.* — R 86 omits the suffixes in *ikm-f* and *titi-f* of B, which is supported by G; the preference must be given to the latter. — For *ṯꜣw* in the Middle Kingdom, cf. *Eloquent Peasant,* R 72 = B 1, 22; other examples, *Westcar,* 4, 2; 12, 17; the geminated form in the epithet of a god "he who snatches away souls", *Harhotep,* 550. Of taking up, seizing, weapons, in N. K. texts, e. g. *ÄZ.*, 44 (1907), 38.

*61-62.* — B "he does not repeat when (?) he kills"; note that has neither the literal meaning "arm", nor yet a derivative sense "stroke", but *wḥm-ʿ* is an idiomatic compound for "to repeat", cf. *m wḥm-ʿ* "again", *Urkunden,* IV, 4. 114. — R 86-87 has the reading "he does not repeat to kill", i. e. he kills once and for all. Both versions are possible, but that of R seems more direct and for this reason superior.

*62-63.* — The sentences "there is none who can turn his arrow, there is none who can draw his bow" are omitted by R, but are probably part of the original text. It should be observed that does not mean "'to escape from" (Erman, "entgehen") but "to make to cease", "check" (Masp., "détourner", Gr., "turn"). — The second clause recurs in the *Amada stele* (line 2), and recalls a passage of Herodotus (III, 21), see Schäfer, *Ä. Z.*, 38 (1900), 66-67.

*63-64.* — B has ; R 87-88, completed by G, gives . The objection to B's reading is that the first clause cannot be brought into relation with the king here described without the violent supplying of a conjunction at the beginning of the second clause; M. Maspero renders (*M. S.*, p. xvi) : "Les archers libyens tournent dos, *car* ses bras sont comme les âmes de la grande déesse." The text of R : "the foreigners flee before him as (before) the might of the Great one" is in my opinion vastly superior.

1. It would hardly help matters to emend *mꜣꜣ-f* for *mꜣ-f* in B 60 = *hꜣ-f* in R 84; for there a similar objection would arise, since *mꜣꜣ-f* precedes in B 59.

*64.* — B ; R 88-89 < > [ ] , the suffix in *ʿḥ3-f* being supplied from G. The reading of R (and G) gives a coherent sense "he fights without end", *m ḫmt* "without" being possibly spelt as in R 68 (see the note thereupon). The reading of B might be rendered : "he fights and plans the end", a meaningless translation[1].

*64-65.* — B ; R, which is here damaged, had a similar text. The earlier translations followed by my own, render : "he spares not, and there is naught left over". But the sense "to spare" is not proved for *s3w* "to keep". One might perhaps suggest "he does not lag" (see below note on B 151). In the negative ought be written .

*65.* — in B is an unusual spelling; R 80 [ ].

*66.* — B ; R 90 which is confirmed by G [ ] . In my translation I have followed B and rendered like my predecessors : "der sich Liebe erobert hat". This involves a questionable use of *iṯ*, and it may be asked whether the preference should not be given to the reading of R, which might be interpreted[2] either (1) "he has conquered through love" or (2) "he excels in love"; for *iṯ* "to excel" with object, cf. *Anast. I*, 5, 2.

*66-67.* — B (sic) (sic); so too R 91-92, except that *sw nt* is lost and that *ḥʿw* is replaced by the correct [ ]. The suffix *-sn* here is used κατὰ σύνεσιν owing to the collective sense of [3].

*67-68.* — "men and women go by (?), rejoicing over him, so long as he is king". In the first place it must be noted that *iwf m stn* cannot be taken as a principal clause, as has hitherto been done; "he is king" would be or ; the words are evidently a temporal qualification of the preceding sentence "while he is king", "so long as he is king". — must, as Sethe points out, be an abstract infinitival form like ; for the plural strokes, see SETHE, *Verbum*, II, § 603. The simple verb from which it is derived is not common : cf. the but half-intelligible epithets of king Dudmose [ ] [4] *Proc. S. B. A.*, 15 (1893), 495 (plate 5); "the southern shrine praises thee, the northern shrine extols thee", PETRIE, *Rifeh and Gizeh*, XIII, F; Griffith quotes a possible demotic example, *Rylands Papyri*, p. 366, and one may perhaps adduce the personal name . The

---

1. M. Maspero reads wrongly in B *ḫmt rn-f* (*M. S.*, p. 8).

2. M. Maspero renders R : "il s'est emparé des affections" (*M. S.*, p. XIV), but I doubt if *m* can be used with *iṯ* partitively, or on the analogy of *sḫm m*.

3. M. Maspero's criticism of the passage (*M. S.*, p. XV) fails through his erroneous reading for in B.

4. Read .

noun *rnnwt* must thus mean "joy", "exultation", and is construed, on the analogy of *ḥ'* "to rejoice" with a following *m*[1]. — The *crux* of the passage is in reality *sw3* [2]. Elsewhere *sw3 ḥr* always signifies "to pass by"; this yielding no meaning here, it becomes necessary to separate *ḥr* from *sw3* and to assign to the preposition its frequent sense of concomitant action "engaged in" *sw3* being interpreted absolutely in a temporal sense[3] "to go by". Tolerable sense is thus obtained : "Men and women pass by (i. e. live and die), exulting over him, so long as he is king."

*68.* — in B is a vicious spelling. — For the image employed, see ERMAN, *Lebensmüde*, p. 48.

*69.* — is the reading of B, and is quite unintelligible as it stands; M. Maspero emends "<his diadems> are on him since he was born" (*M. S.*, p. xv); but "on him" instead of "on his head" is awkward. With the reading of R 93 "his faced was directed towards it (i. e. being king) since he was born" emendation becomes unnecessary.

"he multiplies what was born together with him", i. e. he leaves Egypt more populous than it was at the time of his birth". Cf. the Horus-names and .

*70.* — R 94 appears to have read ; this is less idiomatic than in B, for the construction of which cf. B 187, note.

In of B "how joyful" is an afterthought of the scribe; it is not supported by R 95 nor is an exclamation at all appropriate in this descriptive context.

*71-73.* — B gives (*sic*) ; R is here much damaged, but seems to have had a sign between and , and rightly interprets of B as . Sinuhe has now reached the end of his description of Kheperke, and here goes on to speak of the policy that the new monarch will pursue; this is followed by advice to Amuienshi to cultivate friendly relations with Pharaoh. The translations of M. Maspero and Professor Erman are practically identical : "Il prendra les pays du Midi et ne désire-t-il pas les pays du Nord (ERM., "wird er nicht auch an die nördlichen Völker denken")? Il a été créé pour frapper les Saatiou et pour écraser les Nomiou-shâîou." Now a primary and insurmountable difficulty is that does not mean "désirer" transitively, nor yet "denken an"; everywhere that it occurs it means "to think out", "devise", and though one can devise an action (infinitive) one cannot "devise countries", or at

1. Dévaud discusses the word, *Sphinx*, 13, p. 85-88, identifying it with the hebrew רננות. Curious as is the coincidence of meaning and sound, I do not consider it justifiable to offer an explanation from Semitic for a word that can be explained at least as well from Egyptian itself.

2. Not *pḫr* (so MASP., *M. S.*, p. 90) which, so far as I am aware, is never determined or abbreviated in this way.

3. The temporal sense of *sw3* is not uncommon, and is suggested by the following temporal clause, which qualifies it with precision.

all events that cannot be what is meant here. A further argument against connecting *kꜣ* in with *kꜣ-t* "to devise" is that after the negative (Sethe, *Verbum*, II, § 145) the geminated form would be required[1]. Consequently the division of words to be adopted is *n nkꜣ-f* and R 96 should probably be restored ; *nkꜣ m*, as I have shown, *Admonitions*, p. 101, means "to meditate upon". The most straightforward way of translating these words is to render : "he does not think about the northern lands". To interpret a negative sentence as a rhetorical question because the negation does not seem to fit is a dangerous expedient and one which must always excite suspicion. Here there is an obvious reason why Sinuhe should say that the king has no plans of aggression against Syria : he is no longer engaged in describing the prowess of Sesostris, but is forecasting the king's probable foreign policy[2]; this he does in a manner reassuring to Amuienshi. However if the next sentence be translated : "il a été créé pour frapper les Saatiou et pour écraser les Nomiou-shâîou", it will be seen to stand in a quite intolerable contradiction to what precedes. To this translation I object on several grounds : (1) the description of the king ended *before* the words : "he will conquer the southern lands; why should Sinuhe return to it here? (2) "he has been made" is strange both as an expression (one expects *ḳmꜣ* or *msy*) and in tense ("he has been made" would rather be ); (3) the last sentence so vividly recalls B 17 = R 43, that it is difficult to believe that there is not here also a reference to the "Wall of the Prince". I am thus led to conjecture that at a very early date some such words as < > dropped out of the text before ; one may even guess that the variant which C and G give for *inbw ḥkꜣ* in B 17 is due not merely to mistaken transcription of the hieratic, but to an untimely recollection of this later passage. The sense obtained by this conjecture is good; that Kheperkere can afford to disregard his northern frontier would then be explained : "for the wall of his father has been built to smite the Asiatics and to overthrow the Sand-farers". I am aware that it is a venturesome course to emend the text where B and R are in agreement, as here; but for the present I see no other solution of the difficulties above specified.

*73.* — For of B we have in R 98. I prefer the latter reading, as Amuienshi could hardly be expected to leave his own country to visit the Pharaoh, though it might well be proposed that he should send him an embassy. For the confusion of *hꜣ* and *hꜣb* in Mss., cf. above B 60, note; *Admonitions*, p. 43, the note on 5, 10.

*74.* — *M šny, wꜣ r ḥm-f;* for *wꜣ r*, see my remarks, *Admonitions*, p. 53. — "he never fails to do good"; the double negative (cf. the Greek οὐ μή) is a characteristic Egyptian idiom, cf. *Urkunden*, IV, 519; *Urkunden*, IV, 123;

1. This observation I owe to Prof. Sethe.
2. The change to the future tense marks the end of the descriptive passage.

Louvre C 15; and with other negative words often in *Wenamon*, see Erman, *Ä. Z.*, 38 (1900), 8, footnote 1.

*75-77.* — The elaborate description of the young king Sesostris, extending from B 47 to B 72, somewhat obscures the drift of the dialogue into which it is inserted, and it will be well here to recall the main points. Amuienshi questions Sinuhe as to the cause of his flight from Egypt, and hazards the conjecture that some political event lay at the root of the matter (B 34-36). Sinuhe answers by telling the news of Amenemhet I's death, and then proceeds to give a distorted account of the occurrences which led to his own exile (B 36-43). To this Amuienshi, more interested in politics than in Sinuhe's disingenuous excuses, replies by asking how Egypt fares without its great ruler, of whose decease he has just heard (B 43-45). Sinuhe reassures the prince and announces to him the accession of Senwosret I, whose praises he loudly sings, concluding with the recommendation to Amuienshi to send an embassy for the purpose of conciliating his mighty neighbour (B 46-75). In answer to Sinuhe's long tirade Amuienshi expresses his satisfaction that Egyptian affairs have taken so happy a turn, and urges Sinuhe to remain with him.

*76-77.* — "Well then, Egypt is happy in the knowledge that he (Senwosret) prospers". — For *nfr* "happy", see above B 31, note. — *ntt-si*[1] *rḫt(i)*; doubtless is to be understood as equivalent to "because", cf. below B 168, where the suffix should either be omitted or else emended to . — R seems here to have had a quite different text, but I can offer no explanation of the signs still legible in that manuscript.

*77.* — "Behold thou art here; thou shalt remain with me". So B; the thought seems to be, that Sinuhe might well be happy in Egypt, but that since he is now in Syria, he had best remain with the Syrian prince. — R 103 gives, in the midst of lacunæ, [ ] "establish thyself here [with me]"; this provides a less suitable continuation, or rather contrast, to the preceding sentence, and the text of B is therefore preferable.

*78.* — From this point onwards B is often our sole authority. — The words are repeated, with slight variants, in B 107-8.

*78-79.* — "he allied me with his eldest

1. Note that *-ś* here may be the suffix and not the absolute pronoun, though the latter is more usual after (Erman, *Æg. Gram.*[2], § 411); this is proved by the following examples : "since thou art come in peace", *Ä. Z.*, 19 (1881), 18; *Nw* "dilated is the heart of *Nw*, for that he is one of these", Budge, *Book of the Dead*, 131, 3 (p. 286, line 8 : *dr-ntt-f* is confirmed by the more corrupt version of this sentence, Lacau, *Sarcophages*, p. 213); so too below B 162-3.

daughter". *Mini m* "to attach ... to" is a metaphor from mooring a ship to the mooring-post. So in a different sense "she attached me to (the cult of) the statue of her Majesty", *Urkunden*, IV, 30. Here of marriage, no doubt a deliberate piece of choice diction. — The giving of a determinative to is unusual, and it would not be quite fair to instance such writings as B 239, where *wr* is written with a word-sign. None the less *wr-t* here should undoubtedly be understood as "eldest", not as a proper name.

*82.* — For the dative in , cf. *Shipwrecked Sailor*, 150.

*85.* — "that which accrued to me". *Dmi* means "to touch", and is often construed with an accusative (e. g. B 16. 200); the construction with *r* is used to express a rather different *nuance* of meaning "to become joined to" and the like, cf. "Take it (the eye of Ḥorus) upon thee that it may be joined unto thee, and joined unto thy flesh", *Pyr.* 844; *Totb.*, ed. NAV., 89, 1; *Ebers*, 86, 14. — (? read ) "as the consequence (outcome) of my love" seems quite a likely phrase; however only here.

*86-87.* — For in B we find in R 114; the latter seems to be nothing more than an erroneous writing of *ḥkꜣ*. — In the sentence "he made me chief of a tribe" the last words occasion some difficulty; hardly "in the best part of his land", which would demand as in B 80; more probably it is meant that the chieftaincy bestowed upon Sinuhe was "of the best in all his country", cf. *Shipwrecked Sailor*, 28, "one hundred and fifty sailors were in it of the best of Egypt"; and similarly, *Beni Hasan*, I, 8, 12.

*87.* — *irw ni* "there were made for me", the passive form *sḏm-wf;* so too below B 305 and see SETHE, *Verbum*, II, § 476. — is here in parallelism to *ḫrt-hrw* (B 88) and the word must mean "daily fare" or the like. It is obviously a derivative from "today" and it may be conjectured that for the determinatives should be read , the sign being perhaps due to the proximity of . Should not "daily offerings"[1] also be compared?

*89.* — R 118 has in place of in B. Either reading may

1. Professor Erman derives this word from "to remain", "persist" and speaks of it as "das sogenannte *dauernde* opfer", *Æg. Religion*², p. 60; and in favour of this view it may be pointed out that is so spelt as early as the 12th. Dynasty, cf. NAVILLE, *Temple of the XIth. Dynasty*, 24. On the other hand the word definitely means "the daily offerings" and it would be natural to derive it from . Cf. which is undoubtedly a related word, and for = *mn*, cf. *mni*, = , *Urkunden*, IV, 469.

stand, but perhaps that of R is slightly better, since *ḥrw* recurs in B 90, the next line.

*89-91.* — None of the translators seems to have appreciated the grammar of the next sentence. The presence of *iw* indicates that these words are explanatory of the preceding clause, supplying the information how Sinuhe obtained his venison : — "for men hunted (*grg-t[w]*) for me, and laid (*wꜣḥ-t[w]*) before me, besides the spoils of my (own) hounds". For *grg* "to hunt", transitively, cf. "lions are hunted for thee in the desert", *Sall. II,* 14, 7 = *Anast. VII,* 11, 7; "hunters" (without object), *Totb.*, ed. Nav., 153 A, 21; "good is the catch" over fishermen drawing in their nets, *Thebes, tomb of Puemre;* cf. Coptic ϭⲱⲣϭ : ϫⲱⲣϫ "to hunt" and ϭⲉⲣⲏϭ "hunter". The origin of the idiom seems to be "to set a snare", *Harris 500,* recto, 4, 2. 6. 9.

*91.* — M. Maspero restores the omitted word < >; B has however *ꜥšꜣ-w,* masculine plural, not *ꜥšꜣ-t.* *ꜥIḫt* is occasionally treated as a masculine singular (Sethe, *Verbum,* II, § 14, 3) but I know of no instance where a masculine plural adjective agrees with it.

*95.* — "tarried on my account", i. e. with me. Perhaps one may compare B 172-3. — *Sꜣb-i* "I caused to tarry"; this causative only here.

*97.* — cannot mean : "je réprimais le brigand", "wehrte dem Räuber", for *nḥm* does not signify "to repress" but "to rescue". Translate therefore : "I rescued him who was plundered"; this gives a better parallelism to the preceding sentence, "I gave water to the thirsty, and put the wanderer[1] on his way". Cf. Petrie, *Abydos,* III, 29; and further the name of the goddess.

*97-99.* — "when the Asiatics became overbold (so as) to oppose the chieftains of the hill-tribes, I counselled their movements". The construction of the first words, which do not fit into their place in the context unless translated as a temporal sentence, is not at all natural. *Wꜣ r,* see *Admonitions,* p. 53. — For *štm,* cf. "the insolent man (?) comes to grief (?)", *Prisse,* 11, 13. — For perhaps should be read. — is evidently the little-known verb , of which the earlier instances may mean "to discuss", "argue"; cf. "argue (?) with him after a space", *Prisse,* 14, 8, and the substan-

1. *Tnm* "to turn aside", "go astray", cf. *Pyr.*, 1695; *Totb.*, ed. Nav., 169, 23; *Eloquent Peasant,* B 1, 131. Not to be read *dnm,* as is done Masp., *M. S.*, p. 10.

tive "disputant", "speaker", *ibid.*, 5, 10. 13; 6, 1 (the utterly obscure *ḏ3is* in *Siut,* III, 7; *Rifeh,* I, 18, may be an entirely different word[1]). In Greek times *ḏ3is* is frequently used in the sense of "utterance", "speech" (so already, BRUGSCH, *Wörtb.*, 1693), cf. (sic) "I hear (*ntb-i*) thy utterances", ROCHEM., *Edfou*, I, 209, and similarly, *ibid.*, I, 75, 483; *ibid.*, I, 114; BUDGE, *Meux Collection*, 52, 20; "Isis..." ROCHEM., *Edfou,* I, 149. As a verb "to speak" *ibid.*, I, 327.

*99-101*. — "For this prince of Retenu caused me to pass many years as captain of his host"; indicates that this sentence is an explanation of what precedes.

*101-102*. — ( later inserted) (sic?) (sic); the general sense is clear, but there are certain difficulties of detail. — "against which I went forth"; *rwt-ni* is apparently the past relative form of "to run (?)", *Pyr.*, 743; cf. the pseudoparticiple in *Hirtengeschichte*, 20, and the obscure *Eloquent Peasant*, B 1, 255-6[2]. — The later insertion of *iw* before *ir-ni ḥd-i* (cf. L., *D.*, III, 128 b; similarly, R., *I. H.*, 248, 85; *Piankhi*, 14) renders the construction extremely awkward, for what is required is clearly a principal sentence governing the emphatically-placed words *ḫ3s-t nb-t,* not a subordinate sentence. We must either omit *iw* or else assume an anacoluthon ("Every land to which I went forth — and I achieved my attack, and it was driven from [its] pastures and its wells")[3]. — It is not quite certain whether or should be read in 102; both are palæographically possible. In favour of *im-ś* it might be argued that a prepositional phrase is required to take up the emphasized *ḫ3s-t nb-t;* but this appears to me unnecessary, the sense being quite clear without it, and *iw-ś dr-ti* being obviously an easier construction than would result if *im-ś* were read and *dr-ti* taken as a pseudoparticiple referring to the suffix of *im-ś*. — That is a misspelling of (*dr-ti*, cf. B 182 = *pr-ti,* 2nd pers. masc. sing.) is, I think, evident[4]. — "away from" the Hebrew מֵעַל, cf. such phrases

1. Or it may be derived from the same stem and mean "to contend", the determinative being that of a soldier.

2. Probably to be distinguished from *rwt* "to cease", "to make to cease", though that verb is written *rww* below B 152. — Spiegelberg, *Ä. Z.*, 43 (1906), p. 159, identifies *rwt* here with an obscure verb *rwti*. This however is impossible grammatically, as the gender of *ḫ3s-t* would demand a form *rwti-t-ni*. Nor does the sense proposed by Prof. Spiegelberg "jedes Land, in welches ich floh", suit the present context.

3. A third possibility, though to my mind a very unlikely one, would be to construe *iw ir-ni ḥd-i* as an interposed temporal sentence: "every land against which I went, when I had made my attack, it was driven", etc. One objection to this is that *ir-ni ḥd-i* seems, from the analogy of *ḥd-f ḫpr*, to mean "I made a *successful* attack" not merely "I made an attack"; the former meaning does not fit into a temporal clause.

4. Maspero interprets as ⲥⲧⲱⲧ *tremor* (*M. S.*, p. 161). But *sd3d3*, from which ⲥⲧⲱⲧ is derived, is not a feminine, nor does it ever lack its bird-determinative; and the omission of 3 is not usual at so early a date.

as "copper from the desert": *Israel stele,* 3. — After *smw* the suffix *-ś* might be expected, but is perhaps not quite indispensable.

*103.* — *in-ni,* see above the note on B 30.

*104.* — "their food was taken away"; cf. "I have not taken away food", *Totb.*, ed. Nav., 125, 10. For *wnm-t,* cf. also *Israel stele,* 7; elsewhere only as "fodder" for cattle and horses, spelt , e. g. *Sall. I,* 4, 8; 9, 3; *Leiden* 350, col. 2, 29; *Harris* 500, verso, 1, 5.

*105.* — here probably "my actions", opposed to *sḫrw-i iḳrw* in 106; the earlier translations render literally "my marchings".

*106.* — *iꜣḫ-ni;* R 133 likewise omits the suffix *-i,* though only one more instance of the kind can be quoted from that Ms. ( R 161).

*107.* — , a mistake for , see Sethe, *Verbum,* II, § 264, case 12, o.

*108.* — , erroneously for , which R 134 rightly has.

*109.* — R 135 has for of B. There can be no doubt, I think, that *Tnw* is an error, and not a legitimate variant; still it is curious that occurs instead of *Rtnw* in *Anast. I,* 28, 7. The reason of the corruption is obviously that *tnw* is a very familiar Egyptian word; where the determinative stood in the Ms. copied by the scribe the mistake was particularly easy. — The meaning of , possibly "to flout", "insult", rests on the context here alone.

*110.* — The precise meaning "hero", "champion", for rests on this passage alone; but there are analogous usages of the word. In B 123 clearly means a bull of strength and ferocity beyond the average. In *Anast. I,* 14, 6, *pry* must be rendered "famous"; so too perhaps in *ibid.*, 6, 7. occurs between and in the Golenischeff *Vocabulary* (4, 12), but there is no indication of its meaning there. In the above-mentioned expressions *pr* seems to mean "to stand forth" superior to others; the stem has the same comparative sense in the derivative "more than".

*111-112.* — All translators seem to have regarded *ḥwt-f* in as the *sḏm-f* form of "to smite". This however is quite impossible; *ḥwt,* if connected at all with that verb, could only be the infinitive (Sethe, *Verbum,* II, § 683, 6 b). But the spelling without would be unusual, and the suffix as subject and absolute pronoun as object is hardly to be supported by *m ḥr*[*yt*] *nt mḥꜣ-f sw* in B 124 below. The clue to the right reading is given by "he planned to spoil me", which R inserts, not in the passage corresponding to B 111-112, but in the midst of the account of the combat (R 163). In R *ḥwtf* is infinitive, and therefore has the suffix as object : in B we must emend , the mistake being analogous to for in B 27; for in B 181; for *Eloquent Peasant*, B 1, 78. For the tense *sdm-f* after *ḫmt*, cf. above B 7. — *Ḥwtf* "to plunder" or "to seize as plunder", cf. *Vienna, Saal I, no. 20* (sarcophagus); MAR., *Karnak*, 37, 31-32; *Urkunden*, IV, 138; compare too ϩⲱϥⲧ in Coptic. A faint recollection of our passage may be contained in the corruptly written sentence[1] : (sic) "I have repelled those who thought to plunder me", *Pap. Leiden* 347, 11, 10.

*114-126*. — The speech of Sinuhe is full of philological difficulties, which need discussion point for point. In order to prepare the way for the notes, I here give a translation of the passage as I understand it. "The prince conferred with me, and I said : 'I know him not; forsooth he is no comrade of mine that I should have access to his encampment. Or have I ever opened his gate, or overthrown his walls? (Nay), it is ill-will for that he sees me performing thy behest. Lo, I am like a roaming bull in the midst of a strange herd; the bull of the cattle charges him, the long-horn attacks (?) him. Is the humble man loved as a master? There is no foreigner who can associate with the man of the Delta (?). What can cause the papyrus (?) to cleave to the mountain? Doth a bull love combat (?) and then shall a strong bull love to sound the retreat (?) through the dread lest he might vie with him? If it be his will to fight, let him speak his desire. Is God ignorant of what is decreed for him, or how (else) shall it be known?'" Both Maspero and Griffith have divined the meaning of a part of the passage, but my version of the hardest sentences, from B 120 to B 124, differs entirely from theirs.

*113-114*. — "he conferred with me", cf. *Prisse*, 5, 8. Elsewhere *ndnd* seems always to mean (1) "to ask (about) something", e. g. *ndnd sḫrw Pap. Turin*, 18, 3; with other objects, *Anast. I*, 13, 6; 14, 4; (2) "to ask of () somebody", "to question somebody", e. g. *Anast. III*, 3, 11 = *Anast. V*, 8, 3; *Anast. I*, 12, 5; R., *I. H.*, 26, 12; (3) "to question somebody" (with direct object of person) *Harris 500*, verso 6, 8; *Pap. Leiden* 368, 11; *Max. d'Anii*, 3, 10.

*114*. — "pray", "forsooth" is not common except in interrogative sen-

1. The first sign is cancelled in the original by a stroke, and *sḥm-ni* "I caused to retreat" should probably be read.

tences, but some possible instances have been quoted by Spiegelberg (QUIBELL, *Excavations at Saqqara*, III [1907-1908], p. 81).

*115.* — The word *'f'y* is not known from any other source than the Story of Sinuhe (B115 = R140; B146; B201).

*115-116.* — I understand the sentence as an alternative which might have suggested itself to Amuienshi's mind; the sense of 114-116 therefore, put as briefly as possible, is "I know him not; I am neither his friend nor yet his foe". — This interpretation seems to give the clue to the meaning of (R140 has the same reading) as an enclitic particle "or". Cf. , and compare B126 "Is God ignorant of what is destined for him (i. e. for the champion of Retenu), OR how should one know?" [The construction of *rḫ* in the latter sentence is obscure, but it is evidently contrasted with, and in that sense an alternative to, the preceding *ḫm*.. I am inclined to view these words as a rather subtle way of expressing Sinuhe's confidence that he will win in the fight; Sinuhe puts his trust in God, who alone can know what fate awaits his enemy.] So too in ***Ebers***, 99, 5 : "whatever limb he touches, everywhere he feels the heart; for its vessels (lead) to every member of his : OR (i. e. in other words) it (the heart) speaks from out of the vessels of every member". The example ***Rhind Math. Pap.***, 7 is obscure.

*116.* — *S'* "door" is uncommon; however cf. (= *iw*) *Metternichstele*, 18. — in B is an unknown verb, aud doubtless to be rejected in favour of "to overthrow" in R141; for *šnb* cf. ***Pyr.***, 1236; ***Rifeh***, 7, 48; ***Urkunden***, IV, 64; ***Pianchi***, 95.

*116-117.* — B; R141-142. This sentence tells us the true reason for the challenge which Sinuhe received from the mighty man of Retenu; the latter was jealous, seeing Sinuhe so high in favour with Amuienshi. — ***Rḳ-t ib***, elsewhere only in "victorious.....-ing the ill-willed" ***Mission***, V, 283 P3 = PIEHL, *Inscr. hiér.*, I, 113 χ. — B117 is infinitive, cf. B5. 282-3; R142 has the normal . — in B does not make good sense; it can hardly mean "the commission which he (the hero of Retenu) ought to perform". The variant of R142 is obviously preferable; Sinuhe is talking to Amuienshi "it is ill-will because he sees me performing thy commission(s)". The suffix of *wpwt-f* in B is doubtless borrowed from the preceding , a striking example of the variety of corruption that I have called "the assimilation of pronouns" (see above the footnote to the comment on B2, and also B25, note).

*117-118.* — For the particle *nḥmn* see the note on B46.

*118.* — "cattle allowed to roam freely"[1], see the note on *Admonitions*, 9, 2.

*119.* — That should be understood as *idr* is, I think, almost certain, though the reading in R143 is too doubtful to be adduced in support of it.

*120.* — *Ngꜣw* "the long-horned bull", see B13 note. — *ꜣm rf* only here. — In this lengthy simile Sinuhe expresses his consciousness that he is a stranger among the Asiatics, whose leading men resent his presence as that of a rival.

*120-121.* — B; the text of R145-6 agrees with that of B, so far as it is preserved, only giving the variant[2] for . This word, which doubtless means "a master", "superior", does not occur elsewhere, but has an obvious analogon in . — seems to mean "a man of low station", "inferior", "subject"; cf. below B273; "all men, all scribes, all learned men every poor man and every man of low station, who shall enter into this tomb" *Siut*, I, 223. 225; "I am one bright of face to his inferior, doing good to his equal" *Brit. Mus.*, 581, vertical line 15 = Sharpe, *Eg. Inscr.*, II, 83; "what does thou expend in satisfying thy inferiors?" *Eloquent Peasant*, B1, 94-95. — is imperfect participle passive, see Sethe, *Verbum*, II, § 941. 948. — is probably a compound prepositional phrase containing a substantive "value" (cf. Coptic ϣⲁⲩ, ϣⲟⲩ-) already found in "a block great in value above every thing" *Bersheh*, I, 14, 7. *N šꜣ* is later used with an infinitive following in the sense of "apt to", "serving the purpose of", cf. "goodly negroes from Kush to serve as fan-bearers" *Anast. III*, 8, 6 = *Anast. IV*, 16, 5; "large well-baked loaves fit for the food of princes" *Anast. IV*, 17, 6. On the analogy of this usage *n šꜣ n* may here mean "in the capacity of" "en tant que". This gives good sense "is a man of humble rank loved as a superior?"; for Sinuhe must have appeared to the eyes of his rivals as a low adventurer come to usurp their place[3].

*121-122.* — The next sentences emphasize the disparity between Sinuhe and the people among whom he now lives : "there is

1. M. Maspero reads « le petit bétail domestique, les chèvres » (*M. S.*, p. 68); but apart from the determinative of the bull the word *ꜥnḫw* could not be written with two *w*.

2. The sign \\ however is not certain, and a note of interrogation should be added to my transcription.

3. Gr. rendered " but shall a wretched beggar desire to attain to my fortune ? "; Masp. " ou bien il n'est qu'un hableur de ceux qui sont amoureux des biens qui me sont accrus " (reading *mrrw* *šꜣw* ). In my German translation I gave : " Gibt es einen Bürger, der geliebt wird, weil es der Oberherr befiehlt ? "; but apart from the fact that the sense of this is not very good, *n šꜣ tp-ḥri* and not *n šꜣ-n tp-ḥri* would be required.

no barbarian who can associate with a man of the Delta(?); what can fasten(?) the papyrus(?) to the mountain?" — The translations of my predecessors assume the indefensible reading of for , and has not been recognized. — is a difficult word, hardly to be read *idḥw* (cf. *idḥy* B225); cf. in an obscure context *Rifeh*, 7, 33. — (below B159. 183. 261) is the interrogative "what?"; the interjection *ptri* "behold" does not occur before the 18th. Dynasty. M. Dévaud has sent me an interesting comment on the note upon *Admonitions*, p. 33; he points out that if, as Erman supposes, the word were derived from *ptri* "to see" the omission of would be most striking, and he quotes instances of the spelling for *ptr*, *pti* from the M. R. sarcophagus of *Sꜣ-t-Bꜣstt* (lines 14. 28. 31). Thus he confirms an old hypothesis of mine, that *ptr* "what?" is derived from the combination of the demonstrative *pw-* and the interrogative particle . — *Smn r* "to fasten to(?)"; I can quote no parallel. — ; can this be a writing of ?

*123-124.* — "does one bull love combat, and a fierce bull love to sound the retreat(?) from dread that he (the first bull) might equal him (in the encounter)?" This simile is not difficult to interpret; Sinuhe compares his antagonist to a fight-loving bull, and asks whether he himself, a second bull of far superior kind (*pry*, see above B110, note), is likely to shrink back through fear of defeat. — *Whm-sꜣ* only here — must be read *ḥr (yt)*[1], as the following *nt* indicates; so too B231. 262. 278. 280. For the phrase *m ḥryt nt* see Sethe, *Die Einsetzung des Veziers*, p. 43, note 70 *a*. — In my German translation I rendered "aus Angst vor dem, dessen Ebenbürtiger er ist" understanding *mḥꜣ(w)-f* as relative-form. However this would be somewhat of an anticlimax since *pry* has already implied that Sinuhe is not merely his rival's equal, but his superior. It is therefore better to accept Sethe's version, which has been indicated above. In this case the words mean literally "through dread of his equalling him", and *mḥꜣ* is infinitive; the suffix *-f* after *mḥꜣ* then represents the subject of the infinitive, not its object, as the rule in the grammars would demand. It appears that in the rare cases where the subject of the infinitive must be expressed for the sake of clearness, this subject if pronominal may be represented by a suffix; if there is also a pronominal object to the infinitive this is then expressed by the absolute pronoun, since a suffix cannot be appended to a suffix. As Sethe points out to me, this construction of infinitive + subject-suffix lies at the root of the so-called *sḏm-tf* form. Instances analogous to that which is here discussed are "Truly I know (*rḫ-ni*) that Re loves me beause he has given thee to me", words from a letter of Pharaoh to a favourite courtier, Quibell, *Excavations at Saqqarah*, III (1907-1908),

1. Sethe transcribes the word , to my mind a very unlikely expedient.

p. 80; "He divided the river-valley over its back according to what was performed for the father of my mother by the utterance which went forth from the mouth of Amenemmes I., (read ) namely his making him (apposition to *iryt*) into hereditary prince etc.", *Chnemhotep,* 30. — "to match", "equal" is plainly a denominative verb from "the balance". Only here as a transitive verb in this sense; elsewhere (1) "to adjust", cf. SCHIAP., *Libro d. funerali,* 57, etc. = *Pyr.,* 12. 13. 644; (2) "to counterpoise", cf. "a level (*ḫḫ*) that makes level the two regions, a balance counterpoising the two lands", epithets of the Vizier *Rʿḥtp,* PIEHL, *Inscr. hiér.,* III, 82 (collated)[1]; (3) "to make level", cf. "Tenen levelled its floor" MAR., *Abyd.,* I, 50 *a.* 12; (4) "to be like", followed by , cf. "his sister..... like to her husband in disposition, the lady Teye" *Thebes, tomb of 'Imn-nb;* "the exact counterpart of Baal" GREENE, *Fouilles,* 1, 5; "my hand is like my heart in respect of my valour" *op. cit.* 3,31; "my heart is like to thy heart" *Harris 500,* recto 4, 11; see too *Kuban stele,* 14-15.

*126-127.* — This sentence has already been discussed, see the note on 115-116.

*127.* — "in the night I strung my bow". — For the idiom *sḏr-nt,* see *Schäfer, Ä. Z.,* 31 (1893), 51-60. — *Ḳ*ꜣ*s* only here of stringing a bow; elsewhere "to bind" an ox, DAVIES, *Ptahhetep,* II, 22; a person's arms, *Ani,* 1, 10; "to tie" a rope-ladder, *Pyr.,* 2079.

*127-128.* — is usually rendered "I made ready my arrows". But *wd* means "to cast", "eject", and not "to prepare". It is specially used of shooting arrows, cf. "Sekhmet does not shoot her arrows against me" *Pap. Leiden* 347, 5, 2; "His Majesty shot, and his first arrow fastened in the body of that fallen one" *Urkunden,* IV, 8; other examples *Cairo Statue, nr. d'entrée* 36697; *Rec. de Trav.,* 13, 163, 12 (collated). It will be objected that the nighttime is hardly the fitting occasion to practise shooting; but as Herr Grapow has aptly remarked to me, neither is it the time for stringing the bow, which would naturally be done immediately before the fight in order that the bow-string might be perfectly taut. Thus Sinuhe seems to have tested his weapons while others slept.

1. That *mḫ*ꜣ*t* is infinitive here seems proved by the parallelism; cf. the similar phrases from another portion of the same stele *sic* (read *n wḏ*ꜣ *M*ꜣ*ʿ-t*), BRUGSCH, *Thes.,* 950.

*128.* — "I took out my dagger", i. e. out of the sheath; literally "I gave an opening to my dagger". There is no justification, so far as I can see, for the old rendering "I gave an edge to my dagger[1]". — *Sẖkr* elsewhere "to decorate"; here obviously "to brighten" "burnish" weapons.

*130.* — *ḏdb* properly means "to sting", of a scorpion, e. g. *Metternichstele,* 73. 134. 244; variant *ibid.*, 189; here "to spur on" "incite".

*130-131.* — "it had assembled the tribes of a half of it", i. e. perhaps, half of the surrounding tribes was present. As the text stands can only be rendered thus, see Sethe, *Ä. Z.*, 40 (1902), 94, for the writing of the suffix.

*131.* — The usual translation of "when it thought of this fight, every heart was kindled for me" is rendered impossible by the reasons (1) that R156 inserts a new sentence after *ꜥḥꜣ pn,* and (2) that *kꜣ* never means "to think" *(sḫꜣ),* but "to devise" or "to plan" (see above on B71-73). *Kꜣ-ns* is clearly parallel to *ḏdb-ns* and *sḥw-ns* (B130), and the point in all these sentences is that the rivalry between Sinuhe and his opponent had been schemed and fostered by the people of Retenu themselves; this too had already been implied by the words B113. Translate therefore : "it had planned this combat".

At the end of R155 are traces possibly to be read as in *ꜥḥꜣ pn.* R156 continues thus : "He came to me where I stood, and I placed myself near him". This sentence provides an excellent transition to the narrative of the duel, and is doubtless derived from the text of the archetype.

*131-132.* — "every heart was kindled for me", i. e. was troubled. So in the *Decree of Canopus,* 9 *(iw)* corresponds to the Greek κηδεμονικῶς; on the other hand *Urkunden,* IV, 614 means "their hearts are consumed" with anxiety or fright.

*132.* — "women shrieked". — All previous translators render *ḥm-wt ṯꜣy-w* "men and women", a collocation always represented in Egyptian by *ṯꜣy-w ḥm-wt* (cf. above B67); the inverted order "women and men" would be most unnatural. Doubtless we have here the plural of *ḥm-t ṯꜣy,* a compound expression for "woman" known from *Totb., ed.* Nav., 125, 19, (similarly Petrie, *Abydos,* III, 29). — "to shriek" is a ἅπαξ λεγόμενον; the late word *ꜥiꜥi* "to rejoice" (e. g. Mar., *Dend.,* II, 61 *d.* 70 *c.*; Rochem., *Edfou,* I, 204) can hardly be related to it; nor can it be plausibly identified with , which is used of the beating of the heart, *Ebers,* 41, 21; 42, 9.

---

1. So too my German translation. The word (Mar., *Dend.,* IV, 37, 61; Düm., *Baugeschichte,* 32), ⲥⲓⲛⲉ, *comer,* cannot legitimately be quoted in support of the usual rendering.

*133-134.* — The words [hieroglyphs] have been very variously interpreted. (1) Erman translates : "Giebt es denn keinen andern Starken, der gegen ihn kämpfen könnte?" The sense of this is very poor, and the Egyptian does not say "keinen andern", but "einen andern", which makes all the difference. (2) Griffith's rendering "Is there yet another champion to fight with him?" is too ambiguous to be criticized. (3) Maspero's version is : "Y a-t-il vraiment un autre fort qui puisse lutter contre lui?" If I understand this rightly, it is meant that the men of Retenu cry out in wonderment at their champion's gorgeous panoply, asking "is there any warrior who can fight against such a one as him?" To my mind this is the right view, but it must be admitted that [hieroglyphs] is distinctly perplexing. Two thoughts seem to be confounded : (a) "is there any mighty man who can fight against him?" and (b) "is there another man as strong as he is?" Such confusions are common in every language.

*134-137.* — The early stages of the combat are exceedingly obscure; in order to facilitate the comparison of the two manuscripts I print the text of R underneath that of B :—

B [hieroglyphs] 135 [hieroglyphs] [1] [hieroglyphs]
R [hieroglyphs] 160 [hieroglyphs] (sic) [hieroglyphs] [2] [hieroglyphs]

B [hieroglyphs] 136 [hieroglyphs]
R [hieroglyphs] 161 [hieroglyphs]

B [hieroglyphs] 137 [hieroglyphs]
R 162 [hieroglyphs]

Before proceeding to the discussion of these difficult sentences it will be well to devote some study to the less well-known words and expressions contained in them.

*134.* — [hieroglyphs] (or [hieroglyphs]) in B and [hieroglyphs] in R cannot be read *inb*, as is done by Brugsch, *Wb. Suppl.* 1403 and Maspero, *M. S.*, p. 58, and for two excellent reasons : (1) [hieroglyph] never (unless it be here) has the value *i* before the N. K., and then only in such words as are written in the so-called "syllabic" writing; (2) the value *i* is derived from [hieroglyph] *iw* "island", [hieroglyph] being in this case confused with [hieroglyph] ([hieroglyph]); now in the M. K. these two signs are not yet confused, cf. B 9. 21. 211; R 33 for [hieroglyph] and B 142 = R 168 for [hieroglyph] ([hieroglyph]). Hence I had concluded that [hieroglyphs] must be read *minb*, [hieroglyph] having the same value *mi* as in [hieroglyphs] = [hieroglyphs] *mis-t* and a

1. At first [hieroglyph] was written; then corrected into the right reading [hieroglyph].

2. Or [hieroglyph].

few other words[1]. With regard to the sense of the word neither *Urkunden*, IV, 891 *('Imnmḥb)* nor *Harris 500*, verso 8, 4, permits us to do more than affirm that it is a weapon; Brugsch however suggests that it is identical with (? read ), which is mentioned together with *ʿn-t* "the adze", *mnḫ-t* "the hammer" and *mḏ3-t* "the chisel" in the tomb of Sethos I (see Brugsch, *Wb. Suppl.*, 1403. 234). In this case the word must mean "an axe". To the kindness of M. Lacau I owe the following instances, which afford decisive evidence that both the reading and the sense assigned by me to are correct. In *Mon. de Leide*, III, 24 occurs in a list of objects offered to the dead, in company with *mnḫ*, *ʿn-t* and *mḏ3-t*, i. e. as in the tomb of Sethos I. The name of the axe is written on the M. K. sarcophagus of *Nfri* (*Cairo*, 28088, n° 20)[2]; on the sarcophagus of (*Cairo, Journal d'entrée*, 37566) it is written . The natural transliteration of these spellings would be *minib*, but possibly the employment of was due to the fact that internal *n* is sometimes omitted in writing (so for *ʿnḏ*, for *ḥnḳ-t*, for *msnkt-t* [see Lacau, *Rec. de Trav.*, 25, 152]), as are not infrequently *i*, *w*, and *m*; in this case *ib* for *i(n)b* would be analogous to *mn* for *min* (see above on B87, footnote) or *nw* for *niw*, and could still be read *minb*. This solution agrees better than any other with the obvious and unquestionable relationship of our word to the feminine *mi(n)b-t* in the description above a scene of carpentering in the tomb of Ti (Baedeker, *Aegypten*, 142)[3].

*135.* — "his armful(?) of javelins(?)"; *ḥpt* is not found elsewhere in any similar sense ("embrace" below B143), and for *ns-wt* only one passage can be quoted, viz. "seize your daggers(?)" *Totb.*, *ed.* Nav., 37, 17.

*136-137.* — *Sp n iwtt* (?) "in vain", "to no purpose", cf. *Destruction of Mankind*, 27 (Sethos I). — means "to approach", elsewhere only of persons and usually construed with *n*; with *m* (on the analogy of *tkn m*), *Rifeh*, IV, 45.

---

1. The number of words in which is employed in the M. K. is astonishingly few in number, and from this fact alone it might be concluded that the sign is never merely initial *m*-, but always initial *mi*-. M. Dévaud has recently shown (*Sphinx*, 13, 157-158) that variants of , of and of prove for these words the readings *miḥʿ-t*, *minḫ-t* and *miḥw*. To my mind he does not go quite far enough in his demonstration, for he speaks of these readings as existing « à côté de *mʿḥʿ-t* », *mʿnḫ-t* and *mʿḥw*. But the latter forms are not proved by such writings as and , where is probably to be read *mi*. In order to prove that *miḥʿ-t* was ever pronounced with mʿ, it would be needful to have good instances with written out, dating from a time when was not yet employed for *mi*. Of course I do not ignore the fact that *miḥʿ-t* is derived from *ʿḥʿ*; but my contention is that *mʿḥʿ-t* is a purely theoretical form, and that for *mʿḥw* there is at present no ground whatsoever.

2. In his catalogue *Sarcophages antérieurs au Nouvel Empire*, II, 13, M. Lacau gives a reading which he now shows me to be false. The first sign on both sarcophagi is neither nor , and must therefore be ().

3. It is doubtful whether any importance ought to be attached to the *-t* in the above-quoted example from the tomb of Sethos I.

*134-137.* — We must now return to the question of the sense of this passage. In order to exhibit the diversity of the renderings hitherto proposed, I quote these *in extenso*.

| GRIFFITH | ERMAN | MASPERO |
|---|---|---|
| Then (he took) his buckler, his battle-axe, and an armful of javelins. But thereon I avoided his weapons, and turned aside his arrows to the ground, useless. One drew near to the other and he rushed upon me etc. | Da ergriff er sein Schild und seine Lanze und seinen Armvoll Speere. Aber nachdem ich seine Waffen herausgelockt hatte, so liess ich seine Speere neben mir vorbei fliegen, nutzlos auf die Erde, so dass einer auf den anderen traf. Da kam er auf mich los (?) u. s. w. | Voici, il prit son bouclier, sa hache, sa brassée de javelines. Quand je lui eus fait user en vain ses armes, et que j'eus écarté de moi ses traits sans qu'un seul d'entre eux tombât près de l'autre, il fondit sur moi, etc. |

It will be noted that all versions assume the omission of < > after , and make the next sentence begin with , a familiar collocation of particles. R however does not support this conjecture, which of course arose from the supposition that the verb of the first clause is missing. But is this really the case? It does not seem to have been observed that  may be, not a particle prefixed to the second clause, but the predicate of the first. In favour of this view several arguments may be urged : (1) the particle *ḫr* is elsewhere in B written without the determinative  (cf. B147; *ḫr ḥm* B75. 202)[1]; (2) *ḫr m-ḫt* is, so far as I am aware, only used to usher in an entirely new paragraph or section; it thus corresponds to our "now after.....", as for example in the frequent phrase of Egyptian tales "now after many days had passed"; here therefore, in the midst of the description of the combat, *ḫr m-ḫt* would be quite out of place; (3)  or  of R160 is in either case wrong, but if it shows anything at all, it is that *ḫr* was not regarded as a particle. The cumulative weight of these arguments is considerable, at all events it is enough far to outweigh the alternative view of the passage.

It is true (as was pointed out in the remarks on B71-73) that the agreement of B and R is no absolute guarantee of the accuracy of their text. But their combined authority is exceedingly high, and all other possibilities must be exhausted before recourse is had to conjecture. We shall see that the sense of the context is so obscure that this cannot here be made the decisive criterion as to the correct reading; we must therefore pin our faith upon grammatical analysis, and this demands that *ḫr* should be taken as predicate of the sentence.

It is however hard to see in what sense it might be said of the warrior of Retenu that "his buckler, his battle-axe and his armful(?) of javelins fell" or "had fallen".

1. In B21 = R47  has been shown to be a verb.

The solution of this problem is of course dependent on the interpretation given to what follows. The difficulties of the sentence beginning with *m-ḫt* are quite insurmountable. B and R here differ in their text. B reads, which Erman rendered "nachdem ich seine Waffen herausgelockt hatte"[1] and Maspero "quand je lui eus fait user en vain ses armes"; the causative *spr* occurs nowhere else, and its literal translation opens the door to so many possible interpretations that it is impossible to feel sure that the right one has been chosen. R gives which may possibly be rendered "when I[2] had escaped(?) from his weapons", but there seems to be no way of ascertaining whether this version is superior to that of B or *vice versa.* — The next sentence "I caused his arrows to pass by me[3], uselessly sped" is in itself perfectly clear, but it is not clear whether it is a principal clause, as Erman's translation assumes, or whether we should take it, with Maspero, as dependent on *m-ḫt.* The decision of this question is all-important for the meaning of *ḫr,* since on the former view *ḫr* refers to some incident previous to the failure of the Asiatic to direct his arrows to their mark, on the latter view *ḫr* expresses the consequence or sequel of that failure. On the whole I prefer to construe *rdi-ni swꜣ* as dependent on *m-ḫt;* it seems to me that a principal clause at this juncture would require to be introduced by *ʿḥʿ-n.*

My tentative translation of the passage therefore is as follows : — "Behold, his shield, his battle-axe and his armful(?) of javelins fell, when I had escaped(?) from(?) his weapons and had caused his arrows to pass by me, uselessly sped; while one approached the other[4]". The following sentences go on to describe how the champion of Retenu tried next to rush his adversary, and how he was slain in the attempt. All this throws but little light on *ḫr*. Can it possibly signify that the shield, battle-axe etc. had been let fall, in order that the bow and arrows might be used; and that when these had proved unsuccessful, the Asiatic attempted to close with his opponent without a thought of his accoutrements lying on the ground? If this be the sense of the passage, it must be admitted that the author has been extremely unfortunate in his attempt to convey it. I desist from discussing other possibilities, in the persuasion that no satisfactory or convincing conclusion is obtainable from our Mss.

*137.* — Here R 163 inserts a sentence : ? "thereupon he made....., he purposed to plunder me"; the second half of this addition recalls B 112, where it is perhaps more in place. On the other hand the last stage of the fight might appropriately be introduced by .

B has for of R 164; the latter form is the better, see B 52-53 note.

---

1. For the *sdmnf*-form after *m-ḫt*, see SETHE, *Verbum*, II, § 366.
2. For the omission of the suffix of the 1st person singular, see the note on B 106.
3. For the exceptional position of *ḥr-t* see ERMAN, *Æg. Gramm.*[3], § 365.
4. It seems impossible to refer the last sentence to the arrows, as Erman and Maspero do. *Ḫn*, as we have seen above, is not used of inanimate objects, and its meaning is "to approach", not "tomber près" or the like.

*138-139.* — B "I transfixed him, my arrow fastened in his neck". R164-165 gives [ ] [ ] ..... ..... [ ] which I cannot complete. The objection to this is the presence of the verb *ḫr* "to fall", since it recurs in the following sentence "he fell on his nose". — *St-ni sw,* not "I shot at him" (GR.), but "I transfixed him"; *st* often means "to pierce" in hunting scenes, e. g. *Der el Gebrawi,* I, 3; II, 23; "to shoot at", on the other hand, is *st r,* cf. MAR., *Abyd.*, II, 55, 17; *Stele of the Sphinx,* 5.— For the use of *mn m* cf. *Urkunden,* IV, 8, quoted *in extenso* above in the note on B127-128.

*140.* — B omits the preposition in *sḫr-ni sw* [*m*] *mỉnb-f;* it is correctly preserved in R166. That Sinuhe slays his foe with his own battle-axe is a characteristic trait. So too David cuts off the head of Goliath with his own sword (*I Sam.*, 17, 51); and so Benaiah despatches the Musrite with his own spear (*II Sam.*, 23, 21). — "I raised my war-cry"; *ỉšnn* only here. *Wd* is not uncommonly used with (e. g. *Pap. Turin,* 132, 6) and, more clearly, with (e. g. L., *D.*, III, 195 *a*, 15; *Leiden* 350, recto 3, 5; *Metternich Stele,* 91, 206) for "sending forth one's voice"; by transference, to emit a sound, cf. *wd sbḥ* B265; "I emitted a cry" *Metternich Stele,* 170; "I shake them (the sistra) for thee, and they give forth a noise" ROCHEM., *Edfou,* I, 101.

*142.* — "his slaves mourned for him". probably means "to make a festival", whether one of joy or one of grief. Elsewhere it is only known in a stereotyped phrase with the former sense, cf. "the good god is come, he hath made a triumph with the chiefs of all lands" L., *D.*, III, 121 *b*; similarly *Mission,* XV, 12, 1 (Luxor, with the determinatives ); *Abydos, inscr. dédic.*, 38 (det. ); L., *D.*, III, 166 (Ramesseum, spelt )[1]. GR. probably connected *ḥb* here with *ḥb* "to catch (fowl)", his translation being "I and his vassals, whom he had oppressed, gave thanks unto Mentu"; but this is impossibly hard and circuitous.

*146.* — "I spoiled his dwelling". *Kf* means "to uncover", "unclothe" (also subsequently "to take off" clothes); thence metaphorically "to strip", "plunder", "deprive" (1) "never did I despoil a man of his possessions" *Urkunden,* I, 78; "I have not deprived cattle of their pasture" *Totb., ed.* NAV., 125, *Einl.*, 18; (2) "to despoil", "strip" places, here and perhaps also "and he plundered the dwelling of the Pharaoh" *Salt,* 2, 7.

*147-173.* — The narrative of Sinuhe's victory and of the wealth which thence

1. My published transcription inadvertantly gives for .

2. Note that the words *pꜣ ḫrw n Ḥtꜣ* following the last instance are not the object of *ḥb*, but the subject of the next sentence.

accrued to him is followed by a passage that has hitherto been but imperfectly understood. Sinuhe is usually supposed to be petitioning for his recall : "without any pause or introduction Sanehat begins to quote from his petition to the king of Egypt" (GRIFFITH, *op. cit.*, p. 5242); "dies Gebet (i. e. that of B156) geht allmählich in eine Bitte an den König über und leitet zum zweiten Teil des Gedichtes — der Rückkehr — hin" (ERMAN, *op. cit.*, p. 21, note 4)[1]. Were this view correct, the author of the tale could scarcely be criticized too severely; it may be doubted whether even the deficient literary sense of an Egyptian would have tolerated a petition to the Pharaoh that began "by degrees" and "without any pause or introduction". Nor can this interpretation be reconciled with Sinuhe's professed admiration (B205 and especially 214-216) of the king's intuitive powers in guessing, unaided, the exile's fondest wishes. It is true, this admiration is not very sincere, for it is hinted in B173-174 that Sinuhe had contrived to have his hopes made known to Pharaoh; as it is discreetly put in the Egyptian text "now it had been told the king Kheperkere concerning this condition in which I was". Erman has here an excellent comment, — one curiously contradictory of his remark above-quoted — "man muss sich denken", he writes "dass Sinuhe Mittel und Wege gefunden hat, einen Fürsprecher am Hofe zu gewinnen; dieser hat dem Könige die Hoffnungen und Wünsche des Greises vorgetragen, die in den vorhergehenden Versen ausgesprochen sind" (*op. cit.*, p. 22, footnote 3). When himself addressing the king, Sinuhe of course disguises his own initiative in the matter of his recall, and declares with true Oriental self-abasement that he had been afraid to voice the presumptuous wish which the king had accorded in so magnanimous and unforeseen a manner (B215-216).

The internal evidence of the passage B147-173 is quite decisive against its containing any direct appeal to Pharaoh. There is indeed an obvious avoidance of any such appeal which is not without a certain subtlety of feeling and psychological *finesse*. Sinuhe's wishes are communicated to the reader in the guise of reflexions on the happy issue of his duel. At length the anger of heaven has been appeased, and Sinuhe, heretofore a miserable fugitive, is now a man of wealth among the foreigners (B147-156). Sinuhe next expresses his secret hope that his new prosperity may be crowned by the permission to return to Egypt; "may the god who decreed this flight be gracious", may he bring the exile home, may he cause him to behold "the place where his heart dwelleth" (B156-158). For what, he asks, is more precious than to be buried in the land of one's birth (B159-160). One favour has already been granted — Sinuhe's defeat of the Syrian champion — may it now be followed by a like benefit, if it so be that the god is truly appeased (B161-163). "May the king of Egypt' — note the third person, and the unusual mode of referring to the king — "be gracious to me, may I live through his grace; may I do obeisance to the Lady of the Land who is in the Palace, and may I hear the commands of her children" (B165-

1. I find no explicit statement of Maspero's view of the passage.

167). In support of his request Sinuhe pleads that he is now old and must needs soon die; and lastly he begs that in death he may still be suffered to serve his mistress the queen (B 168-173).

*147-149.* — B; R is here lost. The sentence ends with two relative sentences of which the antecedent is (implicitly) Sinuhe, and the subject the god. (1) *N ṯs-nf im-f* cannot be rendered "for him who trusted in him"; apart from the fact that there is no authority for the translation "to trust in", this translation is open to the grammatical objection that "he who" can in Egyptian only be expressed[1] by the participle *(n ṯs im-f)* or the *sḏmti̯fi*-form (see SETHE, *Verbum*, II, § 742). For *ṯs m* cf. the incomprehensible *Eloquent Peasant*, B1, 124 (= R165-166), and the rather ambiguous examples "combining offices, without....." *Bersheh*, II, 21, *supra*, 7; "I performed many offices without its being grudged to me(?)", *op. cit.*, 21, *infra*, 6. The parallelism of this relative clause with that which immediately follows, and with several that we shall encounter in the next few lines, suggests that *ṯs m* may be an idiom for "to feel anger at", "bear a grudge against" or the like. (2) *Th-nf r k-t ḫ3s-t* "whom he had led astray into a foreign land", cf. B202. — It remains to explain . Sethe suggests that *irtw* (passive) should be read, and that the construction is the same as in B72, i. e. "the god is made to be gracious to him whom"; however this makes but poor sense, and I cannot accept the proposed view of B72 (see B71-73 note). If the reading be correct I should prefer to take it as the *sḏmtf*-form; otherwise might be read. In either case the translation of the sentence will be: "(Thus) has the god done[2] in order to be gracious to him against whom he had been incensed(?), whom he had led astray into a foreign land."

*149.* — "For today is his heart satisfied"; *iw* represents the conjunction "for". A good collection of instances of the phrase *iʿ-ib* is given by MORET, *Rec. de Trav.*, 14, 120-123; the sense seems to vacillate between "to be pleased" and "to slake one's appetite".

*149-154.* — The lyrical character of the next sentences is apparent at a glance; there are four pairs of contrasted sentences, the contrast in the first and second being, as it seems, one of tense, and in the third and fourth pair between the noun *si* and the emphatic pronoun *ink*. The fourfold repetition of *n* in the first clause of all the pairs can hardly be reproduced in English, but should be noted.

| | |
|---|---|
| *wʿr wʿr(w) n h3w-f* | These fled a fugitive in his season; |
| *iw mtrw-i m ḫnw* | now the report of me is in the Residence. |

1. I speak of purely verbal relative sentences; various circumlocutions with *nti* would be possible.
2. Similarly MASP., *C. P.*[2], p. 69.

| | |
|---|---|
| *sꜣꜣ sꜣꜣy n ḥkr* | A lingerer lingered because of hunger; |
| *iw-i di-i tꜣ n gsi-i* | now give I bread unto my neighbour. |
| *rww si tꜣ-f n ḥꜣy-t* | A man left his country because of nakedness; |
| *ink ḥd ḥbs-w pḳ-t* | but I am bright of raiment and linen. |
| *btꜣ si n gꜣw hꜣb(w)-f* | A man sped for lack of one whom he should send; |
| *ink ꜥšꜣ mr-t.* | but I am the plenteous owner of slaves. |

*151.* — The meaning of has hitherto been mistaken; it clearly signifies "to go slowly", "linger", "delay"[1]; cf. "nay, linger here", *Eloquent Peasant*, B2, 127; so too probably *Pap. Kahun*, 3, 30; parallel to , MAR., *Abyd.*, I, tabl. 1; , *Rec. de Trav.*, 26, 234 (religious text M. K.); not clear in the *šwꜣbti*-formula, SPIEGELBERG-NEWBERRY, *Theban Necropolis*, 20, 24. 25. 26. It is just possible that this verb of the 3æ. infirmae class is, in its origin, nothing more than a development of *sꜣw* "to keep", "to beware"; at all events an additional notion of moving cautiously seems to be implied in the frequent epithet *sꜣ iwt-f*[2], e. g. *El Bersheh*, II, 13, 16; *Cairo stele M. K.*, 20538; *Thebes, tomb of Sennofer.* — For , probably a substantival form, see B18-19, note.

*153.* — For the epithet *ḥd ḥbs-w*, see *Admonitions*, p. 27.

*154.* — For *btꜣ* see the note *Admonitions*, p. 108; and compare *op. cit.*, 8, 3, for the sense.

*156.* — is explained by Sethe as *sḏmwf*-form, with assimilation of the ending *-w* to the suffix (*sḫꜣi-i* for *sḫꜣw-i*), see *Verbum*, II, § 458, *ad fin.* I prefer to regard *sḫꜣw* as a substantive (cf. *Prisse*, 15, 5) "my remembrance is in the palace", since the preceding sentences are nominal. Still Sethe is doubtless right in his explanation of the ending; cf. *šn(w)i-i*, *Hirtengeschichte*, 4 (so too read for *Sinuhe*, B201); possibly also = , *Proc. S.B.A.*, 18, 197, l. 10, though this instance is rendered doubtful by the fact that occurs *Siut*, 4, 31. — In it is clear that should be read for .

---

1. I take this opportunity of explaining another misunderstood word with the same meaning, namely . The decisive passages for this verb are "do not linger, thou dost not haste", parallel to "do not be heavy, thou art not light" *Eloquent Peasant*, B2, 104; and "hold him back", *op. cit.*, R123, where B1, 78 has *swdf-k sw.*

2. That this verb is really the verb of motion is proved (1) by , *Cairo stele M. K.*, 20539; L., *D.*, II, 138 *e*, and (2) by such variants as *Rifeh*, 4, 29.

*157.* — , either (1) "may thou bring me home" or (2) "may thou bring me to the palace". On this ambiguity, see SETHE, *Ä. Z.*, 44 (1907), 81.

*157-158.* — "surely thou wilt allow me to see the place where my heart dwelleth". *Smwn* means "surely", "probably"[1] as the following examples show; "He is probably a peasant of his, who has gone to some one else beside him", *Eloquent Peasant*, B1, 44 = R90-91; "peradventure a scorpion has stung him", *Metternich stele*, 188; "turn thy face toward the North wind at the water's brink, haply thy heart shall be cooled in its affliction", *Harris stele* quoted BRUGSCH, *Wörtb. Suppl.*, 1061; "surely he will be content by reason of her praises", *Stele of Nitokris*, 2, (*Ä. Z.*, 35 [1897], 16). Less clear or instructive examples, *Westcar*, 4, 1; *Turin, statue of Horemheb*, 11; L., *D.*, III, 140 *b*, 3 (Redesiyeh; is a faulty transcription from the hieratic); L., *D.*, III, 175 *a*, 7 (Silsileh). — The construction with a suffix is without a parallel.

*159.* — "What can be more important than that I should be buried in the land in which I was born?" Cf. "it is no little thing that thou shouldst be buried, without Barbarians conducting thee (to the tomb)", B258-259. To the Egyptian there was no dread more intolerable than that he might be interred far from his home, and this theme is insisted on in more than one passage below (see especially B190-199). Similarly among the good things that the serpent of the phantom isle wished for his shipwrecked guest is that he may be buried in his own city (*Shipwrecked Sailor*, 169). — That *pw-tr* here and elsewhere in the tale can only be the interrogative pronoun has been demonstrated above, B121-122, note. — The expression *ʿbt-ḥ3t* "burial" is a not uncommon synonym of (below B193), with a similar idea at its base; *iʿb* means "to unite", and the meaning of the phrase is therefore "the union of the body with the earth" or "the tomb". Cf. *Urkunden*, IV, 64; PETRIE, *Qurneh*, 30, 5; *Totb.*, *ed.* NAV., 161; *Paheri*, 8. — For the relative clause *ms-kwi im-f*, see SETHE, *Verbum*, II, § 737, footnote.

*160-161.* — The next sentences are difficult. can hardly be construed otherwise than as a prayer to the god "come to help me", though I can produce no parallel to this use of *m s3-i*. — "that which has occurred is a good event", i. e. "a happy event has occurred", namely Sinuhe's victory

1. So too Sethe, correcting an alternative rendering *nonne?* which I had suggested. Griffith has proposed as an etymology *si-m-wn*, *Ä. Z.*, 34 (1896), 39.

over his adversary and subsequent acquisition of wealth. For the position of *pw* at the beginning of the sentence, cf. "I caused old women to say : this is a happy event", NEWBERRY, *Life of Rekhmara,* 8, 23, corrected from my own copy. Sethe points out that the same construction of *pw* is found in the interrogative *pw-tr,* on which see above; perhaps also compare the proper name . — possibly "I have caused God to be gracious". It is not certain, but at the same time a matter of indifference, whether (with erased) or should be read at the bottom of B 160. The writing of suggests that the scribe was thinking of the word for "offerings"; but it is not absolutely necessary to emend *ḥtp nṯr,* as the verb *di* "to cause" has an alternative construction with object and pseudoparticiple, cf. "I let the earth be strewn upon my hair *(šn[w]i-i)*", below B 201 : "may she cause my statue to prosper and flourish, resting in her temple for ever" *Brit. Mus.,* 81[1]. — "may he do the like so as to make good the end of him whom he hath afflicted". For the optative sense of the verb, cf. *Shipwrecked Sailor,* 20. — *Mi-iḫt* is perhaps a synonym of , not found elsewhere. — *Sfn* is the causative of the rare word *fn* "to be infirm", see *Admonitions,* p. 101. R 188 has preserved the words *r smnḫ pḥwi n sfn-nf* with the significant variant .

In conjunction with one another the four short sentences analysed above yield a tolerably good sense, which may thus be paraphrased :— "Come to help me, o thou god. One good event has already occurred, and I have propitiated the god's anger. May he bestow a like favour in causing me to die and be buried in my own land."

*162.* — "Pitying him whom he had expelled (?) to live in the desert." *'Ib-f mr,* cf. above B 132-133. is a very rare and obscure verb, perhaps meaning in its most literal sense "to press". In the scenes of spinning *Benihasan,* II, 4, 14, a process of a kind not easy to define is described by the word . In *Ebers,* 109, 4, we read "thou wilt find it (*scil.* "the swelling" *'3wt*) going and coming, pressing (?) against the flesh that is under it". Cf. too "he makes a document to exclude (?) him from (the rank of) *ka*-servant", *Urkunden,* I, 13. — Whatever its exact meaning, it is plain that *dkr-nf* introduces a relative sentence of the type of *ṯs-nf im-f* B 148; *sfn-nf* B 161; etc.

*162-163.* — "is he really appeased today ?" For the construction "is it (the case) that....." cf.

---

1. Another curious construction of *di* is exemplified in "causing falsehood not to be said, and truth not to be divulged", literally "I caused falsehood, and (a man) did not say it, truth, and (a man) did not come with it", *Cairo stele M. K.,* 20539, line 8.

[hieroglyphs] "did this thy servant enter into the temple on the twentieth?" *Pap. Kahun*, 32, 6 (context obscure); [hieroglyphs] "has the *m*ʿ*t*- boat been taken upstream by Shetepebre?" *Pap. Kahun*, 33, 12. The suffix in *ntt-f* is discussed in the footnote to my comments on B76-77. The words *in min rʿf ntt-f ḥtp* are virtually the protasis of a conditional sentence of which *sdm-f nḥ n wꜣ* "let him hear the prayer of him who is afar" is the apodosis.

*163.* — [hieroglyphs] "prayer" here and in B213 is masculine, as is shown by the lack of the feminine termination[1] and by the possessive adjective [hieroglyphs]. Elsewhere *nḥ-t* with feminine gender, cf. *Urkunden*, IV, 367; *Harris 500*, recto 7, 4.

*163-164.* — The sentences B162-163 are wanting in R, where the difficult sentence now to be discussed follows immediately upon *sfn-nf*. — The version of B is [hieroglyphs]; R188-189 gives [hieroglyphs]. It seems clear from the outset that [hieroglyphs] must be a relative clause of the now familiar type of [hieroglyphs] (B148)[2], and this enables us at once to reject *ḥw-ni* in R in favour of *ḥw-nf* in B, and to construe "him whom he (the god) had..... (banished [?], oppressed [?])[3]". *Ḥw tꜣ m* seems obviously an idiom for some penalty that can be flicted upon a man, and several obscure illustrations of the expression can be quoted, cf. [hieroglyphs] "To whom speak I today? The oppressor (?) doth wrong, there is no end to it" *Lebensmüde*, 129; [hieroglyphs] "I do not partake of oppression (??)" *Pap. Leiden* 347, 6, 7; [hieroglyphs] below B198-199; a proper name [hieroglyphs], *Cairo stele M. R.*, 20066. — *Wdb-*ʿ may be merely a synonym of *wdb* "to turn", cf. *whm-*ʿ, *ḫsf-*ʿ. — Before *ḥw-nf* (R -*ni*) *tꜣ im-f* B reads [hieroglyphs], but R [hieroglyphs]. We expect *wdb* "to turn" to be followed first by *m* "from" and then by *r* "to", and the reading of R should therefore be accepted; the variant of B may be due to assimilation with the *r* in *r bw in-nf sw im*. — Grammatically therefore we may construe "may he (i. e. the god) turn from him whom he hath oppressed (??) towards the place whence he took him"; this would be, it must be confessed, a very strangely worded sentence. The conjectural sense is either: (1) may the persecuting god leave Sinuhe and return to Egypt; or (2) may the god guide Sinuhe back to Egypt.

---

1. This would not, in the Berlin manuscript, be conclusive of itself, cf. [hieroglyphs], B123-124, note.

2. Unless this view be taken *sw* in *bw in-nf sw im* has no antecedent. — Note that *ḥw-nf tꜣ im-f* cannot mean "the place where....." without a preceding [hieroglyphs].

3. Sethe tentatively suggests "he for whom the earth quaked with him", *tꜣ* being subject; *ḥw* is elsewhere used of more or less violent natural phenomena, cf. *ḥw* "to rain", "to flow". But (1) the combination of *nf* "for him" and *im-f* "with him" is exceedingly unnatural; (2) the analogy of *ts-nf im-f*, *sfn-nf*, etc., leads one to suppose that "the god" is the subject; (3) in B198-199, *tꜣ* is clearly object of the infinitive, though the sense is obscure.

*165.* — Here R190-192 inserts some sentences, too fragmentary to translate, that do not occur in B. — [hieroglyphs] in B is palæographically doubtful, but certainly the reading of the archetype. *Ḥtp-t* is incorrect, and should be emended to *ḥtp-w*.

*166.* — *Ḥnwt-tꜣ* "the queen", see *Ä. Z.*, 45 (1908), 129, note s. — The prominence given to the queen here and in several other passages (B172, 186, 264, 274) is due to the circumstance that Sinuhe had been her special attendant in his youth (R3-4); he hopes, on returning to Egypt, to recover his former position.

*168.* — The determinative of *rnpy* in B is a mistake for [hieroglyph]. — [hieroglyphs] must be taken for [hieroglyphs] "because verily" (see above on B75-77), unless it be preferred to omit [hieroglyphs] as an error.

*168-169.* — [hieroglyphs] may well be a reminiscence of [hieroglyphs], *Prisse*, 4, 3. — On *wgꜣ* see Griffith's note *Proc. S. B. A.*, 13, 74, and for *ꜣs-nf'wi*, cf. above B22 = R47.

*169.* — [hieroglyphs] "weak" like an infant (?), only here; the relation of the word to [hieroglyphs] (e. g. *Siut*, I, 265) etc. is unknown.

*170.* — [hieroglyphs] is an error for [hieroglyphs], cf [hieroglyphs] "thou hast lost (thy) virility" B192; it is not clear whether we have here the *sḏm-nf* form or an intransitive use with dative.

*170-171.* — In [hieroglyphs] we should probably read [hieroglyphs] for *n wḏꜣ*, "death approaches me"; on *swḏꜣ* "death" see the note *Admonitions*, p. 95.

*171.* — The superfluous *n* in [hieroglyphs] can hardly be termed an error; it is an orthographical peculiarity not unknown elsewhere, cf. [hieroglyphs], *Neferhotep stele*, 33, [hieroglyphs], *ibid.*, 31, quoted by Erman, *Ä. Z.*, 43 (1906), 2 footnote; Herr Grapow has shown me other examples from M. K. sarcophagi, e. g. [hieroglyphs] Lacau, *Textes religieux*, 78 = *Rec. de Trav.*, 31, 164. — For [hieroglyphs] read [hieroglyphs].

*171-173.* — I now think that these sentences should all be translated optatively[1]: — "may they bring me to the city of eternity, and may I serve the Mistress of the Universe; o that she may tell me the beauty of her children, and pass eternity beside me." The sense has been almost correctly grasped by Erman, who remarks : "Er möchte noch einmal der Königin dienen, und mit ihr im Tode vereint sein" (*op. cit.*, 22, footnote 2). Only it must be noted that the words *šms-i nb-t r ḏr* are not, as Erman seems to imply, a mere reiteration of the wish of 166, but must, in the position they occupy, express the desire that even in death he may not be divided from his mistress. — Maspero (*C. P.*[3], 70, note 1) understands the words *nbt r ḏr* of a sepul-

1. In my German translation "(bald) bringen sie mich zur Stätte der Ewigkeit" the difficulty of connecting *sb-sn wi* with the foregoing descriptive nominal sentences is very apparent.

chral goddess, the counterpart of the masculine *nb r ḏr;* but he does not attempt to explain the next words *iḫ ḏd-i nfrw msw-s*, which indeed seem inexplicable on this hypothesis. *Nb-t r ḏr* is both here and in B274 evidently the queen (so too Erman and Griffith); as such it corresponds to the name *nb r ḏr* occasionally given to the king, cf. *Millingen*, 2; *Admonitions*, 15, 13.

*172-173.* — [hieroglyphs] "may she pass eternity beside (?) me". So MASP., ERM. rightly. [hieroglyphs] with an object denoting time always means "to pass", "spend"; cf. [hieroglyphs], *Urkunden*, IV, 54, and similarly 61; [hieroglyphs], *op. cit.*, 66; [hieroglyphs], *op. cit.*, 117, [hieroglyphs], *Harris*, I, 1, 2; [hieroglyphs], *Thebes, tomb of Nbwnnf.* — *Ḥr-i* is however a serious difficulty, for which no parallel is forthcoming except *ꜣb-f ḥr-i* B95. We might perhaps translate "may she spend eternity over me", i. e. enjoying my service; but this is a very dubious alternative.

*173-177.* — Sinuhe's reflexions now give place to a few ceremoniously worded sentences relating how the Royal decree for his recall was brought to him.

*173-174.* — Erman is, I think, certainly right in construing [hieroglyphs] as the passive form *sḏmwf*: "now it had been told unto the Majesty of the king Kheperkere concerning this condition in which I was". For the construction, cf. [hieroglyphs] R22-23. GR., MASP., and my German translation less well: "now the Majesty of the king..... spoke". — [hieroglyphs] is of course an error for [hieroglyphs] — *Sšm pn*, see on R18.

*174.* — The construction *wn in..... ḥꜣb-f* is the most ceremonious way of describing actions of the king, see ERMAN, *Äg. Gram.*², § 244; for another example, cf. [hieroglyphs], *Brit. Mus.*, 574 = SHARPE, *Eg. Inscr.*, I. 79.

*175.* — [hieroglyphs] "presents of the royal bounty". *ꜣwt-ʿ* cf. below B211. 245 (in 187 -ʿ is wrongly omitted); the etymological meaning of the expression is "stretching out the arm".

*178.* — Sinuhe's narrative is here interrupted to give admittance to a copy of the royal rescript decreeing his recall from exile (B178-199). This is followed almost immediately by the "copy of the acknowledgement" sent by Sinuhe (B204-238), after which the story is continued in the first person until the end. That these two insertions in no wise militate against the view of the text as modelled on the biographical inscriptions in tombs has been proved by analogous cases dating from the Old Kingdom (R1-2, note). — From this point onwards B is our sole authority, except for two brief passages in which the evidence of late ostraca is forthcoming.

*Mit(t)* in [hieroglyphs] is a masculine substantive, as the following *ni* shows; similarly below B204; *Pap. Kahun*, 9, 2; 12, 1; in the N. K., cf. especially [hieroglyphs], *Sall. I*, 9, 1, a convincing proof of the masculine gender of the word. — For *bꜣk im*[1] see BORCHARDT, *Ä. Z.*, 27 (1889), 122-124; SETHE, *Ä. Z.*, 30 (1892), 126-127. In the best literary texts this expression is followed by the pronoun of the 3rd. person, if the pronoun is in close proximity or at least in the same sentence (so here; below B205. 213; *Pap. Kahun*, 28, 21 = 29, 12)[2]; otherwise the 1st. person is employed (B177; 223). Such an example as *swḏꜣ ib pw n nb-i* [hieroglyphs], *Pap. Kahun*, 28, 6 is a defect of style that would have been intolerable to the author of our tale.

*179-180.* — The scribe of B has attempted (though with but partial success) to preserve the outward form in which royal rescripts were customarily written. From an examination of the decrees of the Old Kingdom (PETRIE, *Abydos*, II, 17. 18; *Ä. Z.*, 42 [1905], 4) it will be seen that the king's name and titles there occupy a vertical line to the right of the text: the latter begins in a horizontal direction with the words [hieroglyphs] (thus reversed), which are at once followed by the titles of the addressee (cf. also *Urkunden*, I, 60. 62. 128). Here the long titles of Senwosret I have overlapped into the horizontal line B180, and the words *wḏ stn* have been connected with Sinuhe's title by the preposition [hieroglyph]. — The flagrant error[3] *'Imnmḥꜣt* for *Snwsrt* (B180) is an overwhelming proof of the ignorance of the scribe of B. — Sinuhe here receives the same title as he held at the time of his flight, namely that of "attendant", "follower" (cf. R2).

*181-185.* — The difficulties presented by the beginning of the decree have baffled all translators; Erman has at least rightly seen that the lines 183-184 allude to the privileges that Sinuhe had foregone through his absence from Court, but his conjecture as to the point of the adjacent context[4] does not appear to me to lay the stress in the right place; the renderings proposed by Griffith and Maspero are open to serious philological objections[5]. The first sentences can be redeemed from utter platitudinous emptiness only by supposing their final words *ḫr sḥ n ib-k nk* to be strongly emphatic; on this view they acquire a real point, declaring that Sinuhe himself alone was responsible for all his toilsome wanderings. I therefore render : "thou hast traversed the

---

1. I fail to understand why *bk* is often read instead of *bꜣk*; surely this is an anachronism so far as texts of the O K. are concerned.

2. This argument alone would suffice to prove that [hieroglyphs] in B235 is not *ṯꜣt-i* "my serfs (?)", but a mistake for [hieroglyphs] "the office of Vizier".

3. It is incredible that this should be anything else but a mistake. Maspero too views it as such (*M. S.*, p. XXXVI), but adds, to my mind quite unnecessarily : "Si pourtant elle (the combination of the cartouches of AI and SI) était préméditée, on pourrait dire que l'auteur, en accouplant ces deux cartouches dans un même protocole, a voulu indiquer le règne commun des deux princes." Apart from all else, Amenemhet was long since dead at the time of Sinuhe's recall.

4. "Der Sinn der Sätze mage etwa sein : dein Vergehen hat sich selbst gestraft; fern von deinem natürlichen Wirkungskreis hast du dein Leben zugebracht", *op. cit.*, p. 22, footnote 7.

5. Both scholars translate *ptri* in 183 as an interjection. GR.'s version of the next sentences is as follows : "thou hast not blasphemed, so also the accusation against thee hath been repelled. So also thy sayings have been respected; thou hast not spoken against the Council of the Nobles". But *mdw-k* can hardly mean "the accusation against thee"; *m sḥ n srw* must surely signify "*in* the Council", in spite of the idiom *mdw m* (*Ä. Z.*, 29 [1891], 49-52); nor does *ltn* mean "to respect". — MASP., *C. P.*[3], p. 71, translates these same sentences as prohibitions, in which case [hieroglyph] or [hieroglyphs] would be required in the place of [hieroglyph].

lands, and hast gone forth from Kedmi to Retenu, and land has handed thee on to land, by the counsel of thine own heart alone". The rhetorical question that follows urges Sinuhe to consider the benefits he has thus sacrificed by his folly: "what hast thou caused to be done unto thee?" The answer is: "thou dost not curse (?), yet (?) thy word is rejected; thou dost not speak in the Council of the Nobles, but thy utterances are thwarted." It may be held preferable by some to understand the verbs in these sentences as having past meaning, but even so this will not affect the fact that they refer to Sinuhe's self-deprivation of the advantages he would have enjoyed, had he remained in Egypt. In line 185 the point that Sinuhe alone is to blame is reiterated in a brief antithesis: "this choice carried away thy heart, it was not in (my?) heart against thee". How well the sense above proposed suits the remainder of the decree will be apparent at a glance.

*181.* — is probably for *dbn-nk*, cf. below B201, and the note on B111-112.

*182.* — *prti*, 2nd. masc. pseudoparticiple, thus defectively written like B193; B257. The following words can in B only be read *m Ḳdmi r Tnw*, but we must emend *r Rtnw*. — In the parallel passage to the *sdm-nf*-form was given (B28); the use of the form (see SETHE, *Verbum*, II, § 311) is too little known for us to be able to judge whether it is here rightly employed or not.

*182-183.* — , cf. *ḥr sḥ n wḥyt-f* B113. The strong emphasis upon these words is possibly indicated by the curious addition of *nk;* the literal translation "by the advice of thy heart to thee" certainly seems to imply that there had been but two actors in the entire drama of Sinuhe's flight and exile, namely himself and his own heart[1]. We shall therefore perhaps be justified in rendering "by the counsel of thine heart alone".

*183.* — "what hast thou caused to be done to thee?" For the use of *ir* in place of *di* "to cause" a few rare parallels occur in the Pyramid-texts (see SETHE, *Verbum*, II, § 150 *b*), and is occasionally employed for in the N. K. (*op. cit.*, II, § 164 *b*)[2]. — The next words contain the answer to this question.

*183-184.* — [3] . The only sentence here that does not contain difficulties of any sort is *n mdw-k m sḥ n srw* "thou dost not speak in the Council of the Nobles". There is just a possibility that the verb might be construed

1. This personification of the heart is quite Egyptian; cf. *Shipwrecked Sailor*, 41-2, and the note thereon in my *Admonitions*, p. 104 *ad fin*.

2. My German translation "Was hast du da getan, und (was) tat man dir an?" assumes a clumsy and improbable ellipse. The renderings of GR. and MASP. give to *pw-tri* the sense of *ptri* "behold", an interjection not used before the N. K. (see note on B121-122).

3. On the strange hieratic determinative given by B to this and similar words, see *Die Erzählung des Sinuhe*, p. 5 top.

as a perfect "thou didst not speak", in which case the allusion would be to the occasion when Sinuhe's affairs were discussed at Court, himself not being present to defend his conduct. But it seems better to take the clause as a generalization, referring to Sinuhe's exclusion from the Council throughout the whole time of his absence. — is a serious difficulty, since in the few instances where the word occurs it has always a *bad* sense. In the extremely effaced text *Rec. de Trav.*, 18, 183, line 33, the words apparently refer to the inundation of the temple of Luxor, and are probably rightly rendered by Daressy "cette situation est une grande malédiction, on ne se souvient pas (d'un fait semblable)"[1]. So too *Piankhi*, 86 "There was none slain there saving the rebels who had blasphemed against God". In the course of the disturbances among the workmen of the Necropolis in the 29th. year of Rameses III a certain man "spent the night cursing the tombs", *Pap. Turin*, 43, 9; and among the sins of another man it is recorded that he "cursed a tomb on the west of the Necropolis", *Salt*, 124, verso 1, 1. Finally, Demotic makes it quite clear that this word is the prototype of the Coptic ⲟⲩⲁ "blasphemia"[2]; see Br., *Wörtb.*, 240; *Suppl.*, 323; *Sethon*, I, 5, 10 (with Griffith's note); *Pap. mag. Leiden*, 19, 15. Apparently the only possible way of preserving its usual sense to *wꜥꜣ* here, is to construe the following words *ḫsf-tw mdw-k* as antithetic to it, i. e. "though thou dost not curse, yet is thy word rejected". — occurs transitively only in one other passage, namely Mar., *Abyd.*, II, 30, 37 (stele of Neferhotep) "he who shall thwart what my Majesty commands"; with *m* "to oppose (?)", cf. , *Prisse*, 13, 11 (perhaps similarly, 14, 3); *ibid.*, 15, 1. 6 are obscure passages. is used for "foes" Nav., *Deir-el-Bahari*, 84, 2; Rochem., *Edfou*, I, 150. 186. Perhaps "secret", "mystery", is connected with the same stem ("that which opposes itself to the searcher", "is elusive"?), cf. R., *I. H.*, 26, 12; *Rifeh*, I, 12; *Anast.*, *I*, 1, 7; *Louvre*, C 232.

*185.* — In the "blank-cheque" word *sḫr* refers to Sinuhe's unresisting acceptance of all the disadvantages above detailed; "this choice" perhaps renders the sense more closely than either "this counsel" or "this mode of life" would do. For the construction see R20-22 note, and for the *sdm-nf* form cf. *ḥkꜣ pn ꜥmwinši rdi-nf-wi r ḥpt-f* B143. — *N ntf m* *rk* might be

1. I quote from my own collation of the passage. Daressy's painstaking attempt to decipher the worn, scarcely visible, signs, is worthy of all commendation. During my recent visit to Thebes I made an effort to revise the text, and was able to correct the published copy in places; a really satisfactory transcript could not however be obtained without good squeezes.

2. *Admonitions*, p. 53, is to be corrected accordingly.

translated either (1) "it was not in (any) heart against thee" or (2) "it was not in my heart (*ib-i*) against thee". The latter version appears to me the more probable, the suffix 1st. sing. being often omitted in B.

*185-187.* — While Sinuhe has been sojourning in a foreign land, the princess Nofru, his former mistress, has become queen of Egypt, her children have grown up and are received at Court. This the king narrates to Sinuhe, urging him to return to his own land, where the favour of the royal princes, Nofru's children, will be restored to him.

*185.* — *Pt-k tn* "this thy heaven", a very violent metaphor for "thy mistress", and a striking example of the artificial style employed in the tale.

*186.* — *mn-s rwd-s* "prospers and flourishes"; the collocation is a very common one, as for example in *Admonitions*, 2, 11; cf. too a quotation contained in the note on B160-161. is a unique and unfortunate spelling, elsewhere being an abbreviation for *dꜣir*, cf. above B50; *Shipwrecked Sailor*, 132. — "today" like simple *min*, cf. *Lebensmüde*, 5; L., *D.*, II, 150 *a*, 16 (Hammamat, *Ḥnw*); *Totb.*, *éd.* NAV., 179, 3; etc.

In the first word is utterly obscure, and almost certainly corrupt[1]. The sense must be "she participates in the kingship of the land".

*187.* — probably meant originally "interior" of a building, and has a wide meaning in the phrase . For the restricted sense "the Court", i. e. the apartment where the courtiers were received, cf. R19; B251. 282. 284; *Louvre*, C174; *Hatnub*, 9, 3. The erroneous writing with becomes a habit in the N. K. and has given rise, in *Pap. Hood*, II, 10, to the monstrous spelling .

is translated in my German version by "du sollst lange geniessen die herrlichen Dinge, die sie dir geben, du sollst von ihren Gaben leben", which differs but little from Erman's rendering. Erman however understands *wꜣḥ-k špss* as "du wirst an dem Trefflichen..... Überfluss haben". There is apparently no authority for this sense of *wꜣḥ*, and of the active meanings of that verb "to place", "to offer", "to add", "to leave" none is here suitable. The parallelism of the verbs *wꜣḥ-k* and *ʿnḫ-k* strongly suggests that the former must here have its common intransitive sense "to endure", "live long", though in this case a preposition (*m* or *ḥr*) must be lost before *špss*. The sense will then be the same as *Westcar*, 7, 21; for the construction see ERMAN, *Sprache des Pap. Westcars*, § 91[2]. — can hardly be

1. MASP.'s suggestion (*M. S.*, p. IX) appears to me far too venturesome.

2. MASP., *C. P.*[3], p. 71, renders « laisse les richesses qui t'appartiennent », reading instead of (= ); so too GR. But even if *ntt* were palaeographically possible, it could not agree with *špss*, which requires either *nti* or *ntiw*; nor would it be easy to parallel the phrase *ntt-sn nk*.

right as it stands, *ȝwt* needing a determinative or complement of some sort; emend *ʿwt-ʿ-sn* as in B 175. 211. 245.

*188.* — For "return thou", cf. B5-6. 19; Sethe however classes this example with some other similarly periphrastic imperatives (*Verbum,* II, § 497). — For the form in a final sentence, see SETHE, *Verbum,* II, § 252, 8, and cf. *Shipwrecked Sailor,* 134. 158.

*189.* — "for now verily"; here again, as in Sinuhe's own reflexions (B159), the hope of burial in Egypt is held out as the chief inducement to return from abroad.

*190.* — "thou hast lost thy virile strength"; for *fḫ-nk* cf. B170, note; *bȝȝwt* is a ἅπαξ λεγόμενον, for which Maspero ingeniously suggests, a postulated derivative of (*M. S.,* p. 83).

*190-191.* — "remember thou the day of burial, and (thy) attainment of the blessed state"; the mental picture here summoned up passes insensibly into a review of the customary rites of burial. — is a common, but not quite easy, phrase; its general sense is very plainly indicated by the following quotation, "I went forth from my house to my tomb, I attained the blessed state" *Cairo stele M. K.,* 20506. The grammatical difficulty consists in the fact that must be given an intransitive meaning "to pass" (into a state), whereas the verb is elsewhere active "to send", "conduct", "pass (time)", except in the proverbial tag "one generation passes, and another springs up, "MAR., *Abyd.,* I, 51, 36; *Inscr. dédic.,* 66; *Harris,* 500, recto 6, 3; M. MÜLLER, *Liebeslieder,* pl. I., l. 2. The hypothesis of a confusion with "to hasten" seems to win support from the occasional appearance of that verb as a variant in the phrase here discussed, cf. *Cairo stele M. K.,* 20506 (quoted above); 20005; and archaistically PETRIE, *Koptos,* 18, 3; *Louvre Apis,* 339 = *Rec. de Trav.,* 22, 178; and a motive for such a confusion might be found in the fact that a very similar phrase in which has its regular active sense "to pass", "spend" time, occurs in the mastabas of the O. K.; cf. "spending the age of blessedness with his god[1]", MAR., *Mast.,* D6; , *op. cit.,* D 38. However against this suggestion must be set the fact that is far more frequent than in the phrase..... *r imȝḫ,* and occurs in texts irreproachable in respect both of age and of orthography, cf. *Siut,* IV, 66; *Benihasan,* I, 24. 41; *Cairo stele M. K.,* 20458. We must content ourselves with the verdict *non liquet.*

*191-192.* —

1. It has been suggested that *r* is here omitted. But (1) the phrase *sb r imȝḫ* is not attested before the M. K., nor has it even then the additional words *ḫr nṯr-f, ḫr nb-f;* (2) the translation "spending the age of blessedness with his god (lord)" is clearly more likely than "passing into blessedness with his lord".

"the nighttime is devoted to thee with oils and with wrappings (made by the hands of *Tȝyt*". *Wdʿ* means properly "to sever"; thence "to divide the true from the false" and so "to judge" persons; lastly "to assign" to a person that which is adjudged to him or falls to his lot by right. For this sense cf. "Ptah assigned to thee thy mouth on the day of thy birth" *Metternich stele,* 147; "my fields are assigned to me in Busiris", *Totb., ed.* BUDGE, 52, 5 = *ibid.*, 189, 6; *Mission,* V, 283 (Amenemhet); similarly *Mission,* V, Neferhotep, pl. 3, second row, left. — The spelling for can be paralleled from *Pap. med. Hearst,* 11, 18; 12, 8. — The goddess *Tȝyt* is known to have been the patroness of weaving; the wish to be swathed in bandages of her making seems to occur in the much-damaged passage *Anast.*, I, 4, 1; and there is an obscure allusion of the same kind *Cairo stele M. K.*, 20565.

*192-193.* — "a procession is made for thee" on the day of interment". *Šms-wḏȝ* is the technical term for the funeral cortège, in which all manner of emblems and strange images were borne upon the shoulders of the servants of the deceased; the words are found in a scene depicting such a cortège in the *Theban tomb of 'Intf-iḳr* (*temp.* Senwosret I.); in two other tombs "a procession consisting of everything (i. e. with all the outfit of the funerary ritual) as is made for the chief courtier" is wished for the deceased, *Urkunden,* IV, 1200 *(Mnḫpr); Rec. de Trav.*, 20, 214 *(Snnfr);* and in yet another tomb an attendant is depicted carrying the *sic* "vessels of the funerary cortège", *Urkunden,* IV, 1023 *('Imnms).*

*193.* — cf. "the sarcophagus of fresh cedarwood, painted and carved with the finest (art?) of the *Pr-nfr*, the mummy-case of refined (?) gold, ornamented with real lapis lazuli", *Louvre,* C 11; the word *wi* is known from no other source. — In the text of B can hardly be correct as its stands; if be the original reading, a suffix must be supplied to qualify it, *tp-f* "its head", i. e. the head of the mummy-case, or rather of the stucco and gilt covering of the mummy. But is it not more likely that *ḫkr* or some such word should be substituted for , as in the Louvre stele above quoted? — By "the heaven above thee", scholars have considered that a canopy is meant, but the reference may possibly be to the conception of the lid of the sarcophagus as symbolizing the goddess Nut, see SCHÄFER, *Priestergräber*, p. 121.

*193-194.* — "thou art placed in the portable shrine". For the writing of the pseudo participle *diti* see above B 182, note; the is depicted *Der el Gebrawi*, II, 7. 10, and is mentioned again in the sentence CHAMP., *Not. descr.*, I, 836.

*194-195.* — For Wiedemann (*Rec. de Trav.*, 17, 2) aptly quotes two later monuments : MAR., *Mon. div.*, 61 = PIEHL, *Inscr. hiér.*, I, 44 (N. K.); *ibid.*, I, 73 (Ptolemaic period). On the evidence of these quotations it is tempting to correct "the weary ones", (i. e. the dead, see *Admonitions*, p. 56) into "dwarfs", this being the M. K. writing of the word *nm(i)* of later periods, cf. above the heads of stunted dwarfs *Benihasan*, II, 16. 32; the passage would then allude, not to a *danse macabre*, but to a dance known as the "dance of the dwarfs"[1]. Among the funerary scenes of the tombs a dance performed by men wearing curious reed-caps is not uncommonly depicted (e. g. TYLOR, *Tomb of Renni*, 12), and the accompanying inscriptions give as the description of these persons a word exceedingly like the term for dwarfs at Benihasan; cf. *Thebes, tomb of 'Intf-ikr;* *Thebes, tomb of the steward and scribe of the corn Amenemhet;* *Paheri*, 5. Unfortunately for the hypothesis of a "dance of the dwarfs", the phonetic writing *mwiw* occurs in a tomb of the M. K. behind the Ramesseum, where the encourages the dancers with the words (QUIBELL, *Ramesseum*, 9). On the evidence above adduced one can only conclude that the archetype of the tale of Sinuhe, or the source from which the sentence was drawn, gave the reading *mw-w*; this unfamiliar word was then misunderstood by the scribe of B, who substituted for it *nnyw*; other scribes however misinterpreted as "dwarfs", of which a modernized spelling was adopted in later quotations of the passage. It is not without regret that we have to replace the "dance of the dwarfs", with its suggestive bearing upon the question of Herkhuf's dancing pygmy, by a "dance of the *Mwiw*" with its inexplicable and unenlightening name.

*195.* — "the offering-table is invoked for thee". Cf. L., *D.*, II, 71 *b*; and similarly L., *D.*, III, 282 *d*; MAR., *Dend.*, I, 32. *Dbḥt-ḥtp* is a term for the altar decked with funerary meal; in a quite concrete sense, "an altar of gold and silver" *Urkunden*, IV, 22. The allusion here is of course to the offerings, which the deceased comes forth to enjoy 'at the sound of the summons of the offerer" (cf. *Turin*, 104; *Leiden* V, 10; *Louvre*, A54. C74; *Mission*, V, 544 [Thebes, tomb of ]).

*196.* — The expression "at the *door* of thy stelae" occurs nowhere else. The stele was itself a false door, and the phrase is therefore not

1. Sethe's explanation of *ir·tw ḫbibi* (*Verbum*, II, § 201) is clearly an oversight. These words cannot be a mere periphrasis of "es wird getanzt", on account of the following substantive. *Ḫbibi* is here clearly a substantivally-used infinitive governing the genitive *nnyw*.

inappropriate, but the proximity of *r rì ìs-k* (B195) suggests that *r rì* may have been borrowed thence. Perhaps should be read, and further the singular *'b3-k*.

*196-197.* — "In the midst of the royal children" naturally means "in the midst of the pyramids" (B301) which the royal children had built for themselves around the sepulchre of the king.

*197.* — clearly means "thou shalt surely not die in a foreign land"; the construction possibly belongs to the type *wn sdm-f;* ERMAN, *Äg. Gramm.*[3], § 239, though an exact parallel is wanting. — For cf. B 259, where *bs* is the infinitive. These examples[1] show that *bs* "to introduce", "be introduced into" (instances are quoted by SETHE, *Die Einsetzung des Veziers*, p. 11, note 39) belongs to the biliteral class, cf. too the frequent heading of temple scenes . This verb is therefore to be distinguished carefully from ⲟⲩⲓⲥⲉ "to swell", "flow forth", which presents all the characteristics of the 3æ. geminatæ class (the infinitive already L., *D.*, II, 149 *f*, 3 [Hammamat, Dyn. 11.]). The meaning "to conduct" to the tomb exemplified in the passages from our tale occurs nowhere else.

*198.* — The allusion to the Asiatic practice of wrapping the corpse in the skin of a ram is interesting, but I find no archaeological confirmation. Maspero rightly quotes *Hdt.*, II, 81, in illustration of the Egyptian's repugnance to woollen burial garments, but at the same time cites a case in which this prejudice was disregarded (*C.P.*[3], p. 73, footnote 1). — "when thy tomb is made(??)"; *ḏr* in this form is utterly obscure, see the note *Admonitions*, p. 28 on the various words from the same stem.

*198-199.* — is another very difficult sentence. For *ḥw-t3* see the note on B163-164. I cannot escape from the impression that these words must summarize what has preceded, and that we ought to translate: "all these things will fall to the ground", i. e. be avoided by thy return. It is true however that (cf. "all these years" *Admonitions*, 13, 2) would then have to be read, and the sense given to *ḥwt-t3* lacks all support.

*199.* — "take thought for (thy) corpse and return". *Mḥ ḥr*, see BRUGSCH, *Wörtb.*, 686-687 and *Lebensmüde*, 32.78. — is evidently the equivalent of , which is so written in the phrase below B259 (see B 159, note); "illness" (BRUGSCH, *Wörtb. Suppl.*, 884) would make but little sense here. — is the *sḏm-f* form optatively used, see SETHE, *Verbum*, II, § 319.

*199-204.* — A brief paragraph describing Sinuhe's feelings on the arrival of Pharaoh's letter.

*200.* — "it was read to me"; so GR. and ERM. rightly. Maspero

1. After the emphatic form with gemination would be needful here if *bs* belonged to the 3æ. infirmae class.

renders "il me fut délivré, remis", giving to *šd* a sense for which I find no parallel; it is however to be remarked that in other old texts *šd* "to recite", "read"[1] either is without a determinative or has ; later exceptionally , e.g. *Anast. V*, 8, 3. — "I threw myself on my belly»; for the writing of *di-ni wi* see B 4-5 note, and for the expression, cf. *Prisse*, 2, 6[2]; *Shipwrecked Sailor*, 161. 166; *Piankhi*, 34. 55. 71; and often. On hearing the words of Pharaoh Sinuhe behaves as though he were actually in the Royal presence. — "I touched the earth", i. e. lay prostrate on the ground; only here and *Shipwrecked Sailor*, 137-138.

*201.* — "I scattered it upon my hair". *Sw* refers to *s3tw* "earth" in the last sentence, the construction being that discussed in the note on B160–161. *Šnby* is, as it stands, a *vox nihili*, and should probably be emended to , see on B156; the scribe was doubtless thinking of "breast", and Maspero actually gives in his critical edition (*M. S.*, p. 17, l. 2). — is a word which we have already twice encountered (B3 and B128); at its third occurrence here the difficult question of the reading can no longer be shirked, and I will therefore outline the results to which a somewhat rapid examination of the examples contained in the Berlin dictionary has brought me. There is not the least doubt that (or ) should be read *sn(i)* in a number of cases, as has long been recognized (see [e. g]. Erman, *Aeg. Glossar*, 105); thus quite certainly (1) when the meaning is "to open", for which we have the old variants and [3]. The determinative , which appears to have been taken over from the word (some kind of bread or cake), has been confused with *š*, whence the writings and for *sn(i)* have arisen. (2) "To pass", Coptic ⲥⲓⲛⲉ : *a*) absolutely, compare *Koller*, 5, 1, with from a collation of Ros., *M. S.*, 125; *b*) absolutely, of time, compare *Canopus* 19 with *Piankhi*, 78; *c*) "to pass by" with direct object; in M. K. (and 18th. dyn.) *always* written , e. g. *Beni Hasan*, I, 8, 8; *Shipwrecked Sailor*, 9; L., *D.*, II, 136, i; *Rec. de Trav.*, 15, 55, 14; in papyri of the N. K. *always* written , e. g. *Pap. Turin*, 44, 11; 42, 6 (of walls); *Anast. V*, 24, 7; *Anast. I*, 21, 3; *d*) "to pass by" with ; the formula (*Pap. Leiden 369*, recto, 4; *370*, recto, 3; *Pap. Bibl. Nat. 197, 4*, 2) offers as an exceptional variant *Pap. Turin*, 114; 115; *e*) "to surpass" with direct object, only examples

1. For the Egyptians themselves there was probably no conscious distinction between these two senses. Doubtless few except the professional scribes were able to read for themselves, so that for the great majority "to read" a letter was the same thing as "to speak it aloud". Similarly ⲱϣ is later the usual word for "read"; thus Smendes causes his despatches to be "pronounced" (*ʿš*) before him, *Unamon*, 1, 5. Similarly in the letters, "I have *heard* (*sdm*) that concerning which thou hast sent to me", i. e. I have noted the contents of your letter (*passim*).

2. The explanation of *Prisse*, 2, 6 given in *Ä.Z.*, 41 (1904), 90 can hardly be defended.

3. The sign in doubtless only a graphic modification of or , just as for *sp.*

with , e. g. *Urkunden*, IV, 102 ; Borch., *Baug. d. Amontempels*, 45; *Anast. V*, 18, 4; *f*) "to transgress"; with direct object, only with , e.g. *Prisse*, 7, 4; *Sall. III*, 2, 4; R., *I. H.*, 239, 33. From these quotations it seems reasonable to conclude that , in the sense of "to pass" and in cognate meanings is identical with , , and that the variation in the spelling depends on the habit of a period or on that of an individual scribe or school of scribes; case *d*) is particularly illuminating. It is however extremely curious to note how the scribe of *Anastasi I* (to quote but one individual case) varies his writing of what we have concluded to be one and the same verb *sn(i)*; for "to pass by" with . he writes 3, 7; in an absolute sense we find 10, 4 (cf. *Koller*, 5, 1; *Pap. Turin*, 46, 15); in "the crossing of *D-r-ʿ-m*" the spelling is 21, 3; in "the crossing to Mageddo" (23, 1) the scribe wrote but then, apparently thinking this wrong, added above the line (similarly 24, 1); in 24, 2 is found in an obscure context. The choice of spelling here seems to depend, not on any difference of grammatical form, but on the meaning. It is at first sight difficult to believe that and in *Anastasi I* can really be the same word, but the evidence that has been adduced from other sources seems to require that conclusion. (3) "to spread", "strew": "to spread out" clothes, *Butler*, 33 = *Eloquent Peasant R*, 49; *Admonitions*, 14, 3; a bed, *Mission V, Neferhotpou*, pl. 3; books, *Rekhmara*, 2, 2; with "extended" claws or wings, Rochem., *Edfou*, I, 306; II, 55; abbreviated as , *ibid.*, II, 65; "thy love is spread throughout the lands", *Cairo Hymn to Amon*, 5, 6; "his rays are extended over my breast (*šnb-t*)", Mar., *Abyd.*, I, 52, 23; and a number of other instances. With this meaning there is no evidence for the reading *sn*. But, as we saw above, particular meanings of the verbal stem *sn(i)* seem to have a specialized orthography of their own, "to surpass" and "to trangress" for example always being written with . We should therefore beware of too great haste in asserting that the reading of "to stretch", "spread" is *sš*, more especially as these meanings might be derived from a primitive meaning "to open", and as we know for certain that the reading of the verb "to open" is *sn*. Provisionally it will be the most prudent course merely to state the two possible alternatives. — To turn now to the three instances in the story of Sinuhe. In R 26 = B 3 may be translated either "my arms opened" or "my arms were spread open"; the example well illustrates the close relationship of the meanings "to spread" and "to open". In B128 I have proposed to render as "I took out my dagger" (to examine it), lit. "I gave an opening to my dagger", in this case being *sn(i)* "to open". It should however be noted that is elsewhere an idiomatic phrase for "to appear", "manifest oneself", cf. "appearing to every eye", *Urkunden*, IV, 495; "thou manifestest thyself in the Boat of the Dawn" *Pap.*

*Berlin 3050*, col. 3, 6; *Miss.*, V 359 (collated); other examples, *Cairo, Hymn to Amon*, 4, 6; NAV., *Goshen*, 1, left; ROCHEM., *Edfou*, I, 110. 148. 231. In the present passage (B201) is "to spread" in the sense of "to scatter".

"I strode round my encampment". MASP. corrects into (*M. S.*, p. 17, l. 2), but this leaves the first *n* unexplained. It is easier to read *dbn-ni*, see B 111-112 note; in B181 is more ambiguous. For *dbn* in simple narrative prose, cf. *Westcar*, 12, 3.

*202*. — "How is this done to a servant whom his heart has led astray into hostile lands?" GR. translates "to the servant, whose heart had transgressed to a strange country of babbling tongue", a rendering which is grammatically defensible, the relative pronoun then being the suffix of (SETHE, *Verbum*, II, § 745). But the analogy of B 148-149 suggests a different explanation, since there can only mean "whom he (the god) led astray[2] into a foreign land", see B 147-149 note. It must be admitted however that the sense "to lead astray" is not supported by any further evidence; elsewhere *th* is "to err", "to transgress" or "to violate". — is understood both by GR. and by MASP. as meaning "of babbling speech", and hence "barbarians"; ERM. leaves the word untranslated. No importance is to be attached to the determinative, apparently without the arms, given to *ḏrḏr-yt* by the scribe of B; as pointed out in my edition of the text (p. 5) this scribe constantly confuses his determinatives, and especially those that represent human beings in various attitudes. When Maspero explains the word to mean "balbutiants comme des enfants" (*M. S.*, p. 183), he seems to attribute more weight to the determinative than it deserves. In all other passages where *ḏrḏri* occurs it has the determinative which connotes not only admiration and respect, but also on occasion fear and dislike (so for example sometimes in ). The verbal stem *ḏrḏr* is rare, and the instances I have collected are all somewhat obscure; nevertheless the sense "to be hostile" seems applicable in every case. In *Sall. IV*, 3, 2 Isis attacks Seth, who has taken the form of a hippopotamus, with her harpoon, until he appeals to her sense of family ties with the words : (read )

1. The original has a sign like but without arms; see below.

2. The grammatical objection to GR.'s rendering of B 148 "who deserted to a foreign land" is that Egyptian must here use the participle , not the relative-form . See SETHE, *Verbum*, II, § 742, for the rule, to which there are no exceptions, so far as I am aware. An apparent exception is *Brit. Mus.*, 614 (new no. 100) = *Piers-Breasted stele*, 8 (collated); *Brit Mus.*, 159; here we may have a ready-made expression — "I was a he-loves-good-and-hates-evil" — analogous to the phrases and quoted by me *Rec. de Trav.*, 26, 14.

"dost thou desire hostility against a maternal brother?" In the difficult passage *Max. d'Anii*, 5, 15-6, 2 advice is given not to speak evil against someone "on the day of thy quarrelling; thou wilt find him good at the time of thy friendship; when troubles come, thou wilt find him ready to bear the(ir) hostility so that it ceases". The phrase occurs twice in the same papyrus (6, 2; 6, 7) in an untranslatable context, where all that can be said is that *ḏrḏr* is an adjective, as in the *Sinuhe* passage. So too perhaps in *Pap. mag. Vatican* = *Ä. Z.*, 31 [1893], 120[1], where it may be an epithet of Seth. In *Lebensmüde*, 116-118 and 123-125, we find two similarly constructed passages, which seem to explain one another. One of these (123-125) runs as follows: "To whom shall I speak today? men have no intimates; a man is treated as a stranger according to (the measure of that) which has (previously) been made known to him", i. e. the greater the confidence which has been shown to a man in the past, the more he is now in these evil times treated as a stranger (*ḫmm*, perfect participle passive, see SETHE, *Verbum*, II, § 927). The other passage (*Lebensmüde*, 116-118) runs: "To whom shall I speak today? companions (lit. "brothers") are evil; men are treated as enemies according to (the measure of the affection (?)[3] (that once was felt for them?). That these two passages have been rightly interpreted seems to be confirmed by the new London parallel text to *Prisse*, II, 1-4, where consideration towards friends is preached; "he who is not considerate to his friends, men say, "He has a selfish[4] character'; the (right) character[5] is the even character with which men are satisfied. There is no one who knows his fortune when he plans for (?) to-morrow[6]. If a second occasion finds him (lit. occurs) in luck, friends say to him

1. This instance I owe to the kindness of M. Dévaud, who also quotes an example from *Butler*, verso, 19.

2. The arms of are omitted by the scribe.

3. The meaning of *mtt nt ib* is not yet established; in the instances at present known to me (*Urk.*, IV, 96. 367. 489. 546) "affection", "sollicitude" "care" are senses which would all suit.

4. The verb *ˁ3b* means "to be pleasant" or the like, cf. *Eloquent Peasant*, R42 = *Butler*, 24; here apparently is meant the man who seeks only his own pleasure.

5. Cf. the closely analogous sentence *sr pw sr sndw-nf*, *Urk.*, IV, 1091, where *sr* is pregnantly used like *k3* here.

6. Cf. the epithets on a stele in the tomb of the royal butler *Dḥwti* (Assassif, discovered 1909).

"Welcome"; the kindly man is not treated as an enemy, he is treated as a friend, if there should be calamity" (*Pap. Brit. Mus.*, 10509, 5, 13-15); here *ḏrḏrt* is constrasted with *'k* as it was contrasted with *snw* in the *Lebensmüde* passage.

*202-203.* — "but verily good is the clemency which delivers me from death"; more literally perhaps "good is the benevolent one, who, etc." — *W3ḥ ib* is a difficult epithet, the complete elucidation of which would need a long discussion; here a few remarks must suffice. That the verb is intransitive, is shown by such examples as ..... ..... N, "An offering which the king gives..... Osiris, may his heart be kindly towards..... N", *Sheikh Said*, 19 (a second example on the same plate, and another *op. cit.*, 28); hence it follows that the comparison with the Hebrew שִׂים לֵב is erroneous. *W3ḥ*, in its intransitive sense, means "to be durable", "lasting"; and hence *w3ḥ ib* may denote a stedfast, complacent attitude of mind. Here perhaps "benevolence", "goodwill" would come nearest to the mark; cf. the epithets "kindly, loving mankind", CAPART, *Mon. ég. de Bruxelles*, fasc. II; *Louvre* C 41; *Anast. I*, 2, 6. So too in *Lebensmüde*, 51, "be so kind, my soul, my brother, to become my heir[1], who shall make offerings and shall stand at the tomb on the day of burial".

*203-204.* — MASP., *C. P.*, p. 77, translates excellently : "Car ton double va permettre que j'achève la fin de mon existence à la cour". It should however be borne in mind that the circumlocution with is merely a respectful way of referring to the Pharaoh; cf. below, B206; *Urk.*, I, 109, and often. — The phrase occurs only here, but there is no reason to emend or the like. — *M ḫnw* might also mean "at home", see above the note on B157.

*204.* — "Copy of the acknowledgement of this decree"; this is the heading of a long section extending from B205 to B238, the counterpart of the Royal decree in B179-199. — The meaning of in the present context is obvious, but only one rather doubtful parallel can be quoted, see my *Admonitions*, p. 108.

The main idea of the section is Sinuhe's feigned astonishment that the great king of Egypt should have taken notice of the flight of a subject so humble as himself. The king is beloved of all the gods, and his power extends over all lands (B205-213); none the less he has discerned the wish of his servant, thus proving his all-wisdom (B213-218). Sinuhe next asks that certain chieftains may be brought to Egypt,

---

1. The original has here several imperfectly written signs, not recognized by Erman. The reading *iw'w* seems to me quite certain, though the determinative and the *m* preceding the word are corrupted almost beyond recognition. — In the preceding sentence 50-51 read "thou wilt not find a place on which to rest in the Amente"; the traces in the original suit the smaller form of *gm* excellently.

perhaps as hostages(?); a difficult passage (B219-223). He then goes on to speak of his flight; this, he pleads, was no deed of his own devising, but was prompted by some irrational heaven-sent impulse (B223-230). In conclusion Sinuhe humbly submits himself to the mighty will of Pharaoh; let the latter deal with him according to his good pleasure (B230-238).

*204-205.* — [hieroglyphs] "the servant of the Palace (?) Sinuhe says". This is, *mutatis mutandis,* the normal beginning of a Middle Kingdom letter. Such introductory words are usually written vertically, the bulk of the letter following in horizontal lines; so at least in the latter half of the XIIth. Dynasty. Between equals the ordinary formula was [hieroglyphs] N [hieroglyphs] "the servant of the estate N says", where *bꜣk n ḏt* is evidently substituted for the true title by a polite fiction which represents the writer as the serf of the recipient[1] (so *Pap. Kahun*, 29, 1; 35, 1.29; 37, 14; a letter from Sakkarah in the Cairo collection adds a title, beginning *bꜣk n pr ḏt sš Nḫt*). In similar manner when the king was addressed a general term for "servant of the Palace" may have been substituted for the precise title of the writer. In my German edition of *Sinuhe* I read [hieroglyphs], basing this suggestion on the mistaken supposition that a definite title belonging to

---

1. The name and title of the addressee may be added in the vertical column, introduced by the preposition [hieroglyph]; cf. GRIFFITH, *Kahun Papyri*, 29, 31; 30, 25; 31, 30, etc.—In support of my contention with regard to this phrase it is particularly to be noted that it is only the writer of the letter who bears the title *bꜣk n pr-ḏt;* the person addressed is correlatively called [hieroglyphs] "his lord".

2. Griffith translates *pr ḏt* by the Arabic term وقف *wakf* "pious bequest". ERMAN, *Glossar*, gives sub voce *ḏ-t* [hieroglyph]: "Stiftung (zum Unterhalt von Gräbern usw.); auch *pr-ḏt.*" I have the gravest doubts as to the accuracy of these renderings. It is not of course denied that the great lords of the Old Kingdom set apart fields and labourers for the continuance of their funerary cult (see for example the contracts *Urk.*, I, 11. 36); the question here is whether the specific term in Egyptian for such funerary endowments was [hieroglyphs]. When for example Zau inspects the carpenters, boat-builders etc., of his *pr-ḏt* (*Deir el Gebrâwi*, II, 10), are we to believe that all these men were artisans belonging solely to the funerary estate? When Ptahhotep counts up thirteen [hieroglyphs] from which offerings were brought to his tomb (DAVIES, *Ptahhetep*, II, 13), are we to imagine that these were separated off from the rest of his property to serve a purely funerary purpose, and that they did not descend to his heirs? Miss MURRAY's article *Proc. S. B. A.*, 17, 240-245 seems to contradict this supposition. To turn from such *a priori* considerations to the philological evidence; it should be carefully noted that [hieroglyphs] ([hieroglyphs]) is often employed alone and is completely synonymous with [hieroglyphs], cf. [hieroglyphs] *Mereruka*, A12, S. wall, compared with [hieroglyphs] QUIBELL, *Ramesseum*, 36 (Ptahhotep); further [hieroglyphs] *Deir el Gebrawi*, I, 7, 23; [hieroglyphs] *op. cit.*, I, 13; [hieroglyphs] *op. cit.*, II, 7; and many similar examples. From this we may conclude at all events that *pr ḏt* does not mean simply "maison éternelle" MASPERO *Études de Myth. et d'Arch. égypt.*, IV, p. 351), but that [hieroglyphs] means "property" of one kind or another; there may be an etymological connection with [hieroglyphs] "eternity", but if so, only in the sense that property is conceived of as a permanent, not a temporary, possession. It seems certain that the Greek statement that the Egyptians called their tombs "eternal habitations" (ἀιδίους οἴκους *Diodorus*, I, 51) has greatly influenced the meaning assigned to *pr-ḏt*; there are however many Egyptian expressions (e. g. [hieroglyphs]

Sinuhe is here needed. The hieratic sign in B is quite unreadable; as it stands it is neither nor nor, as was formerly read, . Possibly we should emend *ʿḥ*[1] "the Palace"; this is Maspero's reading (*M. S.*, p. 17., l. 5).

*205.* — "a very fair welcome", lit. "in most beautiful peace". The phrase *m ḥtp* is an abbreviation of , the formula with which new-comers were greeted. In *Westcar*, 7, 23 the sage Dedi welcomes the prince Hardedef with the words . So here the decree of the Pharaoh is welcomed just as though it were the person of Pharaoh himself[2]. For the addition *nfr wr-t*, cf. QUIBELL, *Ramesseum (Ptahhetep)*, pl. 39.

*205-206.* — The point of the sentence has been missed by all translators : MASP. "cette fuite qu'a prise le serviteur ici présent dans son inconscience, ton double la connaît"; ERM. similarly; GR.'s version[3] is grammatically quite indefensible. To render as Maspero and Erman do is to put into Sinuhe's mouth a remark that is not only pointless but also impossible to connect with what follows. If *rḫ-tw wʿr-tn* etc. simply means "this flight..... is known to thee", clearly Sinuhe must be about to discuss "this flight" in some way. But on reading the next few lines we observe that Sinuhe's flight is entirely forgotten; instead of it we find first a string of epithets in which Pharaoh's favour with the gods is proclaimed, and then a section speaking of Sinuhe's desire for recall from exile and lauding that wisdom that has enabled Pharaoh to become aware of Sinuhe's wish. From a merely external examination of the sentence here discussed it is plain that it is not the words *wʿr-t tn* that are emphatic, but the verb *rḫ-tw* and the subject *in kꜣ-k* at its extreme ends. The points emphasized are (1) that Sinuhe's flight has *become known*[4], and (2) that it has become known to

---

, ) which can be quoted in illustration of *Diodorus*' statement without recourse to *pr-dt*. Surely it is wiser to return to the old view of Goodwin (in CHABAS, *Mél. Ég.*, II, 255-256) and Brugsch (*Dict.*, 1684), and to translate *pr-dt* and its synonym *dt* as "heritable property", "domain". The "domain" of course would not exclude the lands and people set aside for funerary purposes, so that it is no argument to quote against this view such expressions as ; the "domain" of a prince would include not only villages, serfs and artisans, but also his *ka*-servants and even the tomb itself. On any other hypothesis it is difficult to account for the epistolary formula *bꜣk n pr dt*, in which the supposed reference to a funerary endowment seems exceedingly out of place. A still more convincing argument is to be found in the fact that the word "serf", which is obviously derived from *dt*, has no connection whatsoever with the funerary cult; for this word cf. *Eloquent Peasant*, R40; *Sinuhe*, B240; *Pap. Kahun*, 10.11; as title, MAR., *Mast.*, D11 (p. 199); L., *D.*, II, 30; *Berlin*, 1188. 14383.

1. For the reading *ʿḥ* or *iḥ*, not *ʿḥʿ*, *iḥʿ*, see Dévaud's remarks, *Sphinx*, 13, 157.

2. Similarly, when the despatch from Pharaoh is read to him, Sinuhe prostrates himself upon the ground as though actually in the Royal presence (see B200, note).

3. "Known is it to thy Ka that this flight of thy servant was made in innocence"; a primary objection is that *ir-tn* cannot be interpreted otherwise than as past relative form.

4. The point that *rḫ-tw* means "has been perceived", "recognized", not "is known", may perhaps be reinforced by a reference to Sethe's observation that *rḫ* in the sense of "to know" shows a marked preference for "perfektische Formen" (*Verbum*, II, § 761, 2); I should be inclined to reproduce MASP.'s rendering in Egyptian by the words *wʿr-t tn ir-tn....., rḫ-n st Kꜣ-k, nṯr nfr*.

*Pharaoh.* The sentence is in fact almost interjectional : "Become known is this flight, which thy servant made against his will, to thy Ka, thou Good God!" Thus already in the first sentence of the paragraph, already even in its first word the farsighted wisdom of Pharaoh is made an object for marvel, that wisdom which has enabled him to perceive the wish of one of the lowliest of his servants in a distant land. If this view be taken, the opening words join naturally on to the sentences B214 foll.; the intervening epithets serve to heighten the impression that is given of Pharaoh's sublime station, which makes it all the more wonderful that the he has deigned to look upon so humble a person as Sinuhe.

*206.* — In the forms *mrw* and *ḥsw* are puzzling. The sense of the context demands that they should be passive participles[1]; the perfect participle passive would however be , (see Sethe, *Verbum*, II, § 928), the imperfect participle , (*op. cit.*, § 948). Possibly we have here consciously archaistic forms of the perfect passive participle, analogous to the form found in the Pyramid-texts (see *op. cit.*, § 931).

*206-211.* — The list of gods beginning with in 206 and ending with in 210-211 is best taken collectively as anticipating the subject of ; to construe the names with "praised of Month, lord of Thebes, of Amon etc." (so Gr.) spoils the balance between the two phrases "loved of Re" and "praised of Month, lord of Thebes". — The list of gods is a peculiar one; it appears to consist of (1) the gods of the reigning Dynastic family, Re, Month, Amon and Sobk[2], (2) the principal cosmic deities, Re, Horus, Hathor, Atum and his Ennead, and (3) certain other gods, most of whom are connected with distant lands.

*206-207.* — Month is here still the principal Theban god, while Amon is merely the god of Karnak[3].

*208.* — The names are closely connected with one another, and the three last might be thought to be epithets of Sopd were it not for the presence of the determinative after each name. — occurs only here[4]. — is found as an epithet of Sopd in an inscription from Abydos of the time of Rameses II[5], *R., I. H.*, 29 = *Rec. de*

1. I hope to show elsewhere that the relative-form *sḏmw.f* is nothing more than a syntactical development of the passive participles; this is the reason why that possibility is not separately mentioned here.

2. The prominent position given to Sobk may perhaps be used as evidence as to the date at which the story was given its present form. This is a point to which I shall later return.

3. The hieratic form of *ns-t* in B now finds a welcome illustration in the *Carnarvon Tablet*, recto 1, where *ns-t* has a very similar shape.

4. I am ignorant of the grounds for Masp.'s comment (*C. P.*, p. 74) : "on appelait ainsi une forme du dieu Toumou, plus connue sous le vocable de Nofirtoumou."

5. I am indebted to Herrn Grapow for this example.

*Trav.*, 11, 90. Another instance of the god is to be found in NAV., *Goshen*, 5, 4 where he is depicted as hawk-headed, and wearing the double feathers, like Sopd. *Smsrw* is evidently no mere writing of *śmśw*, which is once found (perhaps as a corruption of *smsrw*) as an epithet of Sopd, cf. MAR., *Dend.*, III, 12; were this the case, B would hardly have omitted the determinative . — is mentioned in the *Golenischeff* (*Ritual* M. K.); as a form of Sopd, NAV., *Goshen*, 4, 6; 5, 3; Sopd is often called , e. g. *Pap. Kahun*, 13, 13.

*208-209.* — is quite correctly paraphrased by Maspero with the words "la royale Uraeus qui enveloppe ta tête" (*C. P.*, p. 74), but neither he nor any other scholar seems to have appreciated the difficulty of the word *imḥ-t*. This elsewhere means a sepulchral cavern; it is hard to see why the royal Uraeus should be called *nb-t imḥ-t* "lady of the sepulchral cavern". Now Buto, the Uraeus goddess, enjoyed an important cult at Tell-el-Nebesheh, of which the ancient name was *'Im-t;* it seems an obvious and practically certain conjecture here to emend , cf. , *Tanis*, II, 5 a (now in the Ashmolean Museum, Oxford); similarly *op. cit.*, II, 11, 16 a; *Rec. de Trav.*, 22, 15; MASP., *Mém. s. quelq. Pap.*, 81; MAR., *Dend.*, I, 39 e. — The phrase is obviously a paratactic relative sentence, in which *nti* was felt to be unnecessary; other instances in *Sinuhe* are B262; B159-160. For *ḫnm tp*, cf. ROCHEM., *Edfou*, II, 69; *Leiden*, K13.

*209.* — "the council which is upon the flood" is the curious name given to the divinities attendant on the god of the waters; so in the Nile-stelae, L., *D.*, III, 175 a. 200 d. 218 d; also *Todt.*, *ed.* NAV., 149, 98. 99.

and are doubtless related deities. As the inscriptions of the Wady Hammamat teach us, Min was worshipped in the Eastern desert; he was also identified with Horus under the name of . The god named "Horus dwelling in the foreign lands" seems to be named only here.

*209-210.* — can be paralleled only by NAV., *Deir el Bahari*, 8, 14 = *Urkunden*, IV, 345, where Sethe's collation gives as the reading . If this be right[1] we must in *Sinuhe* emend <*nb-t*> *wrr-t* <"lady of> the crown"; *wrr-t* "the Great one" is not rare as a designation of the Royal crown. In any case Hathor of Punt is here meant.

*210.* — Two celestial deities are named at the end of the list, the well-known goddess Nut and the composite god Har-uer-Re; the latter

1. Naville's edition gives a stroke — instead of the first ; I suspect there may be some correction or restoration in the Deir el Bahari text.

is not mentioned as a deity elsewhere, but occurs as a proper name *Cairo stele M. K.*, 20067. 20080. 20346; *Pap. Kahun*, 28, 4; WEILL, *Insc. du Sinai*, no. 63.

*210-211.* — "the gods of Egypt and of the islands of the sea"; emend and *tꜣ-mri* (as in B276). *Tꜣ-mri* is a name of uncertain derivation often given to the land of Egypt from the Middle Kingdom onwards; the earliest spellings outside the text of Sinuhe are GOL., *Hammamat*, 14 = L., *D.*, II, 149 f; GOL., *Hammamat*, 11 = L., *D.*, II, 149 d; *Cairo stele M. K.*, 20014. The name is preserved as Πτίμυρις in a fragment of Ephorus (no. 108) *apud* Steph. Byz., Δέλτα ..... νῆσος Αἰγυπτου ὡς Ἔφορος, κατ' Αιγυπτίους καλουμένη Πτίμυρις, ἀπὸ τῆς τοῦ σχημάτος ὁμοιότητος : however the statement that Πτίμυρις was a name of the Delta does not agree with the hieroglyphic evidence, in which *tꜣ-mri* is always used for the whole of Egypt, cf. especially the *Decree of Canopus* (passim), where is rendered in the Demotic by the group for ⲕⲏⲙⲉ and in the Greek by Αἴγυπτος or ἡ χώρα. — By the "islands of the sea" the Mediterranean islands are obviously meant, cf. (sic) *Piankhi*, 130; though of course *iw ḏ-wr* does not always necessarily refer to the Mediterranean, cf. *Shipwrecked Sailor*, 85, where an island in the neighbourhood of Arabia is intended.

*211.* — "they present life and strength to thy nose", cf. NAV., *Deir el Bahari*, 21; CHAMP., *Not. descr.*, II, 54; the nose is here regarded as the organ of respiration which receives "the breath of life", not as the organ of smell. — "they enrich thee with their gifts", an usage of *ḥnm* not quite paralleled by any other passage; in such common phrases as *Urk.*, IV, 620 (similarly NAV., *Deir el Bahari*, 18. 94. 96) *ḥnm* means something more than "to furnish", rather "to fill", "endue"; the closest parallel is perhaps R., *I. H.*, 133, 15 (collated). — These sentences are better taken as statements of fact than as wishes (so all the translators), since they continue and amplify the relative sentences *mrw Rʿ*, *ḥsw Mntw* in B206.

*212.* — "the fear of thee is bruited abroad", lit. "repeated" (passive *sḏmw-f*); so ERM., MASP. GR. "doubled", a doubtful meaning of *wḥm*, and one which gives but poor sense, even if the sentence be construed as a wish.

*213.* — "Thou hast subjugated all that which the sun surrounds in his circuit"; is the earliest instance of a very common phrase, e. g. *Urk.*, IV, 82. 102. 283; cf. the almost equally common expression .

*213-218.* — Griffith[1] and Maspero[2] regard the words as the conclusion of a paragraph, since the

1. "This is the prayer of the servant for his master, who hath delivered him from Amenti."
2. "C'est la prière que le serviteur ici présent fait pour son seigneur, délivré qu'il est du tombeau."

next words *nb sꜣ, sꜣ rḫyt, sꜣ-f* are written in red. In this case *nḥ pw* is taken as relating to what precedes, i. e. to the favours bestowed upon Pharaoh by the gods. On this hypothesis the following context becomes quite unintelligible; *sꜣ-f* has now no object, and we are left in the dark as to the identity of "Lord of Perception", and as to what it was that he perceived. In the following clause (B215) the neuter pronoun *st* must necessarily[1] allude to Sinuhe's wish *(nḥ... n bꜣk im)* in B213, there being no other word to which it can refer; we thus are confronted with the amazing sentiment that Sinuhe fears to make heard his wishes on Pharaoh's behalf. The psychology of the passage here becomes so strange that we are forced to seek a different hypothesis.

Erman[2] restores sense to the passage by boldly disregarding the rubric in B214, whereby he is enabled to begin a new paragraph with *nḥ pw*. At first sight it might seem rash to attach no importance to the use of red ink in B214, but an examination of the words rubricized in B187. 225-226. 235. 245. 263 will show that the scribe of B as often as not marks his rubrics in the wrong place. *Nḥ pw n bꜣk im* may now mean "the wish of this thy servant" to return to Egypt; Sinuhe reverts to his own affairs, and it is high time that he should do so. The obscurity that the next lines present is due to Sinuhe's constant preoccupation not to formulate his petition in so many words[3]; the passage in which Sinuhe's desire to return home is first alluded to exhibits a precisely similar spirit (see the note on B147-173). We thus learn how Pharaoh in his great wisdom has perceived the wish of his servant (B213-214, cf. *rḫ-tw* etc. B205); how Sinuhe had always feared to speak it (B215); and how the Pharaoh, a god even as Re, has inspired him with wisdom to adapt his behaviour to the circumstances. Sinuhe explains in the last clauses of the paragraph why it is not needful for him actually to state his wish; "this thy servant is in the hand of one who takes counsel concerning him, I am placed under thy guidance; for thy Majesty is Horus the victorious, strong are thine arms over all lands" (B217-218).

*213-214.* — *Nḥ pw n bꜣk im n nb-f, šd m 'Imn-t* is on Erman's view, which I now regard as proved, the object by anticipation of *sꜣ-f* (B214). *Nḥ* is a masculine substantive, see B163 note, and *pw* is not the copula, but the demonstrative pronoun as in *fnd pw špss* B237. — The construction of the words *šd m 'Imn-t* is difficult; *šd* might be imperative (so Erm.) or else an active participle (so Gr.); hardly, as Masp., a passive participle agreeing with *bꜣk im*, owing to the intervening words *n nb-f*. We thus have to choose between the renderings "save (me) in (or "from") the West" and "who saves (me [?]) in (or "from") the West". Sinuhe's dread of being buried with barbaric funeral rites (cf. B197-199) seems to be alluded to, but the allusion is very obscure. Neither "in the West" nor "from the West" gives a very satisfactory sense for *m 'Imn-t*, and instead of *šd* we might expect *šd-wi*.

*214.* — "lord of Perception", an epithet once applied to Amon

1. Gr.'s translation is vitiated by a misunderstanding of the phrase *m ḥm n stp sꜣ*.

2. "Diese Bitte des Diener's da an seinen Herrn : errette mich aus dem ..... land" — der Erkenner, der die Menschen erkennt, erkannte sie in der Majestät des Hofes."

3. Even if *šd m 'Imn-t* be taken as an imperative this statement will not be contradicted; for the words *šd m 'Imn-t* are to say the least cryptic and ambiguous.

(*Cairo, Hymn to Amon*, 4, 5), is not found elsewhere in reference to the Pharaoh; but *Siꜣ* "Perception" is often named as an attribute of the king, see *Admonitions*, p. 85, for examples. — "who perceiveth (his) subjects"; much obscurity attaches to the word *rḫyt* in spite of Loret's interesting suggestions in *L'Égypte au temps du Totémisme*, p. 36. 38-40; for its use as a more stately synonym of cf. for example *Urk.*, IV, 256. 257. 259. — *Nb siꜣ, siꜣ rḫy-t* is the subject of *siꜣ-f*, preceding it for the purpose of emphasis. Note the jingle with *siꜣ*, a common trick of Egyptian style, e. g. *ḥsy ḥss ḥsyw*, *Eloquent Peasant*, B1, 69.

*215.* — is a stilted phrase for "in the palace", lit. "in the Majesty of the palace"; cf. *Urk.*, I, 139 (Old Kingdom); *Urk.*, IV, 194. 651. 1021; *Ann. du Service*, 10, 153.

*215-216.* — "this thy servant feared to say it, and (even now) it is a great thing to repeat it". The distinction of tense here indicated is not easy to prove, but seems likely from the context[1]. For the construction *wnn-f* + pseudoparticiple *(snd-w)*, see Erman, *Aeg. Gramm.*[2], § 373; for the infinitive after *snd* there seems to be no parallel. — *Ḏd..... whm*, cf. the common epithet , e. g. *Urk.*, I, 132, and the frequent disclaimer in the magical texts *Pap. Turin*. 136, 8; *Pap. mag. Harris*, 9, 11.

*216-217.* — ; all translators have overlooked the fact that *sšꜣ* must be the causative of *šꜣ* (cf. B33) and can therefore only mean "to render wise", "prudent". It follows from this that *bꜣk-nf ḏsf* must be a circuitous way of designating a person; the "great god" is obviously the Pharaoh, *bꜣk-nf ḏsf* can only be Sinuhe. *Bꜣk-nf ḏsf* looks like a relative clause (cf. B147-149, note; B162, note), but *bꜣk* is not found in the sense to "make", "create" a person, so that we can hardly translate "whom he created himself"; this would give point to the comparison with Re, Sinuhe being regarded as a creation of Pharaoh, as mankind is the creation of Re. The only alternative is to take *bꜣk* as participle and to translate "one who works for himself", i. e., one who is thrown on his own resources. A final difficulty is the ambiguity of , which may either introduce the predicate of the sentence ("makes wise"), or else may define *mitw Rꜥ* ("like Re in making wise"); in the latter case, which I prefer, *ntr ꜥꜣ* must be a vocative. Translate therefore "Great god, like unto Re in making wise one who was labouring for himself (?)".

*217.* — "this thy servant is in the hands of one who takes counsel concerning him", i. e. Pharaoh. That is the preposition is obvious when once recognized[2]. — is "to ask the opinion

---

1. Erman renders parenthetically "es ist ja etwas das sich schwer erzählt", an interpretation to my mind very ill-suited to the style of the passage.

2. Erm. leaves the sentence untranslated; Gr. renders "who?" giving to the following words an impossible sense; Masp.'s version is so free as to make criticism impossible.

of", "consult"; the example from the *Kuban stele* quoted below shows that here means, not the "mouth" of the asker, but the "opinion" of him who is asked (*ri* as "saying", "language", "deposition" is well-known); thus the expression is quite analogous to *nḏ ḫr-t*. In *Millingen*, 2, 1, means simply "talk about me"; cf. *Kuban stele*, 11-12, "his Majesty questioned them about this desert". Elsewhere *ḥr* means "on behalf of", cf. "he (Horus) knew that he (Pharaoh) would take counsel on his behalf" *Urkunden*, IV, 807; "he it is who taketh counsel for me in doing all my bidding" L., *D.*, III, 72, 16.

"I am placed under thy power". The ꜣ in *ditwi* ꜣ must be the particle the existence of which was first proved by Vogelsang, *Die Klagen des Bauern* (Inaugural-Dissertation), p. 30-31. This particle is used in a number of well-defined cases (in *ḥwy-ꜣ*, *ḥꜣ-ꜣ*, after *iw*, etc.) but also in others which cannot be classified, as here and in below B260; it seems practically meaningless. — *Ḥr sḫr* "under (i. e. subject to) the power", "guidance", "control" of someone, e. g. *Bersheh*, II, 13, 12; 21, 10; *Siut*, V, 23; *Urk.*, IV, 96.

*217-218.* — here means "for" (cf. B89-91, note; 99-101, note) and the sentence explains how it has happened that Pharaoh in Egypt is able to exercise control over Sinuhe in Northern Syria. — can as it stands only be translated "Deine Majestät ist Horus und die Kraft deiner Arme erobert[1] bis zu allen Ländern" (Erm.). The neuter subject *nḫt-ʿwy* is here awkward, and *iṯ* is never elsewhere construed with. The sentence is greatly improved if we emend, the name of the warlike Horus who smites his enemies (e. g. Weill, *Rec. d'Inscr. du Sinai*, Nos. 7. 18; for *ṯmꜣ ʿ*, cf. *Urk.*, IV, 248); the sentence *nḫt ʿwy-k r tꜣw nbw* "thy arms are strong over all countries" then construes quite easily, such amplificatory clauses being often found after the name of *Ḥr ṯmꜣ-ʿ*.

*219-224.* — A very difficult little section, in which Sinuhe apparently asks that certain chieftains may be brought to Egypt as hostages for Retenu. As we shall see, the words usually translated "to bear witness for Retenu" are extremely uncertain; nevertheless the interpretation here given to the passage, which is that adopted by Masp., Erm., and Gr.[2], seems necessary for two reasons: (1) *in-tw* (B219) can only mean "to be brought" to Egypt; (2) the final words "Retenu is thine, like unto thy dogs" cannot otherwise be brought into line with the preceding sentences.

*219-221.* — must necessarily be emended to *in-tw* (passive), "may thy Majesty command to cause to be brought", i. e. to Egypt. — The names of the three chieftains are indicated as those of foreigners by the determinative. Of the three place-names the first is known from other parts of the tale to have been

1. Gr. "extendeth", Masp. "s'étend", giving to *iṯ* a sense for which is no authority.
2. In my German translation I have wrongly suggested that Sinuhe is here asking pardon for three exiled chiefs; in so doing I have allowed myself to be misled by the name *Ḫnt-kšw*.

in the vicinity of Sinuhe's place of exile (see B29, note), and the last is familiar as a rather vague designation of the country of Syria; for , as we should undoubtedly emend in place of , see MAX MÜLLER, *Asien und Europa*, p. 208-212[1]. The intermediate name is unknown, but must, to judge from its position, be intended as the name of some part of Retenu[2].

*221-222.* — In the sentence we must correct into ; of Maspero's readings *mr-wt* is improbable and impossible. Instead of all translators[3] have read , this being understood by ERM. and GR. as a misspelling of ; but without further determinative is a quite correct writing of *rn-w* "names". As the text stands it seems impossible to do otherwise than to regard (1) *mtrw rn-w,* (2) *ḫpr-w m mrwt-k* as parallel attributes of *ḥḳꜣ-w,* and *nn sḫꜣ* as a brief adverbial addition. *Mtr-w rn-w* is difficult; there is a well-known word meaning "right", "exact", "regular", but it is a question needing careful examination whether this is not to be read *mti* and to be distinguished altogether from *mtr* "to be present", "to witness"[4]. occurs as an epithet in *Brit. Mus.*, 572=*Sharpe,* I, 80; we might guess "celebrated" as the meaning both there and in our tale. — "Who have been in thy love" seems a quite possible Egyptian phrase for "who have always loved thee". — *Nn sḫꜣ* "unremembered" (lit. "there is no remembering") i. e., they have always been well-disposed towards thee, though thou didst not know it.

*222-223.* — For "Retenu is thine (*nk-im-s[y]*), like thy hounds" we have an excellent parallel in "the myrrh belongs to me", *Shipwrecked Sailor,* 151; the idiom *nk imy* is well-known, see ERMAN, *Aeg. Gram.*[2], § 237. — The comparison with hounds at their master's heels is found also in *Millingen,* 3, 1; *Piankhi,* 3.

*223-230.* — Sinuhe excuses himself for his flight from Egypt, denying that it was premeditated or due to some unpleasant situation in which he was placed, but stating that on the contrary it was due to a sudden divine impulse. Compare the similar passage above B38-43.

---

1. The earliest mention of the *Fnḫw* is in a 5th. Dynasty inscription quoted by SETHE, *Ä. Z.*, 45 (1908), 85. 140; von Bissing (*Rec. de Trav.*, 33, 18) is, I think, right in rejecting the comparison with Φοίνικες that is revived by Sethe.

2. The name looks like a compound; for *ḫnt*, a difficult word which might mean (1) fortress, (2) prison or (3) *harim*, see *Admonitions*, p. 48; *Kšw*, the reading of which is none too certain, can have nothing to do with *Kꜣs*, *Kꜣš*, Nubia.

3. The various renderings are as follows :— MASP. "qui sont des princes prêts à témoigner que tout se passe au gré de ton double, et que Tonou ne gronde pas contre toi" *(nn 'ꜣ Ṯnw nk!);* GR. "these are chiefs as hostages that the Tenu act according to the desire of thy Ka, and that Tenu will not covet what belongs to thee in it" (reading *nn sḫꜣ(?) Tnw nk im-s);* ERM. "das sind Fürsten die für Tenu zeugen : es ist voll Liebe zu dir ....."

4. Cf. *mty* in the title *mty n sꜣ*, and *mt-t* "accuracy"; in these words *r* is not written. Nevertheless the question is too complex to be decided without a careful sifting of the evidence.

*223.* — *'Is* in "behold, this flight" is rather doubtful, as does not occur as first word in the sentence before the 18th Dynasty, e. g. *Paheri*, 3; from the 19th Dyn. onwards it is frequent, e. g. *d'Orbiney*, 4, 5; 13, 8; *Piankhi*, 17. 87. 152. In earlier times is used, and it is possible that this should be emended here; though it should be remembered that the use of *isṯ* at the beginning of the sentence assumes a previous similar use of *is*, the particle from which it is derived (see *Rec. de Trav.*, 28, 186). — For emend . — *n ḥmt-i sy* "I did not intend it"[1]; *ḥmt* in this sense is only here construed with a substantival object, elsewhere taking the infinitive, cf. above B111; *Urk.*, IV, 344. 502. Except in the present case, whenever *ḥmt* has a substantive as object, that substantive is a word expressing time and *ḥmt* means "to expect", "anticipate", cf. *Urk.*, IV, 481. 487; *Brit. Mus.*, 581 (with *iy-t*); L., *D.*, 149 f *(ḥnti)*; *Urk.*, IV, 384 *(ḥḥ)*; Rochem., *Edfou*, II, 37 *(ḏt)*; above B64 *(pḥwi)*; in the same sense with *sḏm-f*, above B6; *Urk.*, IV, 367; *Turin*, 154 = *Rec. de Trav.*, 4, 131; *Totb.*, *ed.* Nav., 179, 5.

*223-224.* — *nn sy m ib-i* "it was not in my heart". When the absolute pronoun is used as the subject of a nominal sentence it is always enclitic. In affirmative sentences *mik*, *sṯ* or *sk* is used to support the pronoun, cf. Erman, *Aeg. Gramm.*[3], § 365. 463. 464. In negative sentences the negation precedes it, cf. *op. cit.*, § 515[2]; other examples *Shipwrecked Sailor*, 52. 74. 131; *Ebers*, 108, 20; *Pyr.*, 890 b. When the predicate is an adjective this precedes the pronoun, for references see *Admonitions*, p. 104; Erman, *op. cit.*, § 490 only quotes a very special case.

*224.* — "I did not devise(?) it". For *ḳmd* in this sense only *Totb.*, *ed.* Nav., 30 B, 10 can be compared, evidently meaning there "to invent lies in the presence of the god". This *ḳmd* is not to be confused with (1) the word "to mourn", written in the Pyramid texts, but showing in later times a *d* in place of *ḏ*, cf. Spiegelberg, *Kunstdenkmäler..... Strassburg*, No. 15 a (18th-19th Dyn.); Lieblein, *Le livre que mon nom fleurisse*, p. xxv[3],; spelled , etc., in Ptolemaic times (see Brugsch, *Wörterb.*, 1457; *Suppl.*, 1250; and especially Junker, *Die Stundenwachen*, p. 31); nor yet with (2) "heroic deeds(?)", *Millingen*, 1, 10.

"I do not know what moved me from my place". We must read *iwd-wi*, not *iwdw-i*, since the participle takes as object the absolute pronoun. Egyptian says "who separated me" instead of "what separated me", see above the note on B42-43. The nearest parallel to *iwd* here is the reflexive use "to quit", *Shipwrecked Sailor*, 153.

*224-226.* — The next sentences occur in R65-66, though not in the corres-

1. Note that throughout this explanatory passage the *sḏm-f* form is employed; the *sḏm-nf* form is kept as the narrative tense.

2. does not here mean "es ist nicht vorhanden" as Erman states, but simply "not".

3. I owe this example to the kindness of M. Dévaud.

ponding part of B (i. e. B41). Here B has [hieroglyphs]; R65-66 [hieroglyphs] *Mi sšm* is doubtless practically identical with *mi;* we may translate "after the manner of a dream"; R evidently had a different reading here. — *'Idḥy*, a *nisbe*-form from [hieroglyphs] only occurring here. — [hieroglyphs] is a word for "marshes" or "marshy pools", cf. [hieroglyphs] "I did not fish for the fishes of their swamps", *Totb.*, *ed.* Nav., 125 (Einleitung), 19; except in this passage and in that of our tale it is found only in the phrase *ḥ3-t idḥw* "the Delta marshes", cf. *Kuban stele*, 30; Rochem., *Edfou*, I, 72. 94. 443; II, 66; Düm., *Geogr. Inschr.*, IV, 122; one instance may be quoted where *ḥ3-t idḥ* is opposed to *t3 Sty*, [hieroglyphs] *Turin, statue of Horemheb*, 22. For the writing [hieroglyphs] in B, cf. [hieroglyphs] in B199 for [hieroglyphs] B159. — [hieroglyphs] *t3 Sty*, see *Ä. Z.*, 45 (1908), 128.

*226-227.* — [hieroglyphs] "no one ran *(n sḥs-tw)* after me", i. e., persecuted me; cf. Boheiric ϭⲟϫⲓ ⲛ̄ⲥⲁ. For *sḥs m s3* "to pursue" in a quite different context, cf. [hieroglyphs] "I ran after it (the mare) on foot", *Urk.*, IV, 894.

*227-228.* — [hieroglyphs] is repeated from above B41-42, where it was lacking in the corresponding lines of R.

*228.* — [hieroglyphs] "but my flesh quivered (?)". *Wp ḥr* as conjunction, see Erman, *Aeg. Gramm.*[3], § 455. The next word is evidently corrupt; Masp., emends [hieroglyphs] comparing [hieroglyphs] of B4 = R27, but neither the sense nor the determinative agrees. Perhaps we should restore [hieroglyphs], a reduplicated form of the well-known [hieroglyphs] (see *Admonitions*, p. 44); or else possibly [hieroglyphs] should be omitted and [hieroglyphs] identified with the ἅπαξ λεγόμενον of *Hirtengeschichte*, 4, where [hieroglyphs] must mean something like "my hair stood up" with fright.

*229.* — [hieroglyphs] is an unknown word. — For [hieroglyphs] cf. [hieroglyphs] *Urk.*, IV, 365.

*230.* — For the strange writing [hieroglyphs] parallels are to be found in

1. The rubric here is entirely senseless; see B213-218, note. — The sign [hieroglyph] on the *Piers-Breasted stele* = *Brit. Mus.*, 614 has been misunderstood by its editor and by von Bissing, *Rec. de Trav.*, 33, 23, footnote 3; it is obviously only the determinative of *3bw* Elephantine, which has the same form Petrie, *Dendereh*, 15, 10; the hieratic shapes show a tendency to widen out in the same manner, see Möller, *Hier. Pal.*, I, No. 505. The Hathor [hieroglyphs] on a block from Gebelên (*Rec. de Trav.*, 26, 133) is rather embarassing, as a Hathor of Elephantine is not known from other sources.

*Lebensmüde*, 12. 70; the first of these two examples "behold my soul draws me towards death" also illustrates the sense of the verb here.

*230-231.* — The next sentence is philologically obscure, but its sense may be guessed with great probability from a consideration of the subsequent lines. There Sinuhe first describes in flattering phrases Pharaoh's power over every land, and then declares his readiness to yield up to Pharaoh "the office of Vizier" which he exercises in Syria. Here therefore lit. "I am not high of back" must mean, "I have not become presumptuous through the wealth and position I have acquired in this country" (so too Masp.). For *ḳꜣ sꜣ*, cf. "I am one who represses.......... in him whose back is high, putting to silence him of the loud voice so that he does not speak", *Siut*, I, 229; "abasing the arm of him who is high of back", *Urk.*, IV, 968. — The next words are quite unintelligible to me; literally one might translate "through the fear of a man who knows his land", but the sense of *ḫnt* would be most unusual[1].

*231.* — For instead of *ḥryt-k* see B123-124.

*232-233.* — The sense of has been cleverly guessed by Griffith, who renders, "Behold me in thy palace or behold me in this place[2], still thou art he who doth clothe this horizon". What is meant is that Pharaoh's displeasure can make itself felt whether Sinuhe is in Egypt or whether he is in Asia. is a good instance of the particle *mi*, the development of which has been excellently explained by Spiegelberg in *Rec. de Trav.*, 28, 185-187; he shows that the words , "behold thou", "behold ye" are derived from an old particle (or imperative?) by the addition of the absolute pronoun; hitherto it has been possible to quote only one example with the pronoun of the 1st. pers. singular, namely "behold, I am this illuminated one", *Urk.*, IV, 547[3]. — does not here mean "to clothe" (Gr.), nor yet "vêtement" (Masp.), but "to hide", "verhüllen" (Erm.); for this sense, which is fairly common, cf. *Pap. Petersburg*, I, 174-175[4];

1. Masp.'s reading is impossible palaeographically on account of the clear , and would be hard to account for in any case. Erm. apparently ignores *ḫnt* or *gr* altogether and translates as though the sentence were a proverb : "und wer sein Land kennt, fürchtet sich"; this may be the right idea.

2. So too now Masp., *M. S.*, p. 100, though with the quite impossible reading .

3. Erm. translates "Setze mich an den Hof! setze mich an diese Stätte", evidently thinking of the rare imperative ⲙⲟ (Sethe, *Verbum*, II, § 541). But that word means "take", "receive", not "place", and the proposed sense is very poor.

4. Quoted by M. Golénischeff's kind permission from his unpublished transcription.

[hieroglyphs] GREENE, *Fouilles*, 3, 29; [hieroglyphs] *Urk.*, IV, 840; other examples *Amherst*, 2, 2; MAR., *Dend.*, III, 61 b; ROCHEM., *Edfou*, I, 509.

*234.* — [hieroglyphs] "if thou wilt"; the conditional sentence without [hieroglyphs] is usually written *mrr-k* (see SETHE, *Verbum*, II, § 264, 9), but the shorter form is doubtless due to the position of the word at the end of the sentence. — [hieroglyphs] "when thou biddest", a not uncommon sense of *dd*.

*234-235.* — The sentence [hieroglyphs] is brilliantly translated by Griffith, "Thy servant will leave to a successor the viziership which thy servant hath held in this land". *Ṯꜣt-i irn bꜣk im m is-t tn* was formerly rendered "my serfs whom I have acquired in this place" (so still ERM.)[1]; but no parallel for *ṯꜣt* "serfs" has been produced, and the meaning "acquired" that is given to *irn* is impossible. We should evidently make the slight alteration [hieroglyphs] *ṯꜣ-t* ([hieroglyph] becoming determinative), omit [hieroglyphs], and translate "the office of Vizier". Sethe has recently shown that titles are employed not only as such, but also exceptionally to express the position or functions that they involve (*Die Einsetzung des Veziers*, p. 6. 39), e. g. [hieroglyphs] "behold *the office of* Vizier is not pleasant", *loc. cit.* — Sinuhe's position under Amuienshi is not unaptly compared with that of the Egyptian Vizier.

*236.* — The words [hieroglyphs] can only mean "thereupon men came to this thy humble servant", the idiom here employed (see SETHE, *Verbum*, II, § 551)[2] being always used to introduce some noteworthy event or action in a narrative, cf. the other examples in the story, R156; B241. ERM.'s version, "Man ist zu dem Diener da gekommen — deine Majestät tue nach ihrem Belieben" skilfully conceals the difficulty; but it will be observed that in this translation the first sentence does not really mark a progression in the narrative, but is virtually causal (so MASP., *M. S.*, p. 87, paraphrases "puisqu'on est venu jusqu'au serviteur ici présent"). We have no authority for putting such a construction on the words *iwt pw iry r bꜣk im*, and even if we had, the sense would not be very apparent[3]; the only possible conclusion seems to be that the clause is out of place. This deduction is corroborated to some extent by the fact that some such words are imperatively needed before *rdi-tw iri-i* two lines lower down (B238), where Sinuhe's narrative is resumed. The mistaken position of *iwt pw iry* must however be a very ancient error, since it occurs also in an ostracon belonging to Professor Petrie (No. 12) containing a duplicate of the present passage; in the *Petrie Ostracon* the further corruption [hieroglyphs] ....., with *irn* for *iry r*, is found[4].

1. MASP., *M. S.*, p. 182 has a much more complicated emendation.

2. Sethe is mistaken in saying that with feminine infinitives we should expect *ir-tn* and *iry-t* instead of *ir-n* and *iry*. The relative form and participle here do not agree with the infinitive, but with *pw*. In the present case, literally "a coming it is which was made", *iwt* is logically predicate, and *pw iry* subject.

3. I imagine that what is meant by this translation is: since Pharaoh has once deigned to notice his servant, let him now do as he pleases.

4. The *Petrie Ostracon*. 12 (P.) will be published in the Appendix. — Incidentally both B and P afford

With the omission of *iwt pw iry r bꜣk im* the passage runs quite smoothly : "This thy servant will hand over the viziership which thy servant hath held in this place. May thy Majesty do as pleaseth him, for men live by the breath that he gives." Sinuhe resigns himself completely to the will of Pharaoh, who indeed was considered the arbiter of all men's destiny. — The words are repeated below B263; for the optative form see B160-161 note, and for the idiom "to act according to" see my *Inscription of Mes,* p. 21, note 63. — The hyperbolical saying that men live by the breath that Pharaoh gives may be illustrated by many passages, e. g. *Urk.,* IV, 15. 324. 342. 662. 809; apparently it is the breath of Pharaoh's own mouth that is meant, if we may trust the words "he opens his mouth giving breath to mortals" said of Rameses III, R., *I. H.,* 140, 12-13.

*237-238.* — Sinuhe's missive ends as it begins with the highly flattering assurance that the life of Pharaoh is under the protection of the gods. There is some slight difficulty here in the division of the sentences[1]; the only likely view seems to be to take *fnd-k pw špss* as the object of the *sḏm-f* form , and as a passive participle (or otherwise said, relative form) agreeing with *fnd.* The literal translation therefore is : "Re, Horus and Hathor love this thy august nose, for which Month, lord of Thebes, wisheth that it may live eternally". For both expression and sense of the first clause, cf. "this my nose loved of the gods", *Urk.,* I, 39, and for *špss,* cf. L., *D.,* IV, 57 a (from collation); similarly Rochem., *Edfou,* I, 425; *Inscr. dédic.,* 92. — P has the variant "Re and Hathor", omitting the name of Horus.

*238.* — At this point Sinuhe takes up again the story of his life, the first incidents related being the departure from Yaa and the journey to Egypt. — As it stands in the text of B, the resumption of the narrative is exceedingly abrupt; in place of the simple *sḏm-f* form *rdi-tw,* a more detached and important mode of expression is required. The insertion of from B236 greatly improves the flow of the passage ; see above on B236.

*239.* — "My eldest son having charge of my tribe"; *m sꜣ* is probably a metaphor taken from the herdsman behind his cattle.

*240.* — Masp. (*M. S.,* p. 20, note 1) suggests that is a dittograph; though the supposition is not absolutely necessary, I agree in thinking it

evidence in favour of the view here taken of *iwt pw iry r bꜣk im.* In B the preceding words are rubricized, and though this fact is in itself of little importance (see B 213-218), yet in conjunction with the fact that the line B 235 is a short one, it is evident that the scribe believed he was beginning a new paragraph in B 236; or in other words *rdi-tw ir-y* in B 238 was connected by him with what precedes. So too P, which doubtless was meant to contain one section of the story and not fragments of two sections, begins with the words *iwt.* From the point of view of the scribes of B and P therefore it would be more correct to say that the words *ir ḥm-k ..... ꜥnḫ-f ḏt* (B 236-238) are those which are out of place.

1. Gr. suggests, "O thou who art beloved of Ra, of Horus and of Hathor! It is this thy august nostril that Mentu, lord of Uast, desireth should live for ever." This would require a participle *mrrw* or *mry* or *mrw* (see B 206) instead of simply *mr.* — Erm. renders as I do, but optatively "mögen lieben".

likely, as *(i)ḫt-i nb-t,* but not *wḥyt-i,* is defined by the following nouns *ḏt, mnmn-t* etc. — For *ḏt* "serfs" see the footnote to the note on B204-205.

*241-242.* — simply "southwards", and here doubtless by land and not by water; cf. the famous passage in the stele of Tombos where the Euphrates is called "that circling stream which flows downstream southwards", *Urk.*, IV, 85; cf. too *m ḫd* "northwards", above B16.

*242.* — "I halted at the 'Ways of Horus'". In my German edition I proposed the reading , but have since been convinced by M. Dévaud that Masp.'s reading is the right one; *wdb* could hardly be written without its determinative , see above B163 = R188. *Ḥdb* probably meant originally "to sit" or "settle down", cf. "may he sit upon the throne of Horus according to my wish"[1], *Ä. Z.*, 45 (1908), 125; reflexively, "he seated himself upon the ground and said ah!", *Pap. Kahun*, 4, 5[2]. Possibly the word may be related to the later , the transitive meaning of which ("to overthrow") needs no illustration; for the intransitive use "to be prostrate", cf. Düm., *Hist. Inscr.*, I, 25, 48; also R., *I. H.*, 116; *Anast.*, II, 3, 3. — "the Ways of Horus", a name of the frontier town of , probably near El Kantara; see the article by Erman, *Ä. Z.*, 43 (1906), 72-73, and my note *Literary Texts*, I, p. 29*, note 2.

*242-243.* — For the construction, the subject placed first for emphasis followed by the *sḏm-f* form, see R20-22 note. — *pḫr-t,* the troops stationed at a frontier fortress, "frontier-patrol" (Gr.), cf. *Cat. des Mon.*, I, 155 (Assuan); *Brit. Mus.*, 1177 (Wady Halfa). — is not seldom used of military captains, and specially of the commanders of fortresses, cf. besides the examples above-quoted *Rekhmara*, 5 (Elephantine and Bigeh). — P omits and corrupts *pḫr-t* into .

*244.* — "a trusty head-poulterer". This was apparently a commissariat officer charged with the supply of natural product, such as wild fowl, herbs, salt, etc, ; the list in *Eloquent Peasant* R8-34 gives a good idea of the wares which fell within the province of the ; in *El Bersheh*, I, 22, *sḫty* is the name given to the fishermen. For the *imy-ri sḫtiw*, cf. "thy overseer of fowlers bringing *wrdw*-birds", *Anast. IV*, 3, 9; he is depicted so occupied in *Mission*, V, 589 = *Urk.*, IV, 954; *imy-ri sḫtiw* as title, *Leiden*, V, 102; *Florence*, 1545; *Cairo stele M. K.*, 20520.

---

1. For *mi mrr-i*, cf. *mi mrr b3k im*, *Pap. Kahun*, 27, 4. 17; 28, 2. 5; 29, 9 etc.
2. I owe this example to the kindness of M. Dévaud.

— [hieroglyphs] *ꜣtpw*, similarly abbreviated, *Eloquent Peasant*, B1, 70 (= R115); B1, 276 (= B2, 33). Below in B246 [hieroglyphs] = *fꜣ-ni*.

*246.* — [hieroglyphs] "I mentioned each one of them by his name", i. e., Sinuhe introduced all his Asiatic friends separately to the Egyptian officers. The usual expression is *dm rn n* "to pronounce the name of" someone, cf. below, B260; the construction found here occurs again only in [hieroglyphs] "to deal with the dwellers of the Netherworld, named by their names, recognized in their forms", *Am Duat, Sethos*, IV, 39; [hieroglyphs] "being called by thy name for ever", Davies, *El Amarna*, 2, 21.

The words [hieroglyphs] (repeated below B290) cannot be separated from [hieroglyphs] in B247, and I am now inclined to think that it is the latter which is out of place, since the feasting would naturally take place before starting on the journey, not during it. — For [hieroglyphs] *wdpw* "serving-men", "butlers", cf. the full writing [hieroglyphs] *Pyr.*, 120, 124; also [hieroglyphs] Tylor, *Sebeknekht*, 8, 9 (collated). *Ḥr irt-f* "engaged in his duties", cf. [hieroglyphs] *Urkunden*, IV, 28. The introductory [hieroglyphs] is doubtless explanatory, and therefore *šbb ʿtḫ tp-mꜣʿ-i* must be placed before this clause, not *vice versa*.

*247.* — [hieroglyphs] "they kneaded and strained in my presence"; *šbb* and *ʿtḫ* are probably *sḏmw-f* passives impersonally used. The two words often occur together and express distinct operations in the making of beer (for the methods of brewing see Borchardt, *Ä. Z.*, 35 (1897), 130-131). Except in one passage (*Pap. Hearst*, 14, 10) *šbb* is always named before *ʿtḫ*, cf. *Ebers*, 36, 11; 40, 3; Mar., *Dend.*, III, 80 i (written *šbšb*); IV, 15 *(šbb)*. Combining the hint which the root-meaning of the verb *šbb* gives ("to mix") with the evidence from a sculptured scene in the Cairo Museum (No. 1534), it seems clear that *šbb* indicates the kneading of the barley-bread mixed with water[1]. — The verb *ʿtḫ*, earlier [hieroglyphs] (Dévaud, *Sphinx*, 13, 159), refers to the straining of this softened bread-pulp into a jar, for which purpose a basket was generally used, see the scenes *Cairo*, 1534; Holwerda-Boeser, *Denkm. d. alten Reichs*, 10; Borchardt, *Grabdenkmal des Ne-user-reʿ*, p. 124. — *Tp mꜣʿ* a compound preposition[2] meaning literally "on the temples of", cf. [hieroglyphs] "boats manned and filled with provisions beside my troops of recruits, and soldiers in columns(?) beside it (the statue)", *Bersheh*, I, 14, 7; other examples *Rifeh*, 7, 16; de Morgan, *Cat. des Mon.*, I, 66, 11.

1. The paste thus obtained is called [hieroglyphs] *Destruction of Mankind*, 18; *Pap. Kahun*, 5, 48; *Ebers*, 52, 18; *Hearst*, 3, 2. This is to be distinguished from [hieroglyphs] in the medical papyri.

2. First recognized as such by Erman (Berlin Dictionary manuscript).

*246-247.* — The words *šbb ʿtḫ tp mꜣʿ-ỉ* having been restored to their proper place in front of *ỉw wdp-w nb ḥr ỉrt-f*, two emendations are still needed to bring the following sentence into order. In the first place we must read, with MASPERO (*Rec. de Trav.*, 30, 64), < > instead of merely *šsp-nỉ*, which is meaningless alone. In the second place must be changed into , as GR. first suggested; this town is known from the *Turin Royal Canon* (fr. 64), and from a number of stelae on which it is connected with the royal name Amenemhet (cf. *Cairo stele M. K.*, 20515; *Cairo stele M. K.*, 20516) to have been the seat of the early kings of the 12th Dynasty; and since *Piankhi* 83 places it between (Mêdûm) and (Memphis) it can obviously only be Lisht, where the Pyramids of Amenemhet I and Sesostris I have been discovered (see especially GRIFFITH, *Kahun Papyri*, p. 87-88). — For *fꜣ-nỉ ṯꜣw*, a fairly common idiom meaning "to sail", literally perhaps "to carry the wind", see DÉVAUD, *Sphinx*, 13, 94-97. — , for the *sḏmt-f* form see SETHE, *Verbum*, II, § 353, 13 d α; another instance *Shipwrecked Sailor*, 118.

The entire sentence now runs as follows: — < > < > "I started forth and sailed until I came to the town of Ithtow".

*248.* — cf. GOL., *Hammamat*, 8, 7; *Piankhi*, 20. 89. 100. 106. 147 (always with *ḥḏ* for *ḥḏn*); (sic) *Destruction of Mankind*, 34. How *sp sn* in this expression is to be understood is uncertain; I had conjectured that it was meant to indicate the reading *dwꜣ dwꜣw* "the dawn dawned", but means "early" or "very early" adverbially in *Ebers*, 27, 14; 48, 2; 108, 17; *Zaubersprüche f. Mutter u. Kind*, verso 2, 7. — "and they came and summoned me"; *ỉw* and *ỉꜣš* are the *sḏm-f* form without an expressed subject. — P here reads [ ] [ ], a briefer but equally legitimate version.

*248-249.* — "ten men coming, and ten men going, to bring[1] me to the palace", i. e., ten men came to bring the message and ten escorted me to the palace. For the naive satisfaction of Sinuhe at having so many attendants sent to attend upon him compare the following quotation from the biographical inscription of a prince of Elephantine: "His Majesty caused to be brought to me .......... a dish filled with all kinds of good things, with five uncooked geese upon it; and four men brought it to me", *Ä. Z.*, 45 (1908), 133. — *M* with the infinitive occurs as predicate only with verbs of motion, see *Ä. Z.*,

1. Lit. "in bringing me". English idiom prefers to subordinate two such gerunds to one another, presenting the second as fulfilling the object of the first; so below "stood in the gateway to meet me" *(ḥr ỉr-t ḫsf-w-ỉ)*, B 250; "they go out to illuminate him" *(ḥr sḥḏ-f)*, *Siut*, I, 278.

45 (1908), 134, footnote. — P has the variant [...] instead of [...] and begins a new paragraph with [...].

*249.* — For [...] should be read [...], the former being another good instance of the type of error discussed in the note on B111-112. *Dhn tꜣ* "to touch the earth with the forehead" *(dhn-t)* is fairly common, cf. *Copenhagen stele* = *Ä. Z.*, 34 (1896), 26 (written [...]); *Totb., ed.* NAV., 175, 31; *Destruction of Mankind*, 6; *Adoption of Nitokris*, 5; *Vatican Naophoros*, 3; *Durchw. d. Ewigkeit*, 35; MAR., *Dend.*, I, 63c; ROCHEM., *Edfou*, II, 13. 75. — [...] is of course *imi-tw* "between" (cf. above B5 = R28 and SETHE, *Verbum*, I, 26) and we should therefore doubtless read [...], a plural (or a dual) being needed[1]. *Šsp* is tentatively guessed by MASP. to mean the sphinxes on each side of the palace-gate (*M. S.*, p. 164); this is obviously a probable suggestion, and I believe I am now in a position to prove its accuracy. *Šsp* (later apparently *sšp*) occurs in *L.*, D., III, 63. 64 as collated by Sethe in the sense "statue", "image", statues of Pharaoh in course of completion being described with the words [...] "made into a life-like (?) image portraying the beauty of his Majesty"; cf. too [...] "various precious stones, statues of the king", *Harris I*, 64, 13; sense doubtful, *Eloquent Peasant*, R43 = *Butler*, 25. More frequently the word occurs in the epithet "living image of Atum" applied to the Pharaoh; and in this case a sphinx (or rather lion) on a pedestal, with the head of Pharaoh, is regularly used either as determinative or ideogram in its writing; cf. [...] on an Osiris pillar in the temple of Rameses III at Karnak; [...] *Urk.*, IV, 600; similarly, [...] *Sphinx stele*, 2; without the sphinx [...] *Piankhi*, 1. In Ptolemaic times *sšp ʿnḫ* is written with a single sign, the royal sphinx holding the sign *ʿnḫ*; this writing occurs, as before, chiefly in the epithet *sšp ʿnḫ n ʾItm* (or some other solar deity), but also in some cases where the deity is not quite certainly solar, e. g. *Isis*, ROCHEM., *Edfou*, I, 48 Khnum, MAR., *Dend.*, I, 21b. The epithet *sšp ʿnḫ n ʾItm* seems to give the answer to a much-disputed question, namely as to what it is that the Egyptian sphinx actually represents. Some have said the solar divinity variously named Harmakhis, Khepri, Atum or the composite Harmakhis-Khepri-Re-Atum (*Sphinx stele*, 9); for the literature see NAVILLE, *Sphinx*, 5, 193. Others regard this view as a late and erroneous theory of the Egyptians themselves, the sphinx being originally only the Pharaoh represented as a lion (BORCHARDT, *Über das Alter der Sphinx* in *Sitzb. d. k. Preuss. Akad.*, 1897, following Sethe). If *šsp* in the *Sinuhe* passage means "sphinx", as I have little doubt that it does, it must be an abbreviation for *šsp n ʾItm* "image of Atum", and the tradition that the sphinx was a representation of the Pharaoh in the form of

---

1. Palaeographically [...] is quite possible; my transcription should be amended accordingly.

the sun-god then goes back at least as far as the 12th Dynasty. There is no ground for doubting that both views are right, but neither of them to the exclusion of the other; the sphinx depicts the solar deity incarnate in the king, or the king in the shape of the solar deity[1]. After what has been said, it seems obvious that the words *msw 'Itm* in *Harris*, I, 26, 3 must refer to the sphinxes that stood in the forecourt of the temple of Heliopolis; I quote the passage *in extenso* : — "I have made for thee great monuments in the House of Re of gritstone, children of Atum (sphinxes), being great images excellently sculptured, dragged (thither) and resting in their places eternally in thy great august well-beloved forecourt, carved with thy divine name like heaven ".

Thus the sentence in *Sinuhe,* after emendation, runs and the correct translation is "I bowed my head to the ground between the sphinxes".

*250.* — *sic* "the royal children standing in the gateway to meet me"; *wmt* and *ḥsf-w* would be better spelt and . P has preserved only . — has hitherto usually been translated "das tiefe Gemach[2]", from "thick" (Coptic ουμοτ) on the analogy of *wsḫ-t* "the broad hall"; so STEINDORFF, *Ä. Z.*, 34 (1896), 108; BORCHARDT, *Ä. Z.*, 40 (1902), 48. An examination of the other instances of the word proves that its real meaning is "gateway". (1) In several cases the word is written with the determinative of a gate, e. g. L., *D.*, III, 257 a, 30. In the temple of Hibe the word is used in a dedicatory inscription to describe a pylon, BRUGSCH, *Grosse Oase*, 10. In the great Harris papyrus *wmt* occurs together with words that are known to indicate the parts of gateways, cf. "its (scil. "the wall's") door-posts (?) and gateways of stone of Ayn, with doors of cedar", *Harris I*, 57, 13; 58, 6; similarly 45, 4. A woman about whom prognostications are to be made should stand "in the inner gateway of a portal" (read *sbꜣ*), *Pap. med. Berlin*, verso 2, 1 (so already rightly

1. That (already *Pyr.*) is a lion-god connected with Atum and hence with the sphinxes seems to me, as to Naville (*loc. cit.*), quite evident. Whether the great Sphinx is more solar deity or more Pharaoh is a question which the Egyptians themselves who made it could probably not have answered. Can it be regarded as in any way parallel to the boats of the sun at Abu Gurab ?

2. Another convincing argument against the rendering "das tiefe Gemach" is that *wmt* does not mean "deep", which is in Egyptian *md*, but "thick", "stout", i. e. it is employed in reference to materials of some consistency, but not to air or space.

Wreszinski). In this last instance, which is a particularly good illustration of the Sinuhe passage, *wmt* seems rather the inner part of the gate, the gateway, than the entire structure; and etymologically this must be the precise meaning, though it seems clear that the word was also used more widely. (2) Not to be confused with *wmt* is the related word [hieroglyphs] *wmt-t*, which only occurs in the phrase [hieroglyphs] "the fortification wall" (cf. Coptic ⲟⲩⲟⲙⲧⲉ, arces, propugnacula), *Urk.*, IV, 661. 767. 832. — [hieroglyphs] "to meet", only here; cf. the frequent *m ḫsfw* "opposite" and the note on B2.

The sense here given to *wmt*[1] makes the description of Sinuhe's arrival at the Palace not only comprehensible but vivid. At the threshold he bows down between the sphinxes; and when he rises and passes on into the gateway he is greeted by the Royal children who have come thus far to meet him.

*251.* — "The courtiers who had been admitted into the Forecourt showed me the way to the Privy Chamber". In writing the word [hieroglyphs] the scribe of B has used a strange hieratic determinative; P has wrongly [hieroglyphs]. — In [hieroglyphs] *stꜣw* must be the passive participle; for the phrase cf. [hieroglyphs] *Rekhmara*, 9. — *Wꜣḫ*, see the article by Borchardt, who translates "Überschwemmungshalle", *Ä. Z.*, 40 (1902), 48; further examples of the word *Pap. Boulak* 18, 26, 1; *Rec. de Trav.*, 12, 217; 22, 127; *Cairo stele M. K.*, 20065; L., *D.*, *Text*, II, 192; Mar., *Dend.*, II, 27, 2; IV, 2, 9. Here doubtless is meant the open forecourt surrounded by columns near the main entrance of the Palace. — *Rdit ḥr wꜣt*, see above B96-97. — [hieroglyphs], the inner private apartment of the Pharaoh, where he actually received Sinuhe (cf. B284); see B187 note.

*252.* — [hieroglyphs] "throne", cf. *Pyr.*, 391. 1154; *Urk.*, IV, 342. 349; more often used of the thrones on which the gods sit. — *M wmt nt ḏʿm* "in the golden gateway"; if the text is correct this must refer to a gateway leading out of the *ʿḫnwti* into the private apartments of the Royal family. Borchardt has however pointed out to me that it would be unnatural for the King to sit in the doorway, and Sethe tells me he has long believed the words *m wmt* here to be borrowed from B250 above. This suggestion seems to me extremely plausible[2], the text running much better if we translate : "the courtiers..... showed me the way to the Privy Chamber, and I found his Majesty upon the golden throne"; cf. [hieroglyphs] *Urk.*, IV, 349.

*253.* — *Dwn ḥr ḫt-i* "stretched on my belly"; this phrase only here. — [hieroglyphs] "I lost consciousness in his presence", lit. "I did not know myself", for the spelling of *ḫmn-(i) wi* see B4-5 note. *Shipwrecked Sailor*, 76 has an excellent parallel for this phrase, explained by me *Ä. Z.*, 45 (1908), 63[3]. —

---

1. Masp., *M. S.*, p. 77 has half-recognized the true meaning of the word.

2. I also doubt *wmt* here because *nt ḏʿm* would make it a feminine, whereas it is probably a masculine, the final *t* being radical.

3. Erman (*Aeg. Gramm.*³, § 485) still adheres to the old view of this sentence, which, not to speak of other difficulties, rests upon a misunderstanding of *ḫnmw* (B 254).

P here gives , evidently intending *ḫꜣm-n(i)-wi* "I bowed myself", which would be weak and redundant after *dwn-kwi ḥr ẖt-i;* after *m bꜣḥ-f* P has rightly a verse-point.

*253-254.* — "this god addressed me joyfully". *Wšd* "to address" a person, see ERMAN, *Ä. Z.*, 43 (1906), 6. — *Ḫnmw* has hitherto been translated as having a bad sense, such as "roughly", "angrily"; this was a guess based on the supposition that *ḫmn-wi* refers to Pharaoh's non-recognition of Sinuhe, which is grammatically highly improbable. *Ḫnm* occurs (1) transitively in the sense "to gladden", cf. "the goddess Nub gladdens thee with what thou desirest", *Louvre,* C15; similar examples *Brit. Mus.*, 157. 574; *Cairo stele M. K.*, 20282, (2) intransitively "to be glad", cf. "thy heart is joyful, thou art glad because of him, *Pap. Berlin* 3053, 19, 7; "all thy limbs are glad", *Thebes, tomb of 'I-mi-sbꜣ*. *Ḫnm* "to breathe" may be simply a special use of this word. *Ḫnmw* here is the pseudoparticiple agreeing with *nṯr pn*, in an adverbial sense.

*254.* — "I was like a man overtaken by the dusk". The alternative determinatives and of *iḫḫw*, *ʿḫḫw* (see DÉVAUD, *Sphinx*, 13, 160) would suffice to show that the word must mean "twilight"; usually it is the twilight before dawn, but sometimes, as here, that before dark, cf. "thou sinkest in the Netherworld at the moment of dusk", BRUGSCH, *Grosse Oase*, 25, 15.

*255.* — "my soul fainted", cf. "the soul of him who knows it does not faint", JÉQUIER, *Le livre de ce qu'il y a dans l'Hades*, p. 102. — , for *ꜣdw* emend , see B38-39 note. — *Ḥꜣti-i n ntf m ẖt-i*, see the note on B39, where the same clause occurred.

*255-256.* — Unless be emended before *rḫ-i* ("I did not know life from death", i. e., I did not know whether I was alive or dead), the clause must in my opinion be regarded as the continuation of the previous sentence : "my heart was not in my body, that I should know life from death". This, it must be confessed, seems very unnatural, but it is less artificial than if we render, with MASP. and GR., "I knew the difference between life and death", i. e., I had a foretaste of death

*257.* — For the writing of the pseudoparticiple *iwt(i)*, cf. B182; B193. — "thou hast trodden the foreign countries, thou hast traversed the desert wastes". For *ḥw* "to tread" see *Admonitions*, p. 38; if *wʿr-t* here means "desert wastes" (see B40 note), *ir-nk* must be translated "thou hast traversed"[1], a sense for which see BREASTED, *Proc. S. B. A.*, 23, 237-238[2].

1. The alternative rendering "thou hast made flights" has been felt by all translators to be impossible MASP. proposes "tu as fait des voyages" and GR. (reading *wʿr* for *wʿr-t ?*) "thou hast played the wanderer".

2. In the example quoted by Breasted from Weni the verb means "to work" a quarry, see above B38, note.

*258.* — The sentence is curious in several respects. *Tni* being evidently the subject, *im-k* is not in its usual place, but cf. B136. *Hd* elsewhere means "to push", "attack"; here it seems to have the construction, and roughly speaking the sense, of . Translate : "senility hath assailed thee".

*258-259.* — For the idiom *ʿbt-ḫ3t* "to be buried", see B159 note. In the form of the negation shows that the next word *bs* (see B197 note) is the infinitive and not the passive *sdmw-f* form; and this is confirmed by the sense, *nn* with the infinitive being often used to define the nearer circumstances under which an event occurs, see SETHE, *Verbum*, II, § 550. The whole sentence should therefore be rendered : "It is no little thing that thou shouldst be buried, without Asiatics conducting thee (to the tomb)".

*259.* — The sentence is wholly unintelligible to me; for GR.'s suggestion, "do not, do not keep silence", taking *rk* as the particle and as equivalent to , presents too many difficulties to be regarded as plausible.

*260.* — is probably to be taken as a temporal or concessive sentence, "thou speakest not, when (or "though") thy name is pronounced"; for *dm rn* see the note on B246.

MASP. and ERM. rightly take (read ) as the resumption of Sinuhe's narrative. On the particle *ỉ* see B217 note. *Ḥsf* must here surely have its common sense "punishment" ("I feared punishment"); MASP., *M. S.*, 145 reads *n ḫsf-f*, which he translates "en présence de lui", but *n ḫsf* does not seem to be known with the same sense as *m ḫsf*.

*261.* — is the only possible reading of the hieratic here, but should be emended, as is done by M. Maspero. — The last word of the line is unreadable, but might possibly be a corruption of , the reading given by Maspero (*M. S.*, p. 22)[1]. After the wish "would that I could answer it" we expect some such words as "but I cannot"; perhaps would answer the requirements of the case.

*262.* — Sinuhe seeks to explain why he is unable to answer the Pharaoh[2]. — As the text of B now stands, the sentences are very ill-balanced; and there is the grammatical difficulty that the participle *sḫpr* is written as a masculine, whereas *ḥr(yt)*, to which it must refer, is feminine. It would seem therefore that emendation is necessary; and I think that it is more satisfactory to transpose *mi sḫpr wʿr-t š3ʿ-t*, placing it before *ḥr-(yt) pw wnn-s m ḫt-i* than to alter *sḫpr* into *sḫpr-t*. The text thus obtained is :

1. So too apparently GR.; but cannot be translated, "It was not my act", which would need *pw* at the end of the clause.

2. So ERM.; differently GR. and MASP., who think that the reference is to Sinuhe's flight. GR. renders, "It was the hand of God; it was a terror that was in my bosom, as it were causing a flight that had been foreordained"; but the preposition *mi* can hardly be so meaningless as is here assumed.

"It is the hand of God, like that which brought about the foredoomed flight, it is the fear which is in my body" — *Wnn-s* paratactically in the sense of a relative sentence, see B208, note.

*263.* — more probably "to thee belongs life" than "thou art life"; for this sense of the later absolute pronouns see *Ä. Z.*, 34 (1896), 50; 41 (1904), 135. — *'Ir ḥm-k m mrt-f,* repeated from B236 above.

*263-264.* — (sic) "they caused the Royal children to be admitted". For *rdi-in* we expect , and the position of the *n* in B suggests that the scribe had intended to write this; nevertheless it is not impossible that the ellipse is genuine and correct as it stands.

*264-265.* — The sentence is grammatically susceptible of two translations: (1) "behold, Sinuhe has come as an Asiatic"; in this case is the pseudoparticiple, cf. B257; so Gr.; (2) "behold, this is Sinuhe, who has come as an Asiatic" (so Masp., Erm.); for *mik* in the sense of the French "voici", followed not by a clause but by a substantive, see Sethe, *Die Einsetzung des Veziers*, p. 28, note 134; here can only be the perfect participle active[1]. The surprise of the Queen and the Royal children makes it quite clear that the latter alternative is the right one. — can only mean "whom Beduins created", i. e., the offspring of Beduin parents; so rightly Gr. In my German translation I took *ḳ(m)ꜣm* as a substantive "form" (so Masp., *M. S.*, p. 170) and, emending *m ḳ(m)ꜣm n Stiw,* rendered "in der Gestalt eines Beduinen" (for *ḳ(m)ꜣm* "form" cf. *Rekhmara*, 7, 6. 13; *Kuban stele*, 18); this I now consider very unlikely, since it requires the further emendation of the plural *Styw* into the singular *Sty*[2].

*265.* — "she gave a great cry"; for *wd* of "emitting" sounds, see the note on B140.

*266.* — "and the royal children shrieked out all together", lit. "were in one noise". — is a well-known word for "noise" (e. g. R., *I. H.*, 146, 61; *Israel stele*, 25; Rochem., *Edfou*, I, 212; Nav., *Mythe d'Horus*, 15; 22, 14), the reading of which is still doubtful. Since in *Eloquent Peasant*, R103 is a variant of in B59 it seems possible that *dw-t* is the long-sought reading, in which case it might be derived from (sic) "to call out"; and partial confirmation of this view might be found in , Ros., *Mon. Stor.*, I, 136 (Medinet Habu, collated by Sethe), when compared with *Kuban stele*, 5. It must be admitted however that the Medinet-Habu example might easily be emended into *dni-t*, which would explain the use of the sign . Perhaps after all *dni-t* is the more probable solution of the problem. — For the use of *wꜥ* here cf. , *Urk.*, IV, 18; , *Petrie Ostracon*, 38.

1. So too *ḫpr-t* in the examples *Westcar*, 4, 10; 6, 15 quoted by Sethe; the pseudoparticiple *ḫpr-ti* would have been written out fully in that papyrus.

2. Erm.'s rendering "und zum Beduinen geworden ist" is quite indefensible.

*267.* — "o King, my lord", a common phrase, cf. *Westcar*, 9, 6; *Bersheh*, I, 15; MAR., *Abyd.*, II, 29, 6; *ity* written as here, *Prisse*, 4, 2.

*268-279.* — The Royal Children now make music before the Pharaoh, chanting a song that culminates in a petition for Sinuhe's liberty. It seems very probable that dancing formed some part of the entertainment, though not explicitly mentioned. At all events there must have some mimetic representation connected with the object called , whilst the sistra were shaken in the hand and produced a tinkling sound. The symbolic meaning of the performance has not hitherto been appreciated, and deserves all the more attention as the passage may claim, when rightly understood, to be the *locus classicus* for Egyptian musical entertainments of the kind. I shall try to show that all Egyptian music performed by females and involving the use of the sistrum and *mni-t* was dominated by one idea, namely that the performer is Hathor, the goddess of song and dance, who bestows her favours on the prince before whom the performance takes place.

*268-269.* — All the three objects which the Royal children (probably only the young princesses are meant) bring in their hands are usually considered to be musical instruments. This is certainly true of two of them, the and the (emend thus for ), which are two different kinds of sistrum (see below). It was therefore not unnatural to suppose that the third object named, the , was likewise an instrument of music. This view seems first to have been explicitly taken by Prof. Erman, in his comments upon the passage *Westcar*, 10, 3, where the birth-deities came to the house of *Rʿwsr* and < > "offered to him their bead-necklaces and their sistra". Erman translates, "und sie spielten (?) vor ihm ihre Ketten (?) und (ihre) Klappern (?)", quoting (sic)[1] *Piankhi*, 134 for the sense given to *ms*; this sentence however offers but slender support to the meaning "to play", as it may just as well be rendered "there being brought to me no harp", and the phrase for "to play the sistrum" is elsewhere , see BR., *Wörterb.*, 1316. Apart from the verb *ms* in the *Sinuhe* and *Westcar* passages not a particle of philological evidence has been produced in favour of the *mni-t* being used as a musical instrument, and that supposition rests merely on the fact that it is constantly mentioned together with the sistrum[2].

The truth is that the sistrum and the *mni-t* are always mentioned together, not because they are both musical instruments, *but because they are both emblems of Hathor.* In what seems to be the earliest picture in which *mni-t* and sistrum occur together (see the accompanying figure), the goddess Hathor stands before the Pharaoh

1. Read *bin-t* for *bsn-t*.

2. In *Sphinx*, V, 93-96, M. Loret tries to prove that the *mni-t* is really a kind of cymbals. He seems to be quite aware of the explanation of the *mni-t* as a bead necklace with a counterpoise, but strangely enough does not recognize the incompatibility of this view with his own.

Amenemhet III and offers to him these her emblems; in her right hand she waves the sistrum and with her left hand she lifts and stretches out towards the King the bead-necklace *mni-t* that hangs about her neck[1]. This is clearly the gesture described in *Sinuhe* and *Westcar* by the verb , perhaps the commonest meaning of which is "to present" something to some honoured person, gifts or tribute to the King or offerings to the dead or the gods. The point that the *mni-t* is offered to the King will be amply demonstrated in illustrating the first words of the Princesses' song; here we need only inquire into the meaning of this offering. It seems that the *mni-t*, as a precious ornament worn by the goddess herself, symbolises all the benefits that she has in her power to bestow; in giving the *mnit* she also gives life, prosperity and health. Thus to present the *mni-t* to a person is equivalent practically to offering him the ☥-sign. It is only when this has become clear that we can understand the words "the Golden one presents the *mni-t* to thy nose", DEVÉRIA, *Mémoires et Fragments*, pl. 2; there is no reason for believing that the *mni-t* was supposed to have a fragrant odour, but it is presented to a person's nose because it is synonymous with the breath of life. A similar idea is conveyed too by the words accompanying an unpublished scene in the temple of Sethos I at Abydos; the king receives the sistrum etc. from Isis, who says "receive for thyself the bead-necklace and the sistrum, that they may infuse health into thy flesh[2]". In a scene from Speos Artemidos, Pakht says to the queen : "the *mni-t* is with thee, making thy protection", *Urk.*, IV, 287; this proves that the *mni-t* was supposed, as indeed is everything that comes into close contact with divine beings, to be imbued with magical power. In the light of these quotations it can of course be no accident that after begging the king's acceptance of the *mni-t*, the princesses of our tale go on to say "the Golden one (Hathor) giveth life to thy nostril, the lady of the stars unites herself with thee". Nay, from the last words we may perhaps even

FIG. 1. — From JÉQUIER-GAUTIER, *Fouilles de Licht*, p. 106, fig. 131.

1. Another good illustration of this gesture (one among many) is *Deir-el-Bahari*, 101, where *Wrt-ḥkȝw* offers the *mni-t* to Amon. Sometimes the *mni-t* is not fastened round the neck of the goddess or the singer who represents the goddess, but is held out in the hand; see particularly the early example in the Louvre stele C15 (GAYET, *Stèles de la XII[e] dynastie*, pl. 54), an admirable instance which is conclusive against the supposition that the bead-necklace was jangled to produce a noise as was the case with the sistrum. See too the scene from a coffin in the Bibliothèque nationale reproduced in DEVÉRIA, *Mémoires et fragments* (*Bibl. égypt.*, t. IV, pl. 2), which represents the deceased actually grasping the *mni-t* which the goddess holds out.

2. For this sense of *ẖnm* with object and *m*, cf. B211. However as Schäfer points out, it would be possible to render "unite themselves to thy flesh in health", so that taken alone this quotation would not be conclusive.

conclude that the goddess is actually inherent in the *mni-t* herself; in the late Dendera texts Hathor is not only the "possessor of the *mni-t*" (e. g. MAR., *Dend.*, II, 17c; III, 420), but is herself actually "the great *mni-t* in the house of the *mni-t*" (e. g., MAR., *Dend.*, II, 76. 80; III, 78f; IV, II; and often). Thus even on so purely secular an occasion as that narrated in the tale of Sinuhe song and dance might implicitly be a religious ceremony. Several instances from Theban tombs where Hathor is invoked by the musicians at private feasts will be quoted before we leave the subject.

The religious significance of the as an emblem of Hathor has now been amply illustrated; it remains to prove that in itself it was no more than an ornament for the neck. As such it is described in several places; cf. LACAU, *Sarcophages*, 28027; *op. cit.*, 28092. 28087; MAR., *Abyd.*, II, 55, 25. The best graphic representations of the commonest variety are a relief from the tomb of Sethos I (BEREND, *Musée égypt. de Florence,* pl. I) and another from the temple of Deir el Bahari (ed. NAVILLE, pl. 101). It consists of a thick bunch of stringed beads that hangs heavily on the wearer's breast; before they reach the neck they are caught up and joined together, giving place to single or double strings that pass behind the neck; attached to these secondary strings are two weighed pendants that hang down, as equipoise to the beads on the breast, over the shoulders[1]. The different forms of the *mni-t* depicted on the sarcophagi (LACAU, *op. cit.*, pl. 53. 54), as well as the manner in which the goddesses present it, prove that the beads are the essential part of the object; but the pendant is a remarkable enough part to be sometimes taken as characteristic of the whole, e. g. as determinative in MAR., *Abydos*, II, 55, 25, quoted above, and as amulet. — The fact that the *mni-t* is a kind of necklace was known to Champollion, and has been often repeated since his time (see especially LEFÉBURE, *Proc. S. B. A.*, 13, 333-335); it is to be deplored that this obvious explanation has been obscured by other hypotheses for which there is hardly a vestige of evidence.

Among the appartenances brought by the Royal children there are mentioned beside the *mni-t* two kinds of sistrum, the one written (this reading is more probable than ), and the other (for we must substitute ). So too Thutmosis I offers to Osiris *Urkunden*, IV, 98; and the three objects are several times mentioned together in the texts accompanying scenes of musicians, cf. *Thebes, tomb of Ḳn-imn* (copied by Sethe); BRUGSCH, *Thesaurus*, 1191 (tomb of *Ḥrw-f*); *Urkunden*, IV, 1059, (tomb of Amenemhet). This evidence already suffices to show

1. In some pictures where the *mni-t* is brought to be presented to the king its two ends seem, curiously enough, to pass over one and the same shoulder, not to go round the neck. Contrast however the picture of Hathor as cow wearing the *mni-t* round her neck (NAV., *Deir-el-Bahari*, 104).

that the object written is the sistrum[1] of the shape, while the shrine-shaped sistrum is called *sšš-t*. The inscriptions in the Graeco-Roman temples amply bear out this distinction. For the *sḫm* sistrum[2], cf. MAR., *Dend.*, IV, 26 c; and for the two contrasted, cf. ROCHEM., *Edfou*, I, 167; MAR., *Dend.*, II, 53 b. A good earlier example, MAR., *Abyd.*, II, 55, 22. It would not be difficult to find instances where the determinatives of *sšš-t* and *sḫm* are interchanged, but the bulk of the early evidence and the almost unvarying writing in Ptolemaic times leaves no room for doubt as to which sistrum is which. It is true that is sometimes used as a hieroglyph for *sḫm* (e. g. PETRIE, *Koptos*, 8, 8), but this inaccuracy is not greater than when *ḏ'm* is written with and not with the spiral sceptre *ḏ'm*. That the sistrum is an emblem of Hathor, though not stated to be so by Plutarch in his well-known passage concerning the σεῖστρον (*de Iside*, 63), needs no proof; the sistrum is constantly depicted in Hathor's hands and almost every example bears the goddess' head upon the handle. It is an interesting and perhaps not universally known fact that the sistrum is still used at the present day in the churches of Abyssinia[3].

*269.* — is certainly for "in their hands"; the writing for is probably a mistake, though some partial parallels (18th. and 19th. Dynasty) can be quoted, e. g. NAV., *Deir el Bahari*, 56; L., *D.*, III, 141 b; L., *D.*, III, 140 c, 19.

*269-270.* — The meaning of the first words of the Princesses' song were totally unintelligible to me until Sethe pointed out that *ḫkry-t nt nb-t p-t* is an epithet of the *mnỉ-t;* this point once settled, it forthwith became clear that the King is here asked to accept the *mnỉ-t* borne by the musicians. Among the passages already quoted above we find this sense implied by various expressions: "I offer to thee"; "to thy ka"; or "receive thou". The reading of B is confused by hieratic corrections, but there can be little doubt that the correct text is "thy arms upon the beauteous one", i. e., take the beauteous *mnỉ-t* in thy arms. This view is confirmed on the whole by the corrupt words accompanying a scene at Abu Simbel, where the goddess Hathor stretches out the necklace *mnỉ-t* towards Rameses II; before her are the words , CHAMP., *Mon.*, I, 38 *bis*, 1 (collated). In another similar scene from the

1. My translation "Stäbe" and GR.'s rendering "wands" are accordingly wrong. — MASP. (*M. S.*, p. 22) reads *sšš-sn sššt-sn m's* "their sistra with which they play the sistrum"; but *sšš* does not occur as verb (see above note on B 268-269 *ad init.*). — The hieratic signs for and and are identical with one another.

2. Already known to Brugsch (*Wörterb.*, 1292; *Suppl.*, 1108).

3. The Berlin Museum has a fine specimen of the modern sistrum brought back by Professor Littmann.

4. The sign at the end of B 269 is probably , the at the beginning of B 270 being dittographed.

Rameses temple at Abydos Hathor says, "... I praise thee, my hands holding the *mni-t*, the ornament of the Lady of Heaven, I reward thee with the years [of.....]", *Louvre*, B10-12. Following the latter text we might emend in Sinuhe "our hands hold the beauteous one"; this however involves more serious alterations in the text. It is preferable to retain the second person *ʿwy-k* "thy hands", a reading at least not contradicted[1] by the corrupt Abu Simbel text, the relationship of which with Sinuhe is apparent. — "long-living King", a common expression, cf. for example *Urk.*, IV, 501. 575. 581. 872. *Wꜣḥ* cannot be separated from and joined to the next words, as all previous translators have supposed. — epithet of the *mnit*, cf. Louvre, B10-12 quoted above; the "Lady of Heaven" is of course Hathor, cf. *Mission*, V, 364 (Thebes, tomb of Min).

*270.* — "the Golden one", a common epithet of Hathor; cf. τὴν δὲ Ἀφροδίτην ὀνομάζεσθαι παρὰ τοῖς ἐγχωρίοις χρυσῆν ἐκ παλαιᾶς παραδόσεως, *Diodorus*, I, 97 (quoted by Junker). The earliest examples known to me are in the songs sung by the harpers in the tomb of *'Intf-iḳr* at Thebes (temp. Sesostris I), and on the stele *Louvre*, C15. See too Devéria, *Noub, la déesse d'or des Égyptiens*, reprinted in *Bibliothèque égyptologique*, t. IV, p. 1-25.

*271.* — "the Lady of the Stars (?)", doubtless another epithet of Hathor. The stele *Louvre*, C15 (= Pierret, *Inscr. du Louvre*, II, 30) has as an epithet of Hathor. One of the two texts must evidently be corrected, and provisionally I prefer "Lady of the Stars" to "Lady of the Gates".

*271-272.* — (read ) "the Goddess of Upper Egypt sails north and the Goddess of Lower Egypt sails south, joined and united in the person (?) of thy Majesty", a very artificial and roundabout way of saying that the kingdoms of Upper and Lower Egypt are united under the rule of the Pharaoh. — For *šmʿ-ś* and *mḥ-ś*, names of the Crowns of Upper and Lower Egypt, (which were of course at the same time goddesses) see Sethe, *Ä. Z.*, 44 (1907), 20, who rightly remarks that *mḥ-ś* is here written as though it were derived from *mḥ* "to inundate". — and are pseudoparticiples of the 3rd. person masculine singular, replacing the feminine dual, see Sethe, *Verbum*, II, § 42[2]. — is strange; to say that the Crowns of Upper and Lower Egypt are united "in the mouth of" the Pharaoh is of course nonsense. It certainly seems straining the sense of *ri* to make it mean "the mention" of thy Majesty, i. e. in the title

1. In the Abu Simbel text we may just as well understand, "[thy] hands upon it, the beautiful one (?)" as "[my] hands upon it, the beautiful one (?)".

2. Hitherto had been read, with such translations as "que la science soit établie dans la bouche de ta Majesté". But *twt* cannot possibly mean "établie" (Masp.) or "wohnt" (Erm.); nor yet can we translate "is united with thy mouth", since *ḫnm* or *ꜣbḫ*, but not *twt*, would be employed in a context of the kind. In addition to this, the spelling of *sꜣ* would be most unusual. "Satiété" (Masp., *M. S.*, p. 148) would be *sꜣ-t*, feminine.

given to the King; but this is the only possibility unless we emend "in the name (*rn*) of" or "in the time (*rk*) of" or some similar expression.

*272.* — can, as the text stands, only mean "the papyrus is set upon thy brow", which is meaningless. Both Erm. and Masp. rightly substitute "uraeus" for "papyrus"; we must then read instead of , cf. *Totb.*, *ed.* Nav., 15 A, II, 15; , Rochem., *Edfou*, I, 45.

*272-273.* — "to make distant", "remove", should not be confused with "to go up on high", above R7. — , see the note on B120-121. — The Berlin Ostracon 12379 (OB2)[1] begins with the signs , which must be equivalent to of B. The sentence *ḥtp nk Rʿ nb tȝwi* was absent from OB2.

*274.* — B; [•] OB2 "hail to thee and to the Queen". For *hy nk* cf. Assassif, tomb of *Ḫrw-f* (no. 192), unpublished; , Lanzone, *Domicile des Esprits,* 12th. hour, top row; , *Ritual of Amon,* 19, 6; OB2 substitutes the more usual synonym *ḥnw*. — For *Nb-t r ḏr* as name of the Queen, see B171-173, note.

B; ......... [ ] OB2. The renderings of Gr. and Masp.[1] presuppose the wrong reading for and may therefore be dismissed without discussion. For *sfḫ šsr-k* there is a good parallel in the words "lay to rest (?)[2] the bow, loosen the arrow", *Piankhi,* 12, in an exhortation to desist from warlike thoughts. The thought here too evidently is that Pharaoh should throw off for the moment his bellicose nature, and show a peace-loving and clement disposition by pardoning the exile Sinuhe. *Sfḫ* is obviously imperative as in the *Piankhi* passage, and it seems to follow (1) that *nft* must likewise be an imperative, and (2) that the sense of *nft ʿb-k* is likely to be closely similar to the sense of *šrm pd-t*. The newly-discovered text OB2 helps to support these conclusions, reading *wḥʿ ʿb-[k]* "relax thy horn". I had already conjectured that *ʿb* "horn" is here metaphorically used for "bow" like in *Koller*, I, 8 (on which see my note), and the variant *wḥʿ*, i. e. a verb of which the primary meaning is "to loosen" or "slacken" a rope, is strong confirmation of my hypothesis. in B is, as it stands, an unknown word; I am strongly tempted to read , a rare verb for "to unfasten", "unloose", cf. "thou art bound, and not unloosed", *Pap. mag. Harris,* verso A6; "they unslung their waterskins", *Israel stele,* 6;

1. Gr., "strong is thy horn; let fall thy arrow"; Masp., "ta corne est forte, ta flèche détruit".
2. *Š-r-m* here only in this writing; clearly connected with שלם.

(read ) "thou releasest the horse", *Anast. I*, 24, 5-6; (*sic*) "he who was bound is loosed and freed", *Pap. Turin*, 18+73, 2.

*275.* — B; OB2. Neither text is free from error; in B we must restore an before *nti*, and in OB2 the is missing in <*i*>*tmw*. *'Itmw* seems to be an abstract word meaning "suffocation" or the like, cf. "giving breath to him who is stifled", *Metternich stele*, 88; "releasing him who is confined in suffocation", Petrie, *Koptos*, 20, 9. Cf. also the word *itm* in the sentence , *Pap. Leiden*, 345, recto I, 3.

*275-276.* — (*sic*) B; OB2. The difficulty of these sentences resides in the uncertain meaning of the word *ḫn-t*; and there is also the problem, not quite an easy one, as to which of the two versions is to be preferred. The variants of OB2 are at all events useful as proof that I was on the right tack in translating, "Gib uns unser schönes Fest an diesem Nomaden", etc.; the Royal children clearly demand that they shall be granted the freedom of Sinuhe as a reward for their song and dancing. This point is settled by the second clause in OB2, which may be rendered, "Reward us with Se-[mhyt, the barbarian born] in the land of Egypt"; for *mtn* "to reward" cf. "thou (Amon) rewardest him with many years, that his heart may be glad on the throne of Horus like Re eternally", *Urk.*, IV, 863; similarly "he rewards thee [with] millions ..... ", *Urk.*, IV, 562. Many examples of the verb *mtn* occur in the inscriptions of the temple of Luxor; the substantive *mtn-wt* "reward" is found *Urk.*, IV, 377.

The *crux* of the passage is, as I have said, *ḫn-t*. Erman translated *ḫn-t tn nfr-t* as "dieses Schöne", a rendering for which there is no authority, though the masculine *ḫn pn nfr* could bear this meaning. Masp. and Gr. give respectively "grâce" and "favour", meanings just as little susceptible of demonstration. It is clear that *ḫn-t* here is the same word as occurs in two other passages; one of these is in the list of the festival offerings instituted by Thutmosis III, (*sic*) "what is for the expenses (?) of this festival, 1 measure of wine", *Urk.*, IV, 828; "he instituted new expenditure (?) for his fathers the gods", *Amada stele*, 11-12. The sense "expenses" would also suit both the versions of our manuscripts; in B we should translate, "Give us our goodly expenses in the nomad" etc., and in OB2, "Give us the expenses of this beautiful day"[1]. However the fact that the word *ḫn-t* is in all the cases used in reference to festivals suggests that the meaning "expenses" is too wide; the word may mean specifically "festival outlay", if indeed its sense is not to be sought along some altogether different line of thought. Our evidence is not conclusive.

In B is evidently for , as in *Shipwrecked Sailor*, 7 is for *iswt-n* (see SETHE, *Ä. Z.*, 44 [1907], 80) and as in *Eloquent Peasant*, B1, 7-8 is for *wꜣt-n*. — The use of the preposition *m* in the version of B strikes one as unnatural, but if *ḫn-t* really means "expenses" it might be intended to express what the expenses "consisted of". The text of OB2 is obviously much clearer and better in style; we are here again face to face with the old question — is the easier or the more difficult reading to be preferred? To this question it is perhaps more prudent to give no answer in the present case.

*276.* — For of B see B26 note; it is evident that this word either suggested, or was suggested by, of OB2. — "the son of the North wind" (or simply "of the North") appears to be a playful allusion to the name of Sinuhe on the one hand, and to his wanderings in Northern Syria on the other. A similar antithesis is expressed in the next words "the barbarian born in Ti-muri" (cf. too for the thought B265). Here does not mean "foreign soldier", as GR., doubtless thinking of the late Egyptian "troop", renders; it is evidently the singular of the well-known general name for "foreigners", "barbarians" (cf. B259); cf. *pdti* above B121. — *Tꜣ-mri* was discussed in the note on B210-211.

*277-279.* — The clauses "he fled through fear of thee, he left (this) land through dread of thee" are contrasted with two clauses that follow, "the face of him who has seen thy face does not blanch (?), the eye that has beheld thee does not fear"; Pharaoh, who seems so terrible from afar, is mild and gentle when one is actually in his presence.

*277-278.* — B; was probably the version of OB2. There is not much to be said about these differences. in the sense of "to leave" has been found above B152 (*rwiw*), and apparently occurs only in these two passages. The addition of *pn* improves the text, but [*rwi*]-*nf sw m* is cumbrous. For the writing of *ḥr*[*y-t*] in B see above B123-124, note.

*278-279.* — That in B is a corrupt writing of (see my critical note on the text) is plain, though no confirmation is given by OB2, in which the words are lost. , is a *crux* and may be corrupt. and , it should be noticed, are perfect participles — not "that sees (beholds) thee", but "that

1. *Ḥrw nfr* here means "holiday", "fête", as often.

*once has seen* (beheld) thee"; the imperfect participle would need the gemination[1], see SETHE, *Verbum*, II, § 881. — OB2 read [ ], which is better than *ḥr n mꜣ ḥr-k* in B, where the additional antithesis introduced by the double *ḥr* is disturbing. — For with the dative cf. *Pyr.*, 232; *Rifeh*, 1, 6; *Louvre*, C14; *Ebers*, 51, 22.

*279-283.* — In briefly answering the Royal children the Pharaoh reassures them as to his intentions concerning Sinuhe, and instructs them to wait upon him.

*279.* — "he shall not fear", almost "let him not fear"; the emphatic is not here as in the foregoing sentences used as a strong denial, but rather as an expression of will.

*280.* — is evidently a corrupt sentence. is again here required, and has a very improbable appearance. We might emend "he shall not feel dread (*ḥry-t*)"; for the idiom see *Admonitions*, p. 53.

*282-283.* — For the sentence various translations have been proposed. The grammar is clear; *wdꜣ-w tn* is the plural imperative followed by the absolute pronoun (see SETHE, *Verbum*, II, § 493), and is a spelling of the infinitive (cf. above B5. 117). First of all I must dispose of my own earlier version, "Begebt Euch zur Empfangshalle, dass man ihn lehre, seine Stellungen einzunehmen". This assumes the emendation *sbꜣ-twf*, to which I was prompted by the considerations (1) that *ʿḫnwti dwꜣ-t* as the name of a room or building occurs nowhere else, and (2) that , if to be read *dwꜣ-t*, ought to have the determinative . To (2) the answer may be given that *sbꜣ* itself is only in one somewhat doubtful case (*Prisse*, 17, 12) determined with , elsewhere having as its determinative; and as to (1), the alternative to *ʿḫnwti dwꜣ-t* consists of the absurd supposition that the Royal children were told to go to the very apartment in which they at that moment stood, for B283-284 and B251 make it clear that Pharaoh received Sinuhe in the *ʿḫnwti*. Finally there is the objection that what Sinuhe needed at this particular juncture was not a lesson in Court etiquette, but a bath! We must therefore return to the old view that the *ʿḫnwti dwꜣ-t* is a place distinct from the *ʿḫnwti* in which Sinuhe was welcomed. ERM. translated, "Gebt euch zum Kabinett der Verehrung, damit seine Stellung ihm angewiesen werde", suggesting that the *ʿḫnwti dwꜣ-t* was a department in which the exact rank of courtiers was officially decided. The suggestion cannot be regarded as in itself a likely one, and it is not supported by the subsequent narrative; on the philological side it may be objected that *ḥʿw* "Stellung" would be written . Another rendering that has been proposed by Spiegelberg (*Sphinx*, 4, 140) is accepted by Maspero and Griffith. Spiegelberg thinks that the sentence refers to a formal juridic act by which property was conferred upon Sinuhe;

1. In the late ostracon OB2 however [ ] seems required by the size of the lacuna.

and in support of his translation, "Geht zum Kabinett der Verehrung, um sein Vermögen zu schaffen" he quotes [hieroglyphs], PETRIE, *Denderah,* 15, 19. But (1) *ʿḥʿw* "wealth" is always written with the determinative [hieroglyph] in the Middle Kingdom (cf. [hieroglyphs] above B147; *Lebensmüde,* 33; *Eloquent Peasant,* B1, 105; *Prisse,* 5, 13; 6, 6; 13, 8; *Siut,* I, 247; *Rifeh,* 7, 50), and *r irt ʿḥʿw-f* "to make his wealth" would not be as natural an expression as *r irt nf ʿḥʿw* "to make for him a fortune"; and (2) the proposal rests upon a wrong conception of the events that followed the Royal Audience, as we shall soon see.

Spiegelberg has at least rightly felt that the story must go on to describe the way in which the Royal children carried out the injunction given to them by the King; and he tries to show that the next lines corroborate his translation. In B283-286 we read, "Then I went out from the Audience Chamber, the Royal children giving me their hands; and afterwards we came to the Great Gates. I was taken to (lit. "placed at") the house of a King's son, in which there were precious things". For Spiegelberg the Great Gates *(rwty wrty)* are here the scene of the legal conveyance of property alluded to by the words [hieroglyphs], and [hieroglyph] in the phrase "the house of a King's son" has besides its literal meaning the additional sense "Court allowance" (Hofhalt); the sense thus obtained being that Sinuhe was to receive his pension out of the estate of a certain King's son. Surely this is to read into the text a great deal more than is actually to be found there. In B286-295 I can see nothing more than an elaborate description of the way in which Sinuhe made his toilet; he relates with pride how for this purpose he was installed in the house of a King's son. When it is said in B285, "afterwards we went to the Great Gates", this simply means "we went out of the Royal Palace". For *rwty wrty* as the entrance gates of the Palace cf. especially *Rekhmara,* 2, 5, where it is related that the Vizier, before entering the Palace in the morning to pay his respects to the king, has to wait [hieroglyphs] "in the doorway of the Great Gates", where the Treasurer ([hieroglyphs]), i. e. the chief official of the Palace, reports to him that all is well in the Palace and the Vizier, on his side, reports that all is well in the Residence city. Compare too above R9, where "the Great Gates are closed" at the death of the King. A final objection to Spiegelberg's hypothesis is that it altogether loses sight of the *ʿḫnwti dwꜣ-t.*

This chamber or building is, as I have already said, not known to us from any other text. There is however more than a mere possibility that it may be identical with the [hieroglyphs] mentioned in a common title of the Old Kingdom. The title [hieroglyphs] does not seem to refer to any administrative function but to a high privilege at Court. It is usually appended to the phrase [hieroglyphs] "unique friend" which it follows either immediately (e. g. L., *D.,* II, 34 g. 86 b; MAR., *Mast.,* D6. 38. 49) or separated from it only by the words [hieroglyphs] (e. g. L., *D.,* II, 30. 41. 86 b. 89 a; MAR., *Mast.,* D2, 47. 49) or [hieroglyphs] (*op. cit.,* D38). From this evidence we may conclude, with ERMAN (*Aegypten,* 107), that *ḥry sštꜣ n pr dwꜣ-t* is equivalent to the title "gentilhomme de la chambre du roi". *Piankhi,* 98 confirms this view; when his Majesty came to the temple "his ablutions were made in the *pr dwꜣ-t,* and there were made for him all ceremonies that are made for the King"; cf. too *ibid.*, 103; *Louvre Apis stele* 4 = *Rec. de Trav.*, 21, 72[1]. Hence it seems likely that *pr dwꜣ-t* may mean "toilet chamber", and accordingly we may argue that in telling the Royal children to go to the *ʿḥnwti dwꜣ-t* the King is simply telling them to take Sinuhe to a place where he can wash and dress. — In this case can mean little more than "to wait upon him"; *ʿḥʿw* would be an abstract word for "service", "attendance" and the phrase would be comparable to in B250. Some little evidence may be brought in support of this theory; in *Weni*, 9 we read "I acted so that his Majesty praised me, in acting as escort, in preparing the way of the king, and in attendance (upon him)[2] (?)"; and in the Middle Kingdom (*Cairo stele M. K.*, 20540. 20542; DYROFF, *Grabsteine, aus ..... München*, no. 8) fem. (*Cairo stele, M. K.*, 20026. 20476 ( ); *Louvre*, C196; *Turin,* 107) designates a low station in life that may perhaps be translated by the word "attendant".

My tentative translation is therefore: "Go ye to the Chamber of Adoration to attend upon (?) him." Whatever may be thought of the comparison with and of the guess as to the sense of *ʿḥʿw*, it must at least be admitted that the sense proposed answers the requirements of the story far better than any previous attempt to explain the passage.

*283.* — For the *sḏmt-f* form see B4-5, note: for *rwty wrty,* see the last note.

*284.* — Read instead of of the manuscript; for the phrase *rdi-t ni ʿwy-sn*, cf. *Pyr.*, 555 b; *Harhotep,* 510; *Millingen,* 1, 7; and often.

*285.* — For the unusual position of *mḫt*, cf. , DE MORGAN, *Cat. des Mon.*, I, 66. — "splendid things", "luxuries", see *Admonitions*, p. 25.

*285-286.* — The is certainly a "bathroom", such as has recently been found in El Amarna; see *Mitt. d. deutschen Orient-Ges.*, no. 34, Sept. 1907, p. 25. The word *sḳbbwi,* which must literally mean "how cooling!", is known from the title , MAR., *Mast.*, D47 (p. 308); *Thebes, tomb of the Vizier Dꜣg* (no. 103).

*287.* — "figures of the horizon" must mean painted images of the gods (so MASP.); *ʿḫmw* (or *ʿḥmw* or *ʿšmw*, literally "falcon-shapes", cf. ⲁϩⲱⲙ : ⲁϩⲱⲙ "eagle", as name of the bird once in hieratic, *Pap. Salt.*, *825*, 8, 1) is often

1. Cf. too "A Royal offering to the southern and northern *itr-t*, that they may make for thee a house of ablutions (?) .....", *Bersheh*, II, 7. — The meaning of *pr dwꜣ-t* in the phrase (PETRIE, *Koptos*, 9 and often) is quite obscure.

2. This translation is of course not fully assured; Breasted rendered "in making stations".

so used, e. g., *Urk.*, IV, 607; *Amada stele*, 9; other examples, *Stele of Tutanchamon*, 15; L., *D.*, III, 140 c, 9.

*287-288.* — For the position of *im-f* in the sentence compare B 81-82[1]. — The reading of "precious things" (e. g., L., *D.*, II, 22; *Mereruka*, C4, north wall and south wall; *Urk.*, IV, 515; and especially *Turin altar* = *Trans. S. B. A.*, III, 112) is still quite uncertain[2]; occurs as adjective in the words *Weni*, 38.

*288.* — "clothes of Royal wear (?)"; is often a word of vague meaning very similar to, e. g. *Urk.*, IV, 60; *Urk.*, IV, 118; probably however we should emend "of byssus", "fine linen" (Coptic ϣⲛⲥ). — The construction of *ḥbsw* etc. depends upon the way in which the words *ni-swt srw mrr-f* in B 299 are taken; see next note.

*289.* — In my German translation I separated the words from what follows, taking these words and the preceding *ḥbsw nw šs stn* as further subjects of the sentence; but to make the balance of the clause satisfactory some genitive is urgently needed after *ʿntiw tp-t.* In addition to this, the translation which in that case has to be given for *srw ni-swt mrr-f m ʿ-t nb-t* ("Beamte des Königs, die er liebte, waren in jeder Kammer") does not make very good sense. I therefore return to the old view which makes of *ni-swt srw mrr-f* genitives following *ʿntiw tp-t* ("frankincense and fine oil of the King and the courtiers whom he loves"); on this view *m ʿ-t nb-t* is predicate both to *ḥbsw nw šs stn* and to *ʿntiw tp-t stn srw mrr-f.* In any case must be emended to.

*290.* — , repeated from B 246 above. — , literally "they let years pass over my flesh", i. e., I removed the grime of years from my skin; the goodly unguents and apparel of Egypt made Sinuhe appear years younger. — is perhaps the *sḏm-f* form with an ellipse of the subject "they"; but it might also be 1st. person singular, *rdi-i* "I caused". — For , not "limbs" but "flesh", "skin", see Montet, *Sphinx*, 13, 1-11.

*291.* — The words are usually guessed to mean "I was shaved, and my hair was combed[3]". This translation cannot be far wide of the mark, but both *tꜣ* and *ʿʿb* are unexampled in the senses here assigned

1. There is no reason to construe *nt-pr-ḥḏ* as a compound substantive meaning "things from the treasury", as was proposed by Erman, *Ä. Z.*, 34 (1896), 51.

2. The question is not necessarily dependent on the reading of the title. For the latter I prefer to retain provisionally the transcription *sḏꜣwti* proposed by Crum and confirmed by Spiegelberg; for Spiegelberg's new suggestion (*Proc. S. B. A.*, 27, 287) that *ḫtmwti* is to be read I see no ground whatsoever.

3. As Spiegelberg has pointed out (*Sphinx*, IV, 141), it is related by Diodorus (I, 48) that the Egyptians let their hair grow long throughout their absence from Egypt. However I cannot see that this passage confirms the statement of the Greek historian; if Sinuhe's hair is long, it is because he has conformed to the habits of the barbarians.

to them. elsewhere means "to pluck" or "to seize"; and here it might refer to depilation. is probably akin to "to join", "unite", and "to heap up (corn) with the aid of a pitchfork", references for which are given by SETHE, *Verbum*, I, § 148, and ERMAN, *Ä.Z.*, 46 (1909), 97.

*291-292.* — The sentence "a burden was given to the desert and clothes to the Sandfarers" is an amusing example of the artificial style often adopted by the author of our tale. The burden given to the desert is of course the dirt which Sinuhe's ablutions removed from him, and the clothes given to the Sand-farers are Sinuhe's discarded Asiatic garments. — Notice that a considerable number of the sentences from here onwards until the end of the tale begin with the word . Sinuhe is no longer relating his life progressively, but *describing* the favours he received. is here, as below B295. 305, the passive form *sdmw-f;* contrast "I gave" in B294. — is elsewhere the freight of a ship (*Shipwrecked Sailor*, 162; *Anast. VIII, passim.*) Hitherto has been the accepted reading, but in addition to the hieratic evidence, which is decisive, there is no good authority for such a feminine word with the meaning "dirt", "foulness"; ⲥⲓⲃ *pediculus, rubigo* (compared with *sb-t* here by ERMAN, *Aeg. Glossar*, p. 103) may well be the Coptic equivalent of *Admonitions*, 2, 8 (see my edition pp. 26. 113).

For "to clothe" (originally *šd*), cf. *Pyr.*, 416; *Copenhagen stele* = *Ä. Z.*, 34 (1896), 27; *Zauberspr. f. Mutter u. Kind*, 6, 7; MAR., *Abydos*, I, p. 40, *b*.

*293.* — For cf. MAR., *Abydos*, II, 33. Note that the verbs "to anoint" may be construed (1) either as here, cf. too *wrḥ im-s*, B295; *Totb., ed.*, NAV., 125, Nachschrift, 3; (2) or else with a direct object, cf. *Urk.*, IV. 482; *Leiden* K9; and similarly *Mission*, V, 426. 428.

*294-295.* — Here we have a sentence containing a similar thought to that of B291-292. The words "I gave the sand to those who are in it" is peculiar inasmuch as a phrase is unknown; cf. however *ḥriw-šʿ*. — Are we to infer from the words *mrḥ-t n ḫ-t n wrḥ im-s* that the Egyptians preferred for their bodies oil made from animal fat?

*295-297.* — The sentence (Ms. ) presents difficulties. GR. takes as a proper name, rendering "there was given to me the house of Neb-mer (?), which had belonged to a Companion". A better suggestion, in my opinion, is that of MASP., who gives as his version "on me donna la maison qui convient à un propriétaire foncier qui a rang d'ami", the sole objection to this being that the expression occurs nowhere else. I am greatly tempted to substitute for it , a title which we know from R1 to have been conferred upon Sinuhe. — *M wn mʿ smr* means more probably "such a one as a courtier possesses" than "which had belonged to a courtier" (GR. and ERM.); for the text goes on to relate that "many workmen built it, and all its woodwork was newly appointed". We must not allow ourselves to be misled either by *srwd* or by *m mꜣw-t* in B297. Both these words are ambiguous; *srwd* is indeed very often used of "restoring" buildings that had fallen into decay (e. g. *Sheikh Said*, 30; *Urk.*, IV, 102. 390. 879; *Harris I*, 9, 6; 49, 12), but sometimes appears to mean simply "to supply", "establish" (e. g. *Pyr.*, 1868; *Cairo stele, M. K.*, 20512); *m mꜣw-t* is rarely employed in the sense "anew" (of things renewed, cf. *Anast. I*, 26, 6), but far more frequently with the meaning "newly", "expressly" *(passim)*. — The subject of the sentence "many workmen built it" is very confusedly written, and as the facsimile clearly shows, the first sign has been altered and partly deleted. There is very little reason for reading the hieratic sign as a ram (thus MASP., *M. S.*, p. 85; MÖLLER, *Hierat. Paläogr.*, I, no. 140, footnote). As it stands, the sign is illegible; but its lower part, which is intact, suggests that is to be read. Thus we should obtain as the reading , a not impossible variant of , the word which we should naturally expect in this context.

*297.* — Instead of we should probably read , the analogy of (B295) and (B300) requiring here the passive form *sḏmw-f*; the reading given by SETHE, *Verbum*, II, § 476 and MASP., *M. S.*, p. 24, is palaeographically impossible.

*298.* — "meals", cf. "there were given to me meals of meat and fowl", *Urk.*, I, 139; "a bull was slaughtered for my meal", DYROFF, *Grabsteine aus..... München*, no. 3; and in the common formula of the funerary stelae, *Louvre*, C60; C55; C202; *Stockholm*, 55.

*299.* — For the phrase "to make delay" instances are quoted by SETHE, *Die Einsetzung des Veziers*, p. 32, note 149.

300-308. — There follows the description of the tomb which was built for Sinuhe. For this section there is a parallel text in the late Ostracon no. 5629 of the British Museum (here called L). Of the numerous variations which L displays some are simple corruptions of the readings of B, but others are clearly derived from a different original text. In a few places, as we shall see, L has clearly preserved the better readings.

*300-301.* — B; L. The version of B, "a tomb was built for me", is perhaps rather more natural than "[my tomb was] built" in L, and *m ḳꜣb* in B might be preferred to *m ẖnw šnw n* ("in the midst of the circle of") in L on account of its greater brevity.

*301-304.* — The respective readings of B and L will best be displayed by printing the two versions one above the other :—

B (302)
L

B (303)
L

B (304)
L

It is apparent at the very first glance that L here corrects two glaring errors of B. That the "overseer of the treasurers" should draw designs in the tomb of Sinuhe is sheer nonsense, and hence of L must take the place of in B. In the next clause is evidently[3] a corruption of (so L), due to the similarity of and in hieratic. On the other hand , which occurs in L not only here but once again later on, is a transparent mistake for , the hieratic easily decomposing into . It will further be noted that B twice has the word where it is absent from L, and L has the same word once where B omits it; at its fourth occurrence, in both manuscripts are in agreement. The point of these sentences is probably that the best workers in each craft (i. e. the overseers) helped in the construction of Sinuhe's tomb, and therefore the word ought perhaps to be retained throughout. It would possibly relieve the stiffness of the text thus obtained if we omit in the first instance: this is quite plausible, as in the text of L is qualified by the words "who build tombs", i. e. the workmen who constructed Sinuhe's tomb were practised hands.

Let us now discuss the other divergences between B and L one by one. Neither "took its ground" (B) nor "they divided its walls" (L) gives good sense; but the composite reading "divided up its ground", i. e. "plotted out its foundations", seems to yield a quite suitable meaning. The twofold in L adds to the clearness of the text. in B is quite a correct form, as the verb belongs to the class of the 3ae. infirmae (SETHE, *Verbum*, I, § 396); but is the infinitive in *Admonitions*, 11, 3, as well as here in L. *Ntiw* in B is superior to the singular *nti* given by L. Between *ḥr ḥr-t* (B) and *r ḥr-t* (L) it is hard

1. Corrupt signs, from which the reading indicated seems recoverable.

2. is repeated by dittography at the top of B 303.

3. I have pointed out in my palaeographical note that cannot be read, as MASP. and the other translators had supposed. Besides this the word *ḥrtiw-nṯr* (literally "necropolis people") always means "stone-masons", not "sculptors".

to choose. Lastly, [hieroglyphs] of B is less easily explicable than [hieroglyphs] of L, which would refer to *mr* "the pyramid" (B300); perhaps for that very reason *rs* is the better reading.

The sole difficulty of vocabulary in the passage is the phrase *ḥr ḏꜣ-t tꜣ rs* (or *rf*), concerning which Dévaud has recently written in *Sphinx*, 13, 118-120. The translation "crossed the land concerning it", proposed by Masp. and Erm. and adopted from them by myself, is a correct literal rendering of the text (for *ḏꜣ tꜣ* in this sense see e. g. *Pyr.*, 1215 a); but the passages quoted by Dévaud and others supplied by the Berlin dictionary show that we have here to do with a more indefinite metaphorical meaning "to occupy oneself with" something, or in a bad sense "to interfere with". For the good sense the only example seems to be that in our tale, which we must now translate "busied themselves with it". In a bad sense, cf. "As to this my tomb, let me be buried in it with my wife [hieroglyphs] "without any people being allowed to interfere with it", *Pap. Kahun*, 12, 12; the bird-catchers and salt-gatherers etc. shall be allowed to exercise their profession [hieroglyphs] "without interference from anyone" R., *L. H.*, 257, 6 = de Morgan, *Cat. d. Mon.*, I, 119[1]; [hieroglyphs] (read [hieroglyphs]) [hieroglyphs] "any man who shall interfere with this my stele", *Cairo stele, M. K.*, 20458; the Theban temples, [hieroglyphs] "all their..... are consecrated and no one may interfere with them", L., *D.*, III, 257 a, 24; lastly, with ellipse of [hieroglyphs], cf. [hieroglyphs] "if thou examine a man with an ulcer on his right side, under his ribs[2] but not interfering (with them)", *Ebers*, 41, 5-6.

The entire passage may now be conjecturally restored and translated as follows :—

[hieroglyphs] "The masons who build tombs marked out its ground-plan, the master-draughtsmen designed in it, the master-sculptors carved in it and the master-builders who are in the Necropolis busied themselves with it".

*304-305.* — B has [hieroglyphs]; this is on the whole confirmed by the reading [hieroglyphs] of L, which has no variant of value. [hieroglyphs] here clearly means the funereal furniture[3], such as was usually buried with men of

1. There is another rather similar instance in the tomb of Nebamon at Gurna (no. 90; *Brit. Mus Add. Mss.*, 29823 sheet 84).

2. *Ḏrw* is the "paroi costale" (cf. *ḏr-t* "wall"), as I hope to prove elsewhere.

3. *Ḫ'w* (written here as above B 129; outside *Sinuhe* B always with [hieroglyph] not [hieroglyph]) is of course very common with the meaning "weapons"; but it is also found signifying (2) the "tackle" of ships (e. g. *Mission*

distinction. can only be the imperfect passive participle (SETHE, *Verbum*, II, § 954), the pseudoparticiple from this verb being written in Middle Kingdom texts (SETHE, *op. cit.*, II, § 135); the predicate of *ḫ'w nb* and the following words is therefore *ir(w) ḫrt-f im*. — The word here written must be identical with , as no other *rwd* denoting a part of the tomb is known; for *rwd* "staircase", "shaft" the writing with *w* is sometimes found. e. g. *Pyr.*, 279c: *Cairo stele, M. K.*, 20512, though the Pyramid texts already seem, curiously enough, to connect the word with *rd* "leg", cf. *Pyr.*. 1090c. That *rwd* means the "shaft" of the tomb seems decisively proved by the words *Siut*, I, 308. "Staircase" was doubtless the original meaning, and in fact the burial chambers of mastabas of the 1st to 3rd Dynasties are approached by descending staircases. Later when the staircase was replaced by a shaft, the word *rwd* was still retained, although its literal sense no longer applied; cf. our use of the word "pen", French "plume", etc.; so too the literal meaning of *mr* in B300-301 must not be pressed, mastabas being more probably meant than actual "pyramids".

Translate therefore: "all kinds of furniture which are brought to the tomb-shaft, its (i. e. the tombs) requirements were supplied therewith[1]".

*305-306.* — B; L. It does not seem possible to derive any good readings from L; is certainly a corruption of , but in B is better; is again here to be emended to , see above B301-304 note. — In B both and are doubtless the passive *sdmw-f*, and that follows in each case is the dative. — "tomb-garden", see Maspero's instructive note *C. P.*, p. 82 and the examples of , in this sense quoted by me *Ä. Z.*, 45 (1908), 129. — *M ḫnt r* I take to be a compound preposition "in front of", though I can produce no other example of this[2]; after *dmi* we should probably understand the suffix of the 1st. person singular.

---

V, tomb of Neferhotep, pl. 3, *Pap. Turin*, 54, 15); (3) more rarely in a general sense "utensils"; thus the tree says to the beloved one, "Send out thy servants before thee *Turin Love-songs*, 2, 9.

1. GR. translates, "and all the instruments applied to a tomb were there employed". MASP., *C. P.*, p. 82 gives, "Je donnai le mobilier, faisant les agencements nécessaires dans la pyramide même"; but he seems to have changed his view, since in *M. S.*, p. 157 we find registered an otherwise unknown word "les matériaux de choix (?)". ERM. offers no explanation of the passage.

2. So ERM.; GR., far less probably, "the land in it better than a farm estate". MASP. (*C. P.*, p. 82) renders "avec des terres prises sur les bois royaux et un bourg", reading ; MASP. can indeed point to in L in support of his version, but the spelling of *ḫntl-š* in B would be most abnormal, and this word, as I have shown in *Ä. Z.*, 45 (1908), 129 never means "estates" before the 18th. Dynasty, but is always a title.

*307.* — The phrase recurs in an 18th. Dynasty text (*Urk.*, IV, 1200) quoted in the note on B192-193 above.

*307–308.* — "overlaid" with gold, cf. *Shipwrecked Sailor*, 64; *Harris*, I, 30, 5; perhaps too *Deir el Gebrâwi*, II, 19; *Benihasan*, II, 4. The word properly means to "sweep" or "brush over" something, cf. "Make her sit on ground swept with the eaves of beer", *Pap. Kahun*, 6, 15; other examples *Ebers*, 97, 17; 98, 7. An obscure metaphorical use in *Prisse*, 12, 3[1]; Sethe compares cagp (cegp) : capg *verrere* (*Verbum*, I, § 260).

*308.* — B; L gives the phonetic spelling "its apron". The metal *ḏ'm* is here apparently distinguished from *nb* "gold". The theory of Lepsius that the word means electrum rests on no evidence whatsoever. In poetical texts *ḏ'm* is a simple synonym of *nb* "gold". Here it might be meant that whereas the statue itself was only overlaid with "gold", the apron was solid gold. The difficult question of the precise meaning of *ḏ'm* requires careful study. Some good criticism will be found already in Chabas, *Études sur l'Antiquité historique*, 2nd. ed., p. 17-64. — B; L has the inexplicably corrupt version

*309.* — In the version of B emend for . On the word *šwȝw* see *Admonitions*, p. 24, and for the construction of *iry nf mit-t* see Sethe, *Verbum*, II, § 899. The sentence is quoted in the form Mar., *Karnak*, 37b, 7 (statue of *'Imnḥtp* son of *Ḥpw*). L has here , and clearly read *m tȝ pn r ḏr-f* "in all this land" at the end of the sentence, though there is not room on the ostracon for the restoration of [*m tȝ*] as well as [*mit-t*]. The addition is superfluous.

*309-310.* — The words are translated by Gr., "Thus am I in the favour of the king until the day of death shall come"; so too Erm. and Masp. It is plain however that this rendering is merely an attempt to avoid the difficulty of making Sinuhe recount his death; and it is open to the grave objection that a clause beginning with must be the continuation of the descriptive passage that precedes[2]. The difficulty disappears as soon as it is recognized that the story is written in the form of a funerary biography (see on R1-2); Sinuhe speaks out of his tomb, and there is therefore no reason why he should not narrate his own death. — L, which had the reading instead of *ḥr ḥswt*, continues with thoughtlessly substituting *mini-nf im-f* for *n mini*, though the first person is obviously required.

1. The determinative of the arrow is of course derived from *sšr*, *šsr* "arrow", and we must beware o transcribing it , as done by Masp., *M. S.*, p. 25, by confusion with *sḫkr* "to ornament".

2. Otherwise we should have *ḫr wnn-i* or *ḫr mtk-wi* or the like.

*311.* — B ends the text with precisely the same colophon as is found at the conclusion of the *Prisse*, of the *Lebensmüde* and of the *Shipwrecked Sailor*. L substitutes the formula characteristic of Ramesside manuscripts, namely [hieroglyphs] cf. *d'Orbiney*, 19, 7; *Sall. II*, 3, 7. 8; 11, 5; 14, 11; *Pap. Turin*, 138; [hieroglyphs] *Anast. III*, 7, 10; *Pap. med. Berlin*, 21, 10. [hieroglyphs] here means "it has arrived", i. e. the book reached its conclusion; for the form *sḏm-f pw*, see ERMAN, *Aeg. Gramm.*[3], § 356.

## III

### THE DUPLICATE TEXTS

The story of Sinuhe has incidentally afforded striking confirmation of the proverb that it never rains but it pours. M. Maspero's edition first made known M. Golénischeff's papyrus fragments (G). The important Ramesseum papyrus R followed close at the heels of G, and laid upon M. Maspero the unpleasant necessity of remodelling part of his work when it had already gone to press. Before the appearance of my photographic facsimile other fragments of R emerged, and a few more annoying scraps have since, I regret to say, come to light so as to render my book incomplete. A few words on a Berlin ostracon (no. 12341, published *Hierat. Pap. a. d. kön. Museum*, III, 42) were not at my disposal when I dealt with the passage to which they refer in the *Recueil de Travaux*. Two other ostraca discovered by me in the Berlin and Petrie collections respectively could fortunately be utilized for my commentary, while some other tiny fragments recently found among Professor Petrie's ostraca could not be so used. At the last moment, when the manuscript of this portion of my work was already in the hands of the printer, news came from Berlin of yet two more ostraca found in the course of this year's excavations (1913) at Der el Medineh. I am deeply indebted to Dr. Möller, not only for providing me with annotated photographs of these, but also for generously permitting me to publish them here.

A new list of Mss., replacing that contained in my former work, is necessitated by these recent accessions to our knowledge.

The Mss. of the tale now known are as follows :—

B. — Pap. Berlin 3022, for all information concerning which see GARDINER, *Die Erzählung des Sinuhe*, p. 4.

A. — The Amherst fragments, really part of B; see *op. cit.*, p. 5.

R. — The Ramesseum papyrus, see *op. cit.*, p. 3-4. More recently some new fragments have come to light, containing additions to R98-101 and R107-111; unpublished hitherto, but incorporated in the text below.

G. — M. Golénischeff's papyrus, now in Moscow; see *op. cit.*, p. 5. Collated by me from a photograph in the Berlin Museum.

C. — The Cairo ostracon 27419, see *op. cit.*, p. 5. The original has been collated by me.

BERLIN OSTRACON 12379 (OB[1])

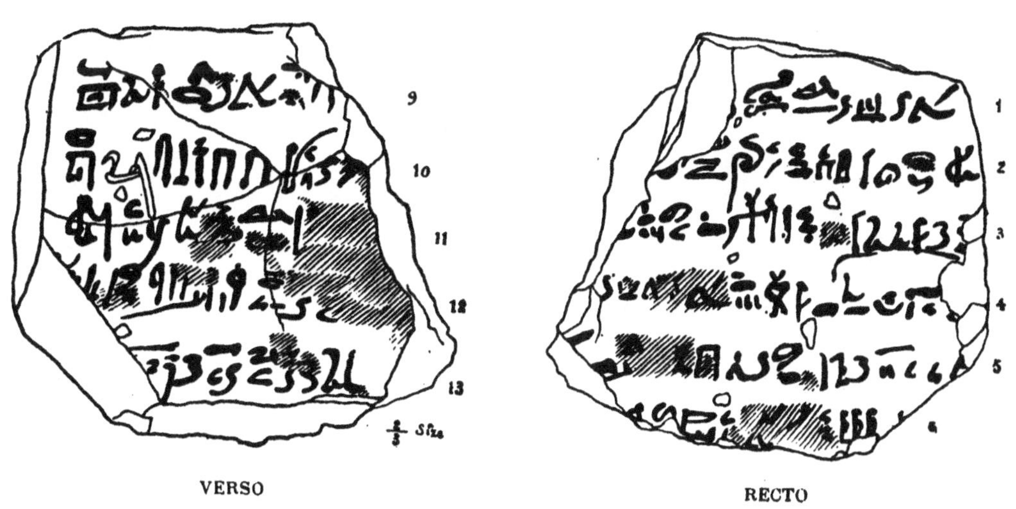

VERSO RECTO

PETRIE OSTRACON 12 (OP[1])

L. — The London ostracon 5629, see *op. cit.*, p. 5. Collated with the original in the British Museum.

OB$^1$. — The Berlin potsherd or ostracon P 12341, published in facsimile and transcription in *Hierat. Texte aus den königlichen Museen,* III, 42 (appeared in 1911). The *recto* contains accounts from about the end of the Hyksos period. The *verso* has, in the same writing, a few words from the much-disputed passage R 58-60 = B 34-36. This I discovered too late to utilize for my commentary as it appeared in the *Recueil de Travaux.*

OB$^2$. — Berlin ostracon P 12379, a piece of limestone discovered by me in July 1911 among the ostraca brought back by Dr. Möller in the preceding season. This bears in bold 19th. Dynasty hieratic a duplicate of parts of the passage B 273-279. Utilized in my commentary, and published in facsimile in the accompanying plate.

OB$^3$. — Berlin ostracon P 12623, a large piece of inscribed limestone found by Doctor Möller near the tomb of Sennozem (no. 1) at Der el Medineh (spring 1913). The writing is not unlike that of C, and belongs to a 19th. or 20th. Dynasty hand. The *recto* contains the greater portion of R 1-19, and the *verso* a more damaged duplicate of R 49-68 = B 25-44. This valuable new document is published for the first time in the following pages, from photographs and notes provided by Dr. Möller.

OB$^4$. — Berlin ostracon P 12624, a smaller limestone fragment discovered at the same time and place as the preceding, which it resembles in its handwriting. A duplicate of R 38-51 = B 13-27. Publication as last.

OP$^1$. — A small fragment of limestone with a few words from the passage R 47-50 = B 22-25. From the Petrie collection (no. 58), date about Dynasty 19-20. Not utilized in the commentary.

OP$^2$. — Petrie ostracon 12, a small limestone fragment found among a large collection entrusted to me by Professor Petrie; soil-stained, and faint in places. The writing is of the 19th. or 20th. Dynasty; the *recto* contains portions of B 236-245, the *verso* portions of B 248-253. Utilized in my commentary and here published in facsimile.

OP$^3$. — A small chip of limestone, with some words from B 250-256 discovered in 1913 among Professor Petrie's ostraca (no. 59). Probably 19th. or 20th. Dynasty. Not utilized in the commentary.

By the newly-discovered parallel texts the synoptic table of correspondences in my Berlin volume (*op. cit.*, p. 7) is rendered incomplete; but it is also rendered unnecessary by the text that is given in the following pages. This only includes those parts of the tale where duplicates exist. For the rest recourse must be had to my facsimile edition. A few errors in the latter are corrected below, and the reasons for the corrections are as a rule indicated in footnotes. Restorations are in square brackets. Signs underlined, as well as the verse-points, are in red.

R

G

C

OB³

---

R

G

(sic)

C

OB³

---

R

G

C

OB³

---

R

G

(sic)

C

OB³

---

1. Here and in the corrupt writing of *rpʿtt* below ◯ is made like hieratic ▬.
2. The correct N. K. form, see MÖLLER, *Paläographie*, II, no. 423.
3. See Additional Notes on R 1.
4. So Sethe proposes to restore.
5. Added in red above the line.
6. My interpretation (see note on R 3) of the corrupt signs in C is proved by OB³ to be erroneous; see Additional Notes on R 3.

R

G

C

OB³

---

R

A(m)

G

C

OB³

---

R

A(m)

G

C (sic) (sic)

OB³

---

R

A(m) ends.

G

C

OB³

---

1. [hieroglyph] above the line.

2. Originally [hieroglyph], then corrected in red into [hieroglyph].

R

G

C

OB[3]

---

R

G

C

OB[3]

---

R

A(n)

G

C

OB[3]

---

R

A(n)

G

C

OB[3]

---

1. Here no verse point.
2. A tiny trace.
3. See Commentary on R 10.
4. These signs on a flint in the limestone.
5. Added above the line in red.
6. is here almost like a small .
7. Above the line , corresponding to the reading in C, is here added in red.

R 13
A(n)
G
C (sic) 3
OB³ [1] [2]

R 14
A(n)
G [3]
C
OB³ 10

R [4] 15
A(n)
G 9
C (sic)
OB³

R 16
A(n)
G
C
OB³ [5] 11

1. 𓏲 is a red correction over black \\. — 2. No more than this can be lost. — 3. So, not ʿnḫ wḏ; snb as Maspero gives. — 4. Quite a different sign from [hieroglyph] R 69. — 5. This sign, which is borrowed from sḏr(t), is surrounded by a number of red dots to indicate that it is an error.

R 17

A(n) ends.

G 10

C

OB[3]

---

R 18

A(o) [1]

G

C [2]

OB[3] 12

---

R 19

A(o) ends.

G 11

C

OB[3] end of recto.

---

R 20

A(p)

G

C

---

1. Like ⲙⲙⲙ.
2. This word is a correction.

R

A(p)

G

C

---

R

A(p) ends after some illegible fragments of signs.

G

C

---

R

A(q)

G

C

---

R

A(q)

G

C

---

1. So Dévaud rightly; see Additional Notes on R 20-22.
2. *Sic*, but corrected out of some other group.
3. Added later below of *hꜣbw*.
4. A correction here; (?) confused with the following sign.

R

B

G

C

R

B

G

C

R

B

G

C

R

B

G

C

R

B

G

C

1. [hieroglyph] in red above the line. — 2. A ligature, and therefore just possibly for [hieroglyph]. — 3. [hieroglyph] added later.

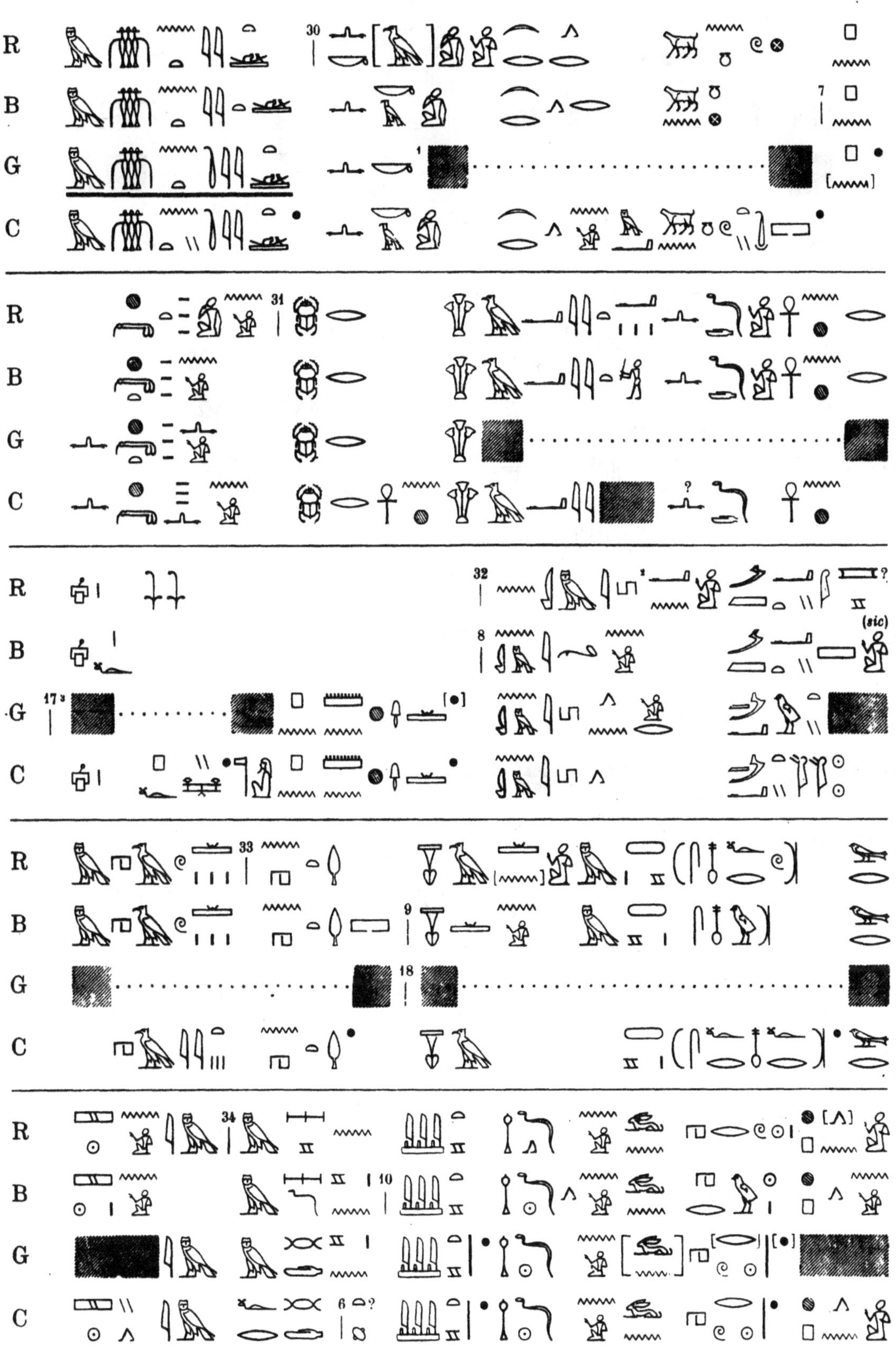

1. Tail only. — 2. This sign has everywhere been substituted for the incorrect [hieroglyph], see on B 8 (p. 15) footnote 4. — 3. Here begins the second page of G.

R 35 36

B 11

G 19

C

---

R 37

B 12

G

C

---

R 38

B 13

G 20

C 2

OB⁴ 1 (sic)

---

R 39 40 3

B 14 15

G

C

OB⁴

---

1. In my autographic transcription wrongly .

2. is a correction, apparently out of ; but doubtful.

3. My former reading (?) is less probable.

R 41
B 16
G 21
C
OB[4] 2

R 42
B 17
G
C 7
OB[4]

R 43
B
G 22
C
OB[4] 3

R 44
B 18
G
C
OB[4]

1. The 𓏏 is a later addition, as the colour of the ink shows. — 2. above the line. — 3. The lower part of the sign is much altered; beneath there is something like 𓈉 — not 𓏪.

R 45

B 19

G 23

C

OB[4] 4 ?

R 46

B 20

G

C

OB[4] 5

R

B 21

G 24

C (sic) 8

OB[4] (sic) 3

R 47

B 22

G the fragments of page 2 end here.

C

OB[4] 6

1. [sign] added later. — 2. See R 33. — 3. Erased traces of some red signs. — 4. [sign] wrongly omitted in my autographic transcription (Dévaud).

R 48

B 23

C

OP[1]

OP[4]

---

R

B 24

C

OP[1]

OB[4] 7

---

R 49

B 25

C

OP[1]

OB[4] 8

OB[3] 30[2]

---

1. 𓏲 is an addition, as the blackness of the ink and the position show.

2. A considerable number of lines are lost between the last line of the existing *recto* (l. 12) and the beginning of the *verso* (l. 29). Of l. 29 only a few illisible traces remain.

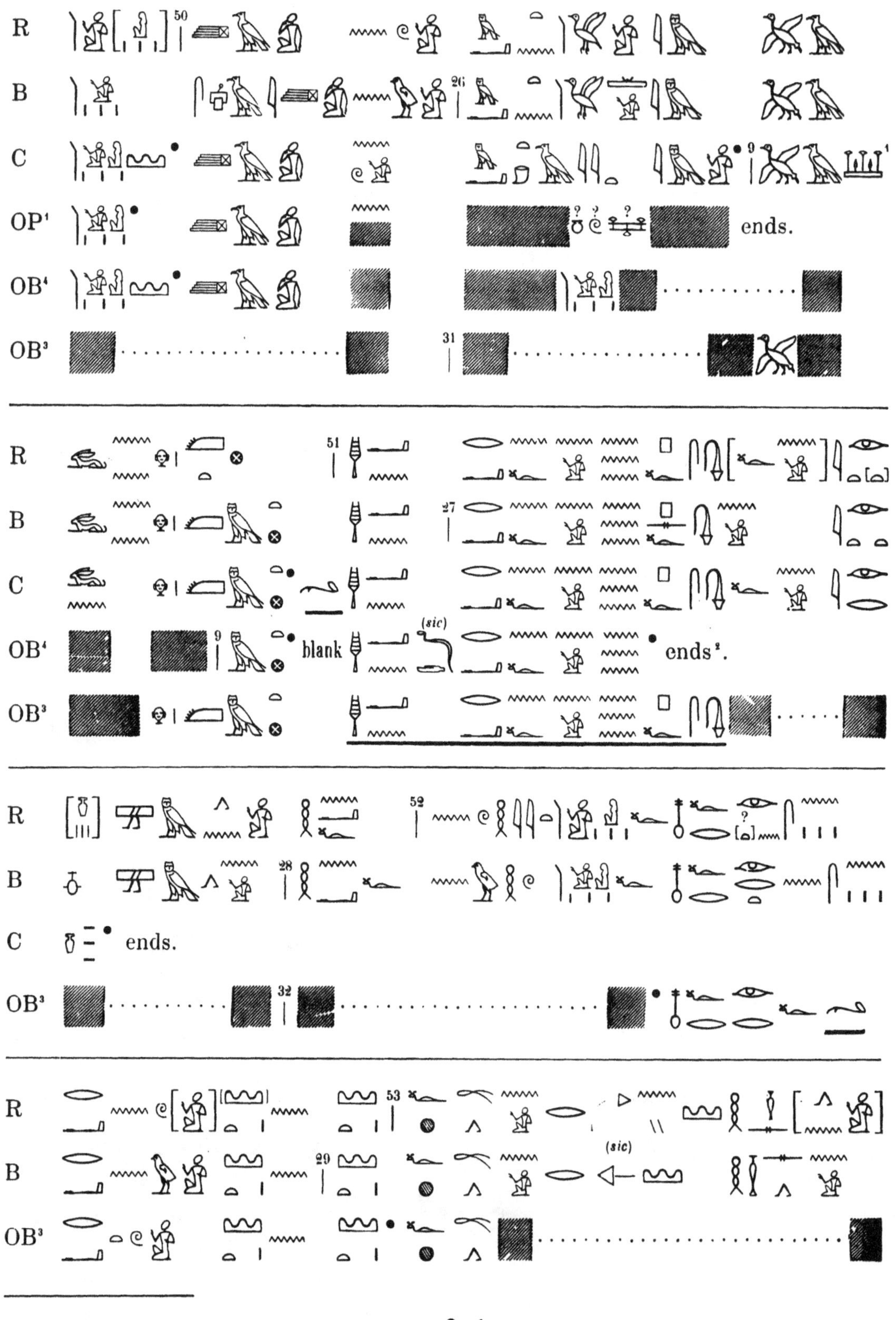


1. [hieroglyphs] has arisen from a corrupted dittograph of [hieroglyph].

2. Here is added in red the date when the ostracon was written :— [hieroglyphs].

R 54

B 30

OB³ 33 (sic)

R 55

B 31

OB³ (sic) (sic) 34

R 56

B 32

OB³ [1]

R 57 ?

B 33

OB³ 35

R ? ? 58

B 34

OB³ 36

OB¹

R 59

B 35

OB³

OB¹

1. is corrected out of .

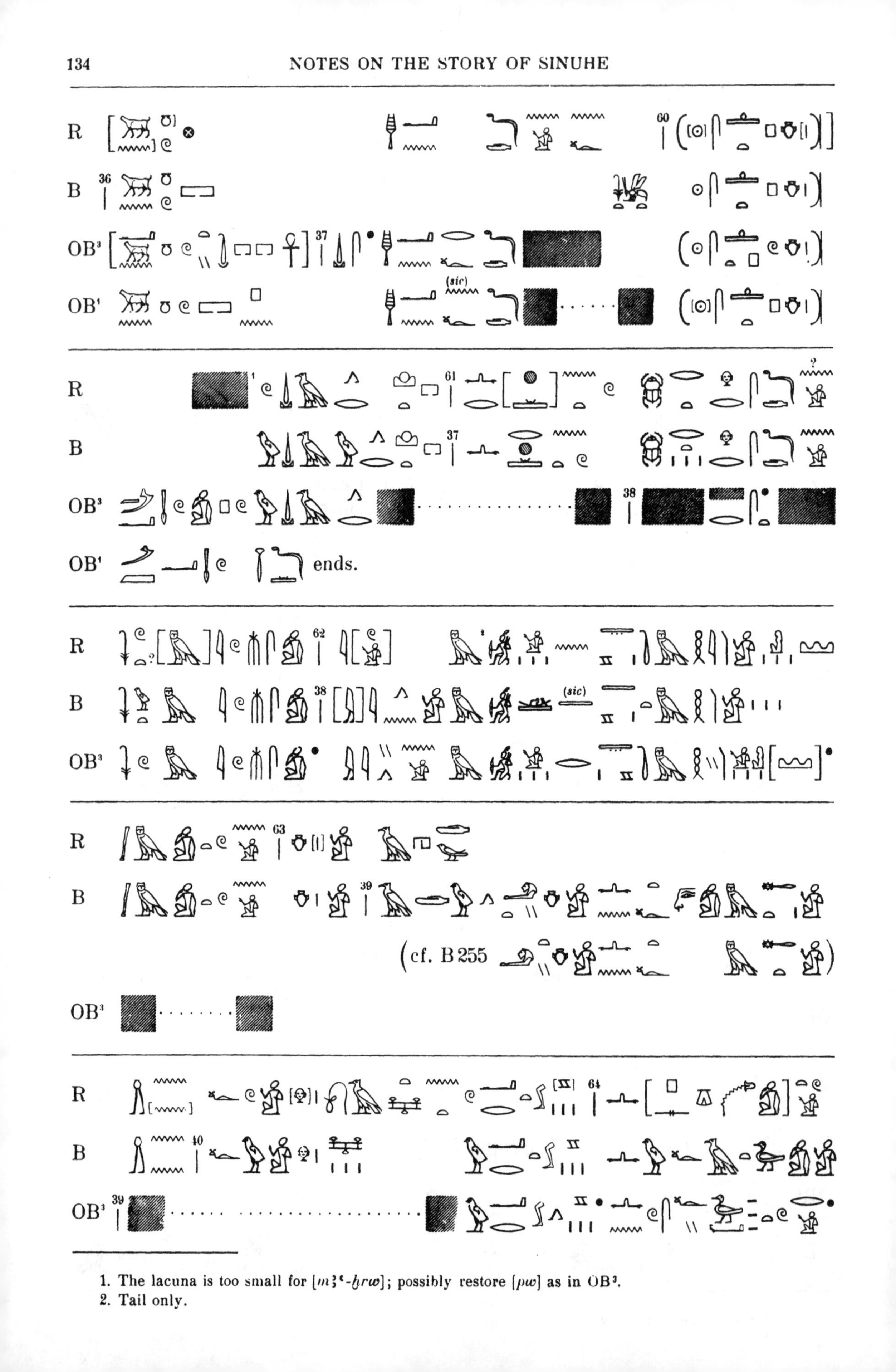

R 60

B 36

OB³ 37

OB¹ (sic)

R 61

B 37

OB³ 38

OB¹ ends.

R 62

B 38 (sic)

OB³

R 63

B 39

(cf. B 255 )

OB³

R 64

B 40

OB³ 39

1. The lacuna is too small for [*m*ꜣꜥ-*ḫrw*]; possibly restore [*pw*] as in OB³.
2. Tail only.

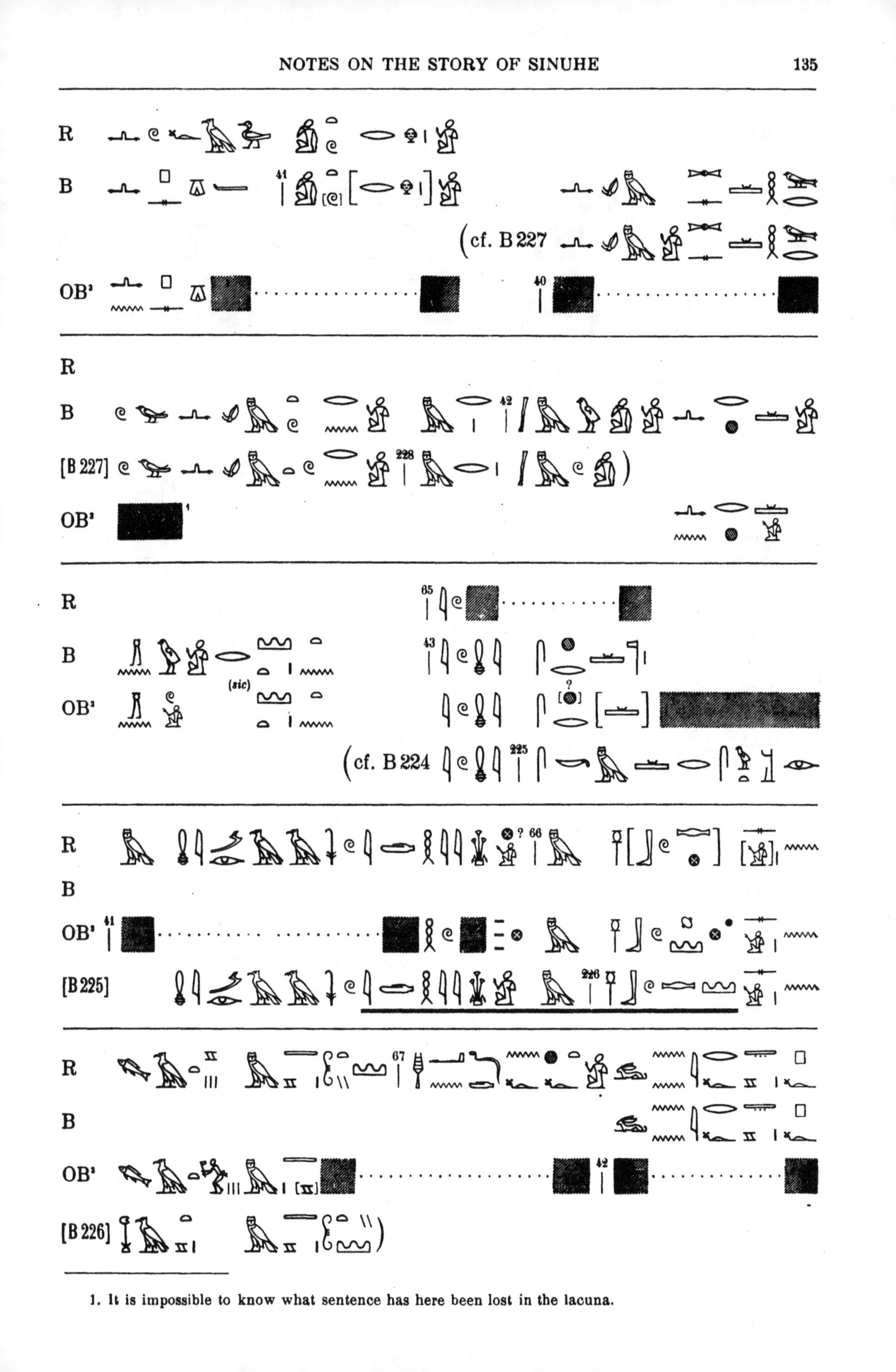

R

B 41 42

(cf. B 227

OB³ 40

---

R

B 42

[B 227] 228 )

OB³ 1

---

R 65

B 43

OB³ (sic) ?

(cf. B 224 225

---

R ? 66

B

OB³ 41

[B 225] 226

---

R 67

B

OB³ 42

[B 226] )

1. It is impossible to know what sentence has here been lost in the lacuna.

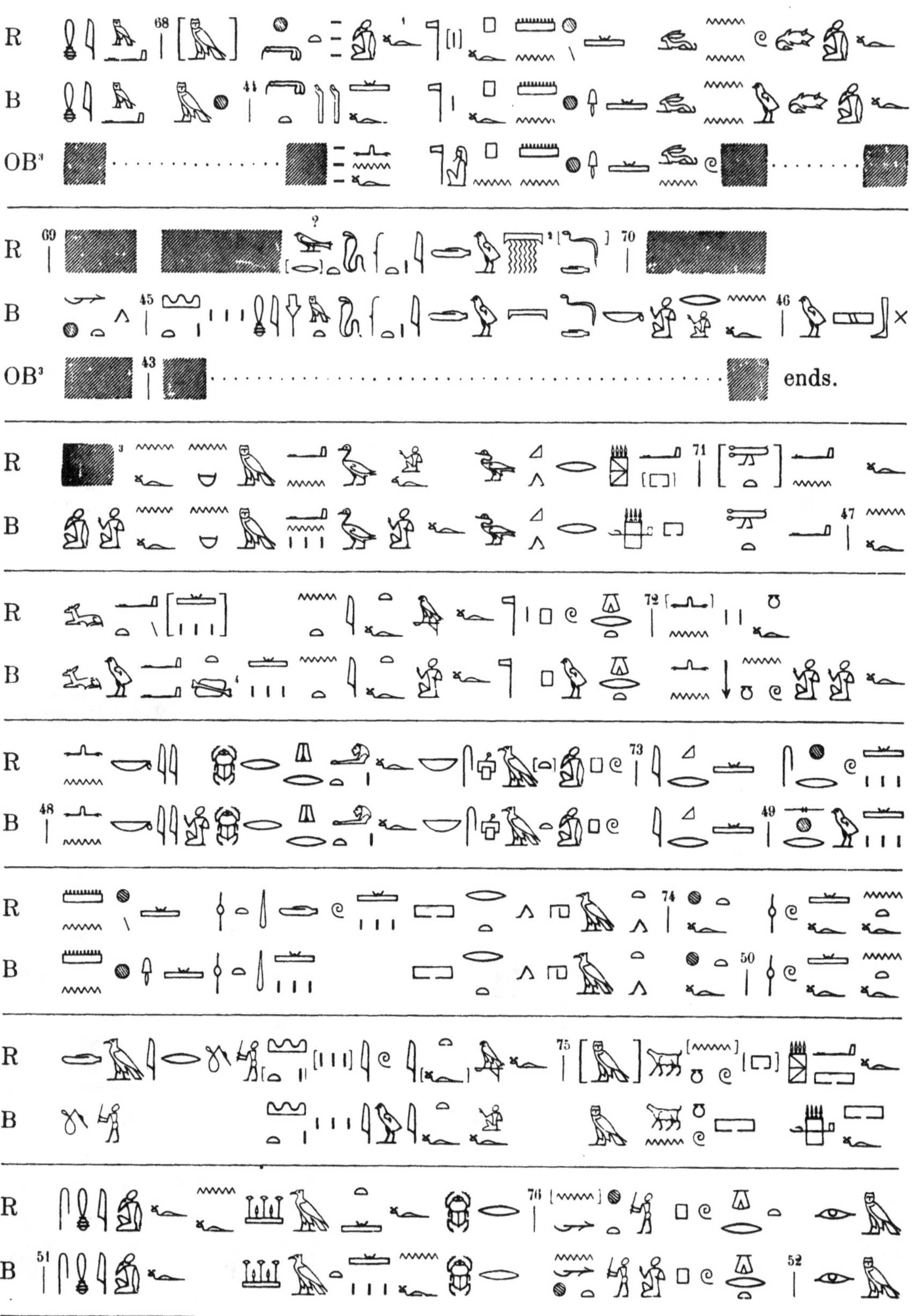

1. A tiny, but certain, trace; not recognized in the photographic edition.
2. In the facsimile publication wrongly [sign].
3. Not sufficient space for exactly the same reading as B.
4. The actual sign in the Ms. is like hieratic [sign].

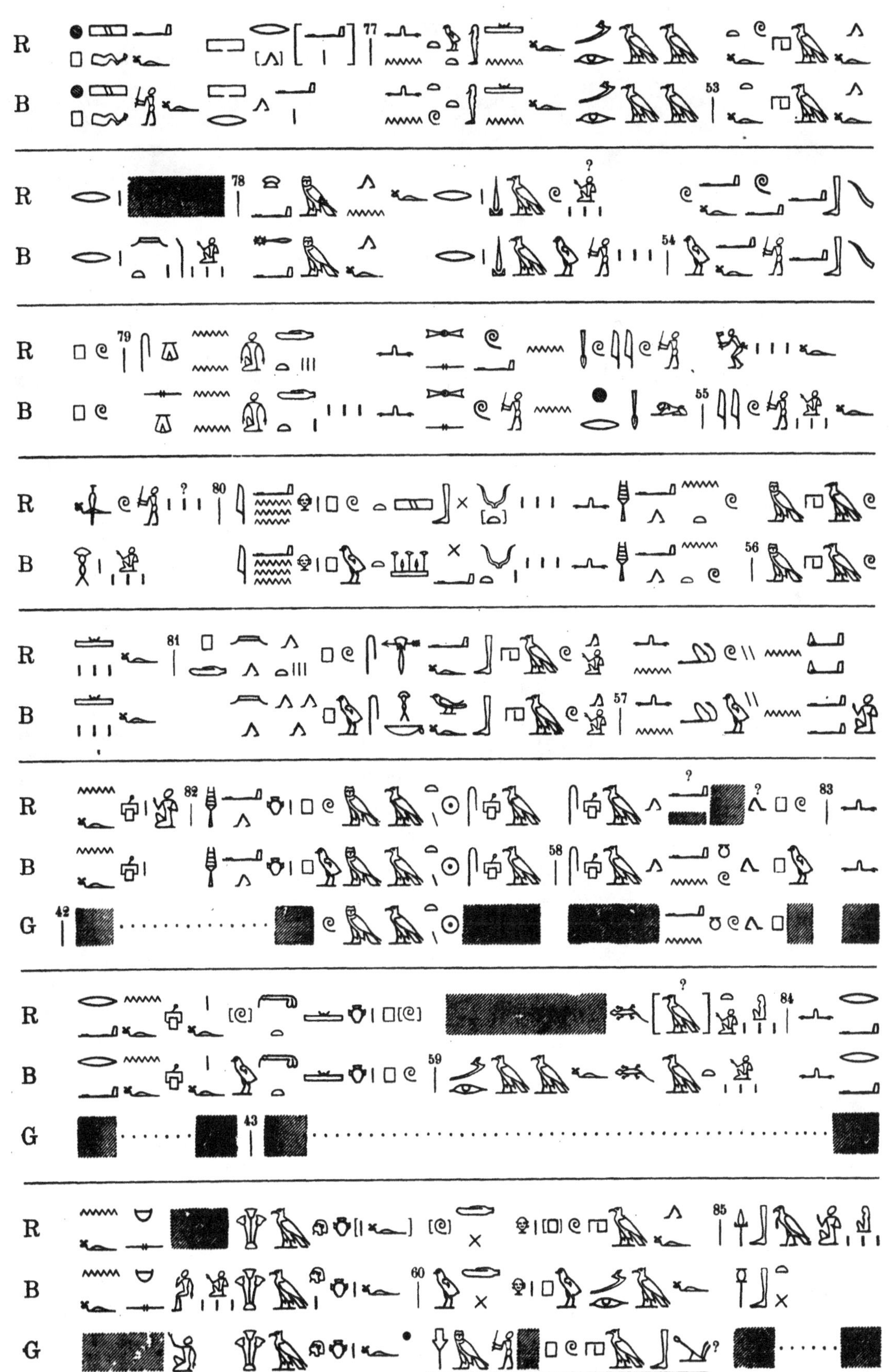

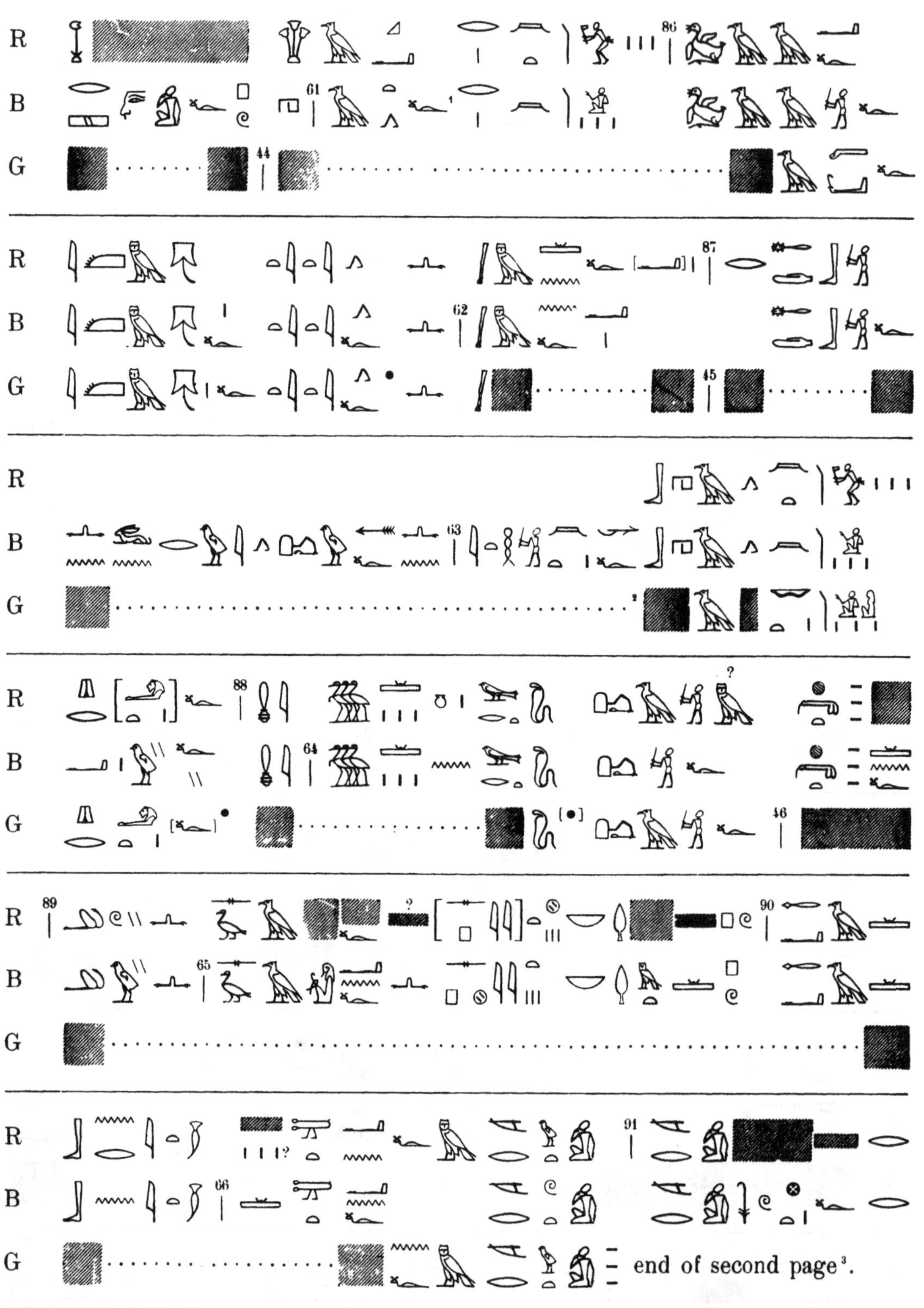


1. [sign] has been later added.

2. G must have contained the words omitted by R.

3. Two signs [signs] are preserved at the beginning of the last line of a third page, and probably belong to some word that would fall between B 90-100.

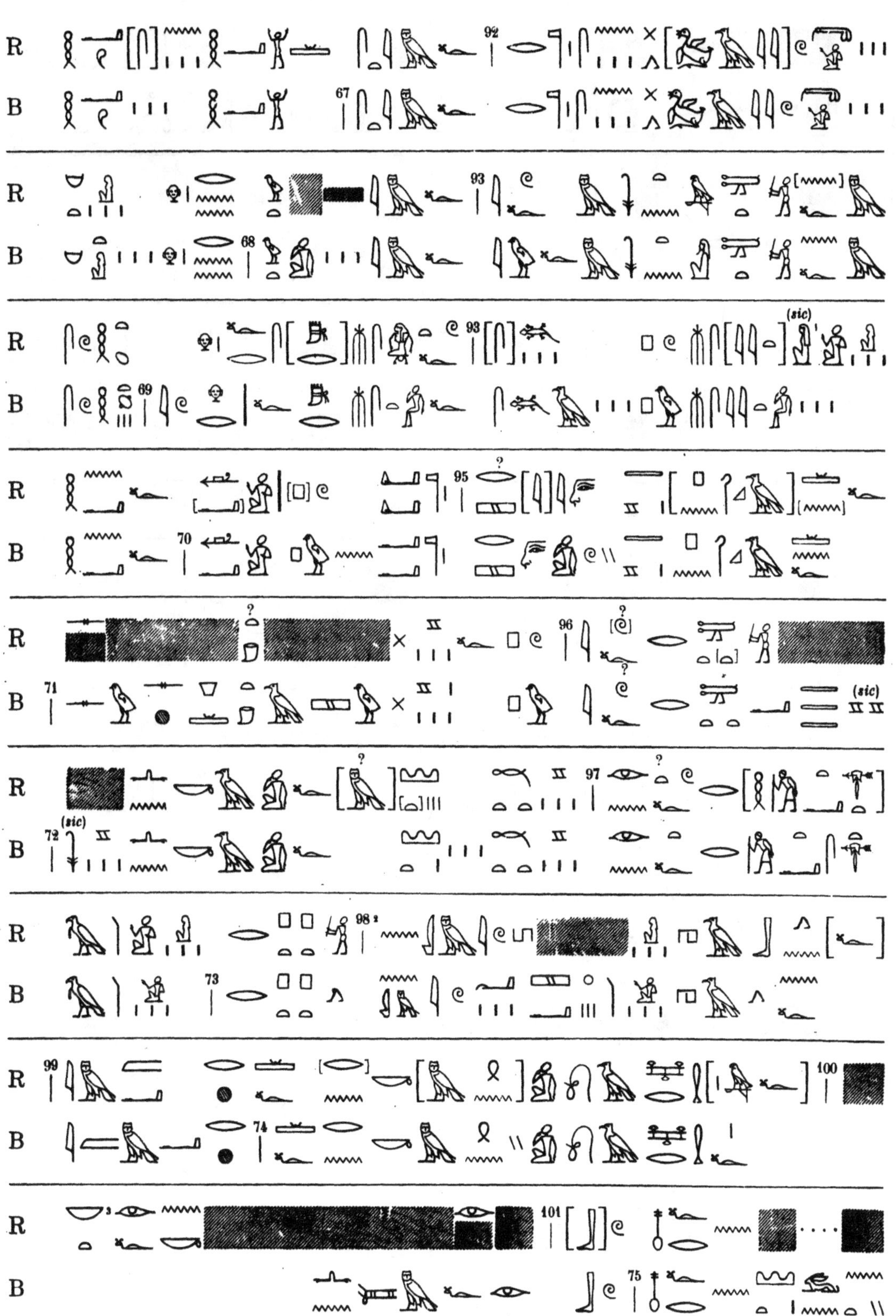

1. The large form employed above R 3, 4.

2. In the sentences that follow (R 98-111) I incorporate the fragments of R recently found and not included in my photographic edition. — 3. [sign] is not quite certain.

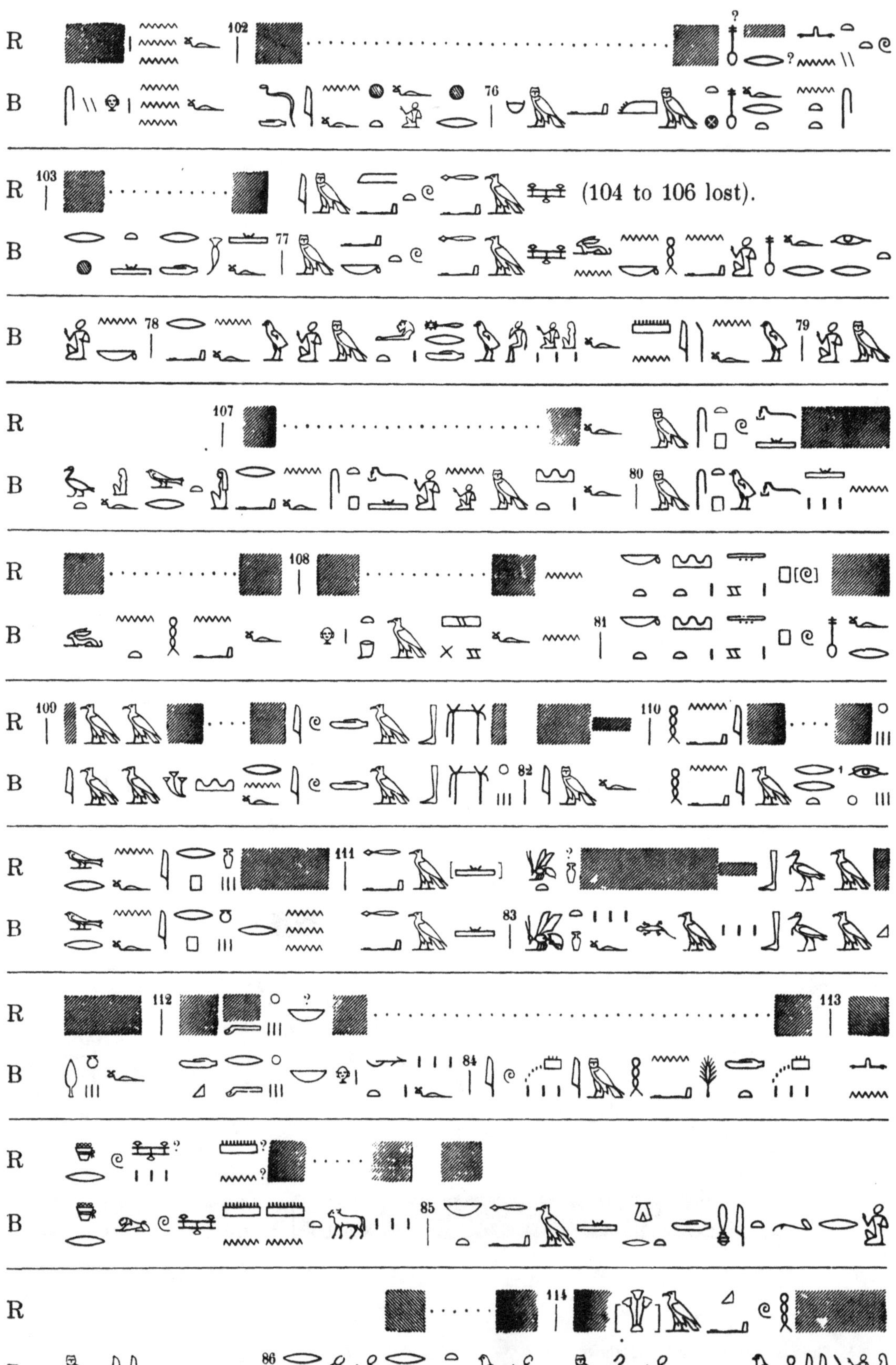
R
B
R
(104 to 106 lost).
B
B
R
B
R
B
R
B
R
B
R
B
R
B
R
B

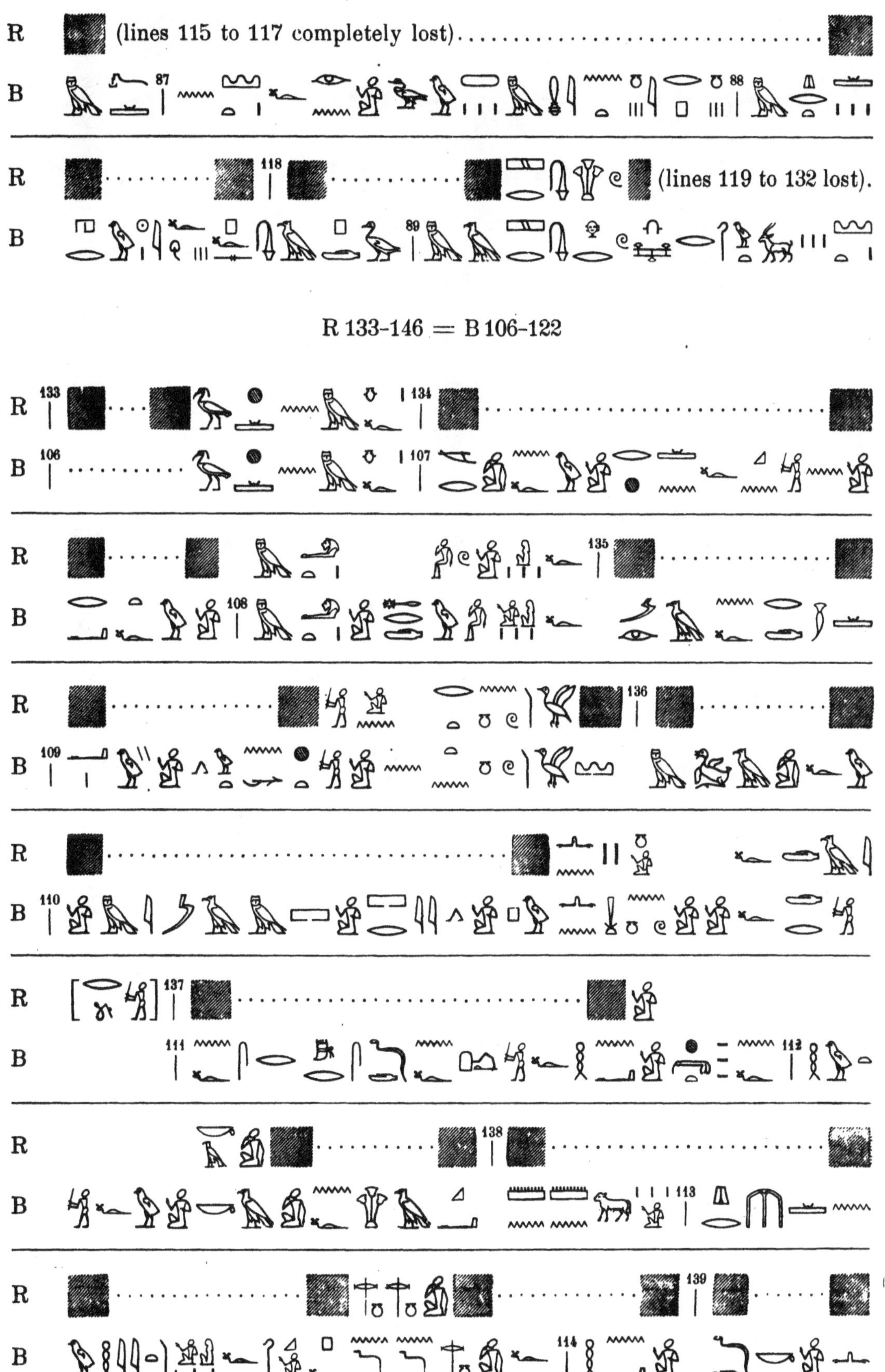
R (lines 115 to 117 completely lost)
B 87 88
R 118 (lines 119 to 132 lost).
B 89

R 133-146 = B 106-122

R 133 134 135 136 137 138 139
B 106 107 108 109 110 111 112 113 114

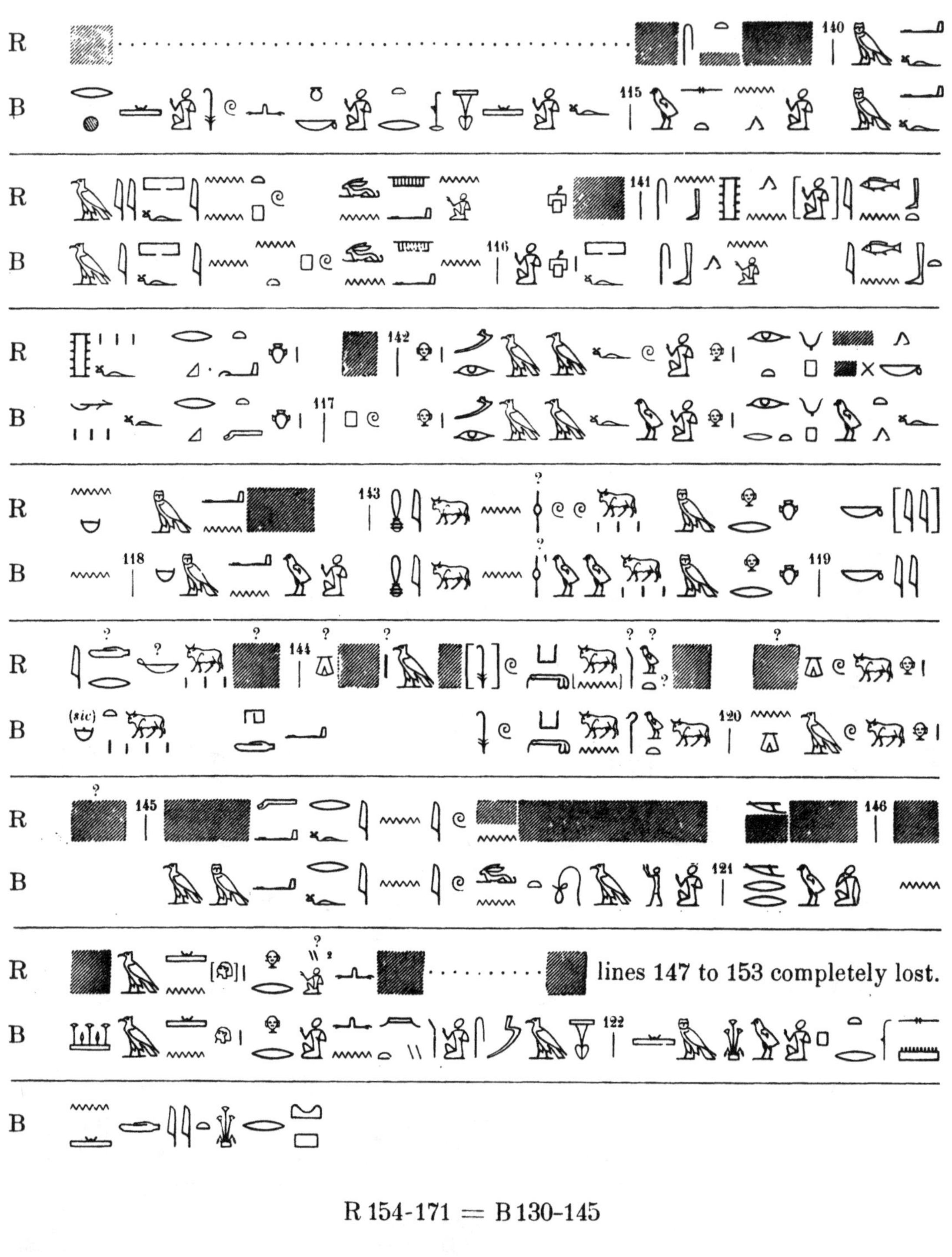


R 154-171 = B 130-145

R 154 155
B 130 131

1. M. Dévaud proposes to read *hcw*; see the Additional Notes on the passage.

2. Or perhaps [hieroglyphs] as in R 161

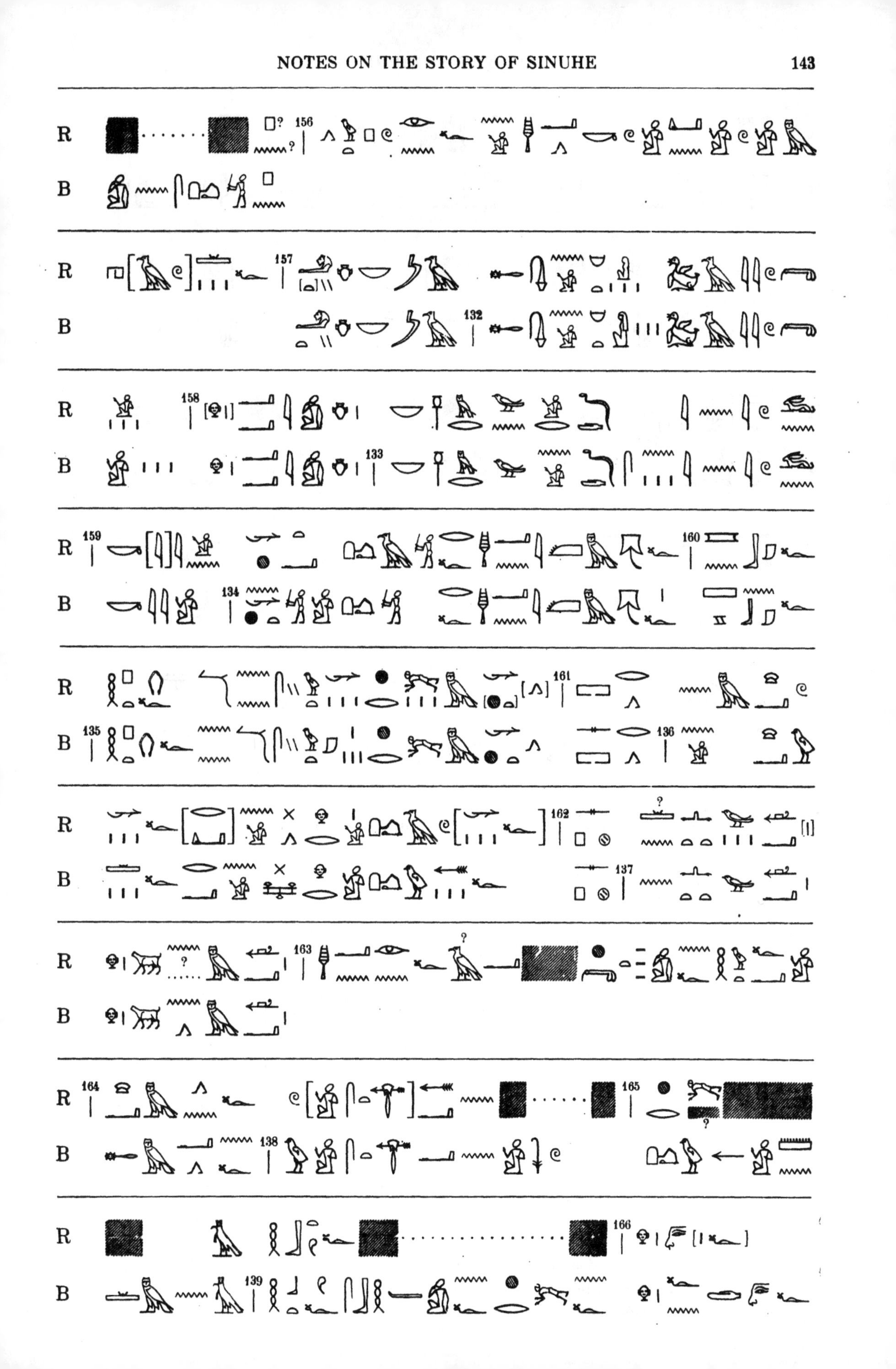

R ... ? ? 156

B

---

R 157

B 132

---

R 158

B 133

---

R 159 160

B 134

---

R 161

B 135 136

---

R 162

B 137

---

R 163 ?

B

---

R 164 165 ?

B 138

---

R 166

B 139

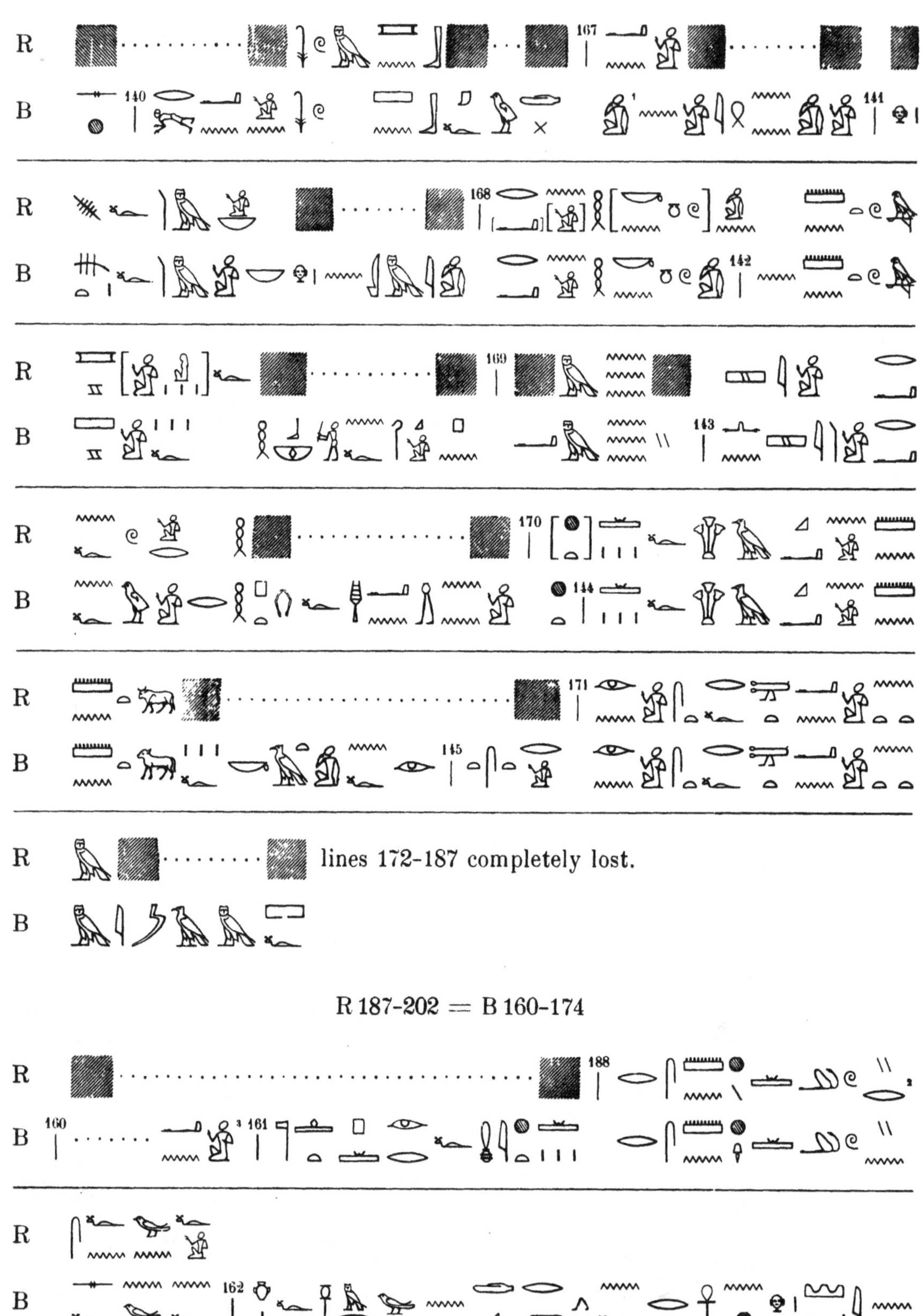


1. My autographed transcription gives erroneously [hieroglyph].
2. So, and not *n* as given in the autographed transcription.
3. Apparently intentionally deleted.

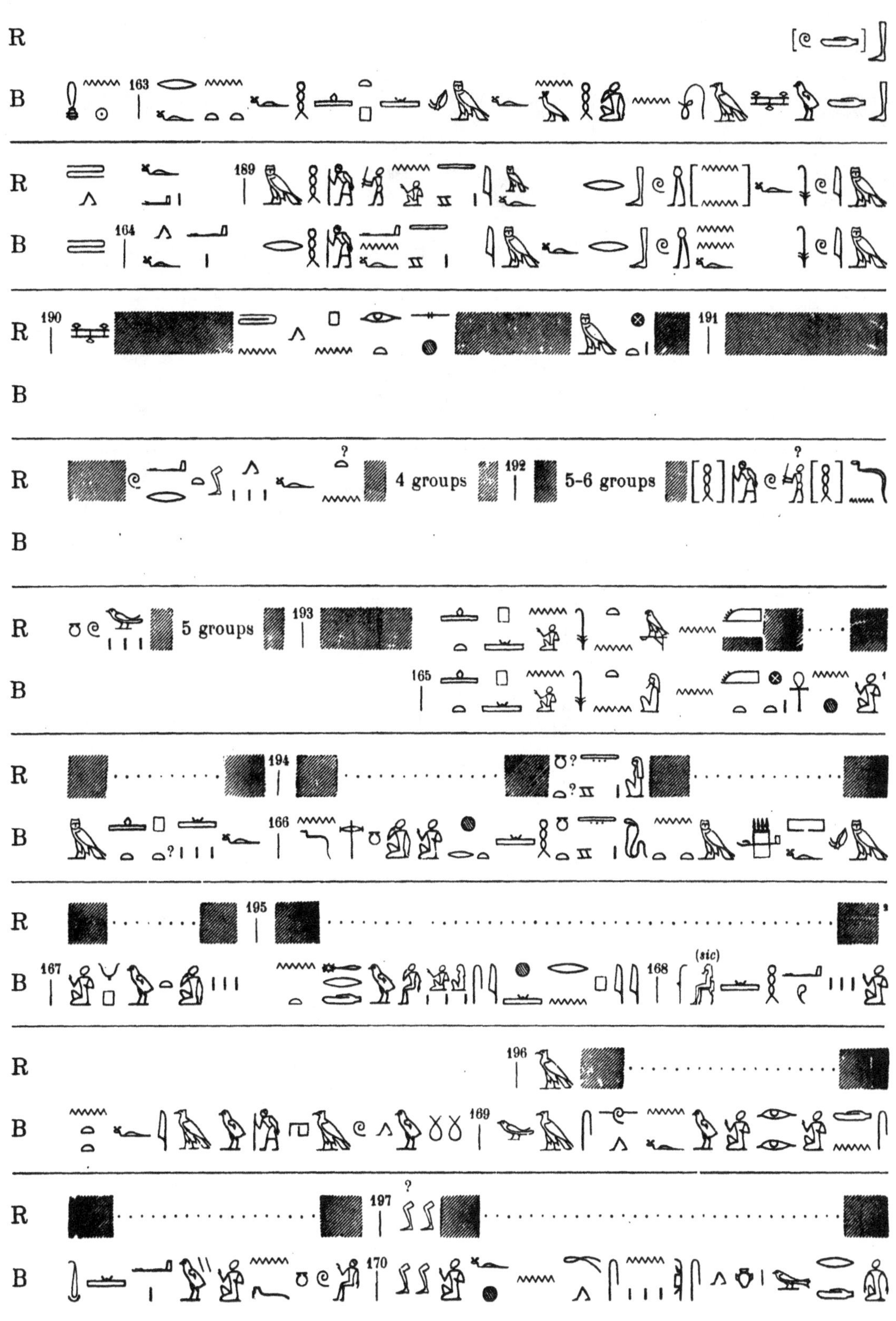

1. [hieroglyph] not quite certain, added later.

2. The lacuna is no larger than here indicated.

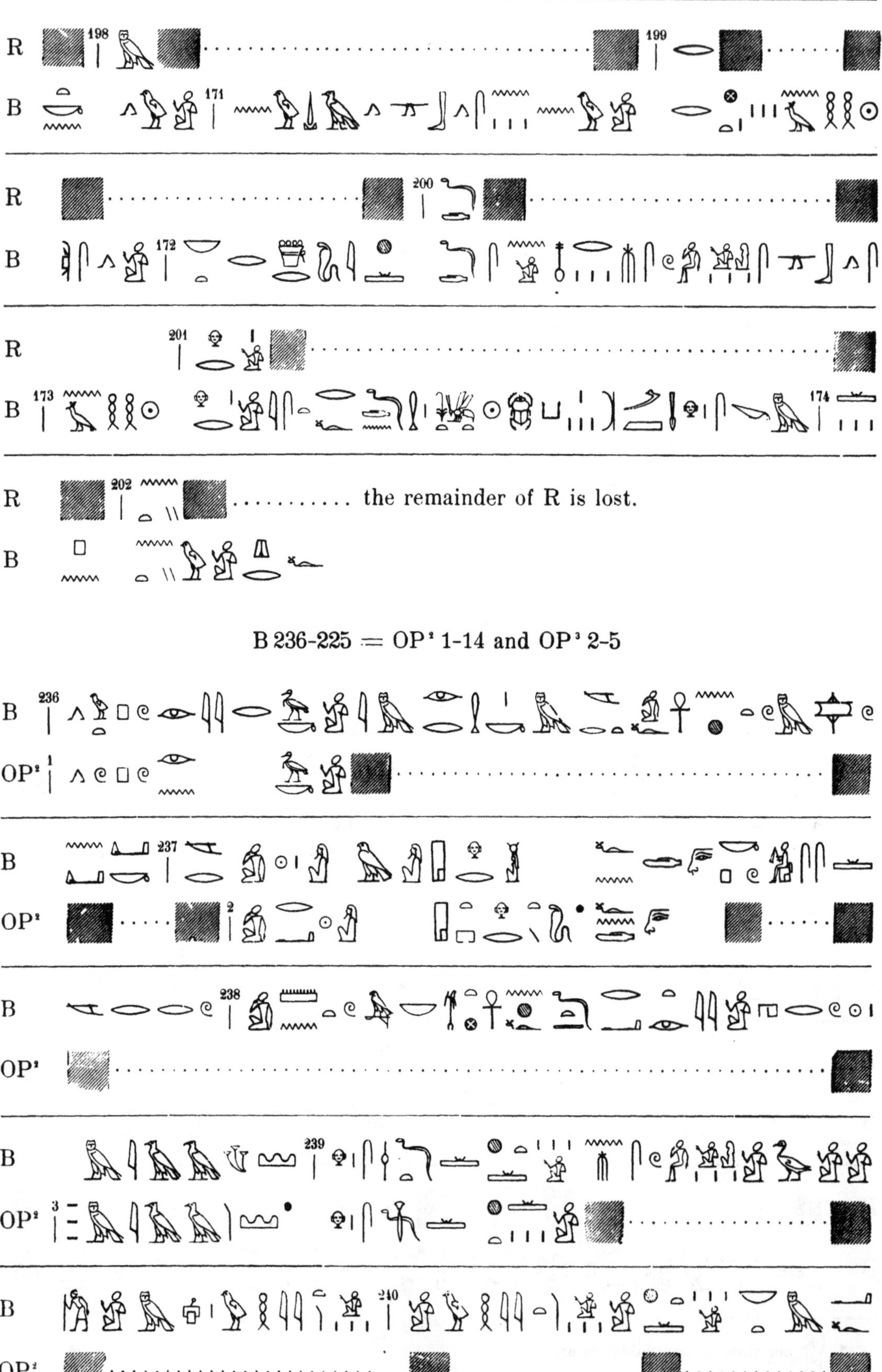
R
B
R
B
R
B
R
the remainder of R is lost.
B
B 236-225 = OP[2] 1-14 and OP[3] 2-5
B
OP[2]
B
OP[2]
B
OP[2]
B
OP[2]
B
OP[2]

B 241

OP$^{2}$ 4

B 242 [1]

OP$^{2}$

B 243

OP$^{2}$ 5

B 244

OP$^{2}$ 6

B 245

OP$^{2}$ 7 Two (?) lines lost at end of recto.

B

B 246

B 247

B 248

OP$^{2}$ 9 [2]

B 249

OP$^{2}$ 10

1. Autographed transcription wrongly ; see Commentary.

2. Beginning of *verso*.

B [1] 250

OP² 11

OP³

---

B 251

OP² 12

OP³

---

B 252

OP²

OP³ [2]

---

B

OP² 13

OP³ 3

---

B 253

OP²

OP³ 4

---

B 254

OP² 14 Two (?) lines lost at end of verso.

OP³ 5

---

1. So better than of my facsimile edition; see Note on B 249.

2. Unintelligible signs, like the cursive ligature for ; as correction above the line a stroke like hieratic .

B 255

OP[3] ........ ........................ ends[1].

B 272-280 = OB[2] 1-7

B 273

OB[2] 1 ..............

B 274

OB[2] [•] ....

B 275

OB[2] 2 ?

B (sic) 276

OB[2] 3

B 277

OB[2] ......... 4

B 278 [2]

OB[2] [*n ḥryt-k*] 5

B 279

OB[2] ......... 6 [ ] .........

1. Illegible traces of a sixth line.
2. Ms. [hieroglyph], clearly a corruption of [hieroglyph].

B 280

OB' 7 ends.

B 300-311 = L 1-8

B 301

L 1 [ ]

B ?

L 2

B 302

L

B 303 (sic)

L 3

B 304

L 4

B 305

L

B 306

L 5

1. For the exact signs of the original see the facsimile and the transcription accompanying it.
2. This is, in late-Egyptian B hieratic, an easy corruption of .

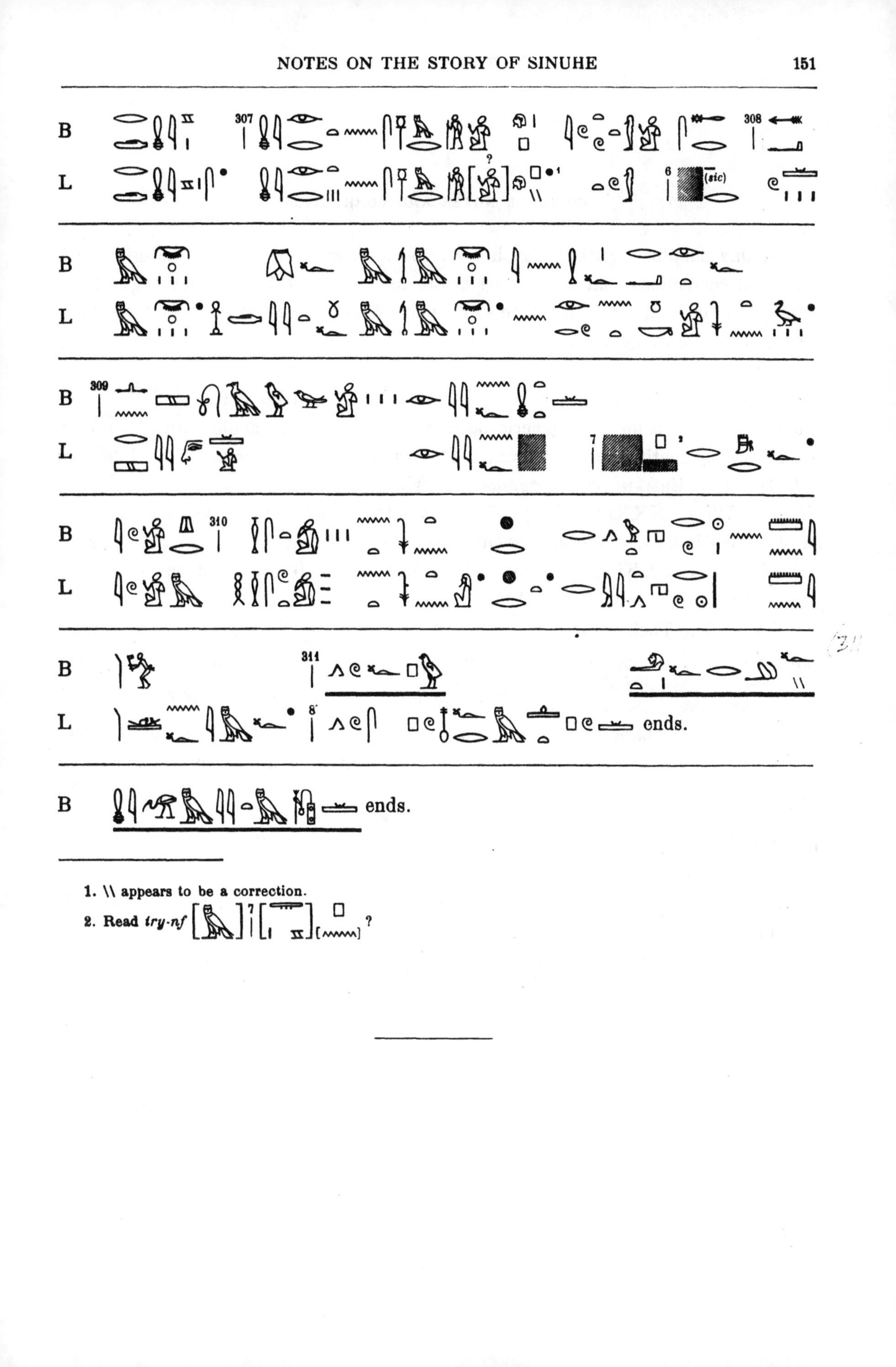

B 307 308

L ? 1 6 (sic)

B

L

B 309

L 7

B 310

L

B 311

L 8 ends.

B ends.

1. \\ appears to be a correction.

2. Read *try·nf* [ ] 7 [ ] [ ] ?

# IV

## ADDITIONAL NOTES AND CORRECTIONS

In this chapter I gather together all the additional illustrative material, new ideas and corrections that have come before me since the Commentary began to be printed. I am particularly indebted to Professor Sethe and M. Dévaud for their helpful and valuable suggestions.

R 1. — I do not now believe that the damaged sign in the title (R) can be the fish; before the generic determinative we should rather expect a specific determinative such as [ ]. The word should moreover be read *'ḏ*, not *'nḏ*, see now ERMAN, *Zur ägyptischen Wortforschung*, III = *Sitzb. d. k. Pr. Akad. d. Wiss.*, XXXIX [1912], 959.—Note the position of the verse-point in G and C. Can it be that the scribes of these Mss. interpreted as two titles, "Territorial Governor and King in the land of the Asiatics"? If so, it need hardly be said their view must be secondary and erroneous.

R 3. — The Theban tomb of (no. 172; *circa* Tuthmosis III) contains fragments of an autobiographical stele in which the narrative begins , perhaps a conscious reminiscence of our tale; for as the later writing of see *Ä. Z.*, 45 (1909), 27.—The new Rameside text OB[3] proves me to have erred in my emendation of the corrupt version of C. Evidently as given by OB[3] was the prototype of C's reading, the corruption of which into was possibly due to the influence of the common expression "Palace".

R 4. — G and OB[3] add the word *m3'-ḫrw* to the names of kings throughout; C is free from this addition to the original text.

R 5. — The name of the pyramid of Amenemmes I at Lisht has long been known, cf. a title on the stele *C 2* of the Louvre, dated in the 9th year of Sesostris I (PIERRET, *Rec.*, II, 108 = PIEHL, *I. H.*, I, 4 = GAYET, *Stèles*, 2).

The Queen was, it is interesting to note, the sister or half-sister of Sesostris I, being like him one of the children of Amenemmes I. It does not seem impossible that this may be the Queen whose tomb was found by Ebers at Deir el Bahri (see GAUTHIER, *Livre des Rois*, II, 121-122); the titles in this tomb are (from notes kindly lent to me by M. Golénischeff).

R 7. — For *sḥr-f* Sethe suggests "er wurde entfernt", "raptus est ad cælum"; but there is nothing to indicate that the word is a *sḏmwf* passive, and the determinatives are against identifying the word with (B 272) "to remove". OB[3], which deliberately corrects *sḥr-* into shows that the latter was a recognized reading, and no mere corruption peculiar to C; was doubtless understood, "he was caused to mount to the sky". In the well-known quotation of the entire passage in the inscription of Amenemhab (*Urkunden*, IV, 896) we find *sḥr-f* and not *sʿrw-f*, an additional proof, if any were needed, of the superiority of this reading.

For the idea involved in this description of the deceased king's apotheosis, and for parallels, see my letter to M. Cumont in *Revue de l'Histoire des Religions*, LXIII (1911), 209; a further instance on the ostracon published by M. Daressy (*Rec. de Trav.*, 34, 46), .

R 8. — On *sgr*, 3-rad. verb "to be still", see now further Vogelsang, *Kommentar zu den Klagen des Bauern*, p. 55.

R 9. — Cf. *Book of overthrowing Apophis* (ed. Budge), 5, 13; I owe the reference to M. Dévaud.

R 11. — The second hand in OB[1] confirms C in its reading *ꜣm(w)*; probably this is a later writing of .

R 13-14. — OB[1] shows no trace of the sentence inserted by R, and it thus becomes more and more probable that this is an interpolation; Sethe points out that it adds nothing to what is already implied in the preceding words.

R 15. — With regard to the origin of I still (see *Rec. de Trav.*, 28, 186) hold it probable that this is derived from [2], the first *s* falling out in consequence of the disagreeable sequence of consonants *sts*; in (R 24) the same reason for change does not exist, and is probably a later *Analogiebildung*.

R 18. — OB[1] confirms the view that the suffix in *sšmw-sn* of C is faulty.

R 20-22. — In connection with the interchange of and , cf. the Bubastite inscription, *Rec. de Trav.*, 16, 57, in the last few lines of which is repeatedly written for . For other writings of see now Erman, *Gramm.*[3], § 512. Vogelsang (*op. cit.*, p. 103) has recently suggested, with good show of reason, that the verbal stem connected with this negative word is "to reject". The proper transcription of the emphatic form still remains problematic.

*Sin* "to delay" turns out to be a commoner word than was suspected. I have shown *Ä. Z.*, 49 (1911), 100-102, that *sin n* is a well-attested phrase meaning "to wait for".

not is, as Dévaud has pointed out to me, the correct reading in R 21; this possibly archaic writing occurs elsewhere only in *Prisse*, 11, 6, but cf. *Song of the Harper*, 5 (Thebes, tomb 50).

4-5. — Add to the examples of the *sḏmtf* form absolutely used in our tale B 283; so too for instance twice in Garstang, *El Arabah*, 5; *Shipwrecked Sailor*, 54.

---

1. (OB[1]) is a very easy corruption of in hieratic; the converse error in C 5, *ad finem*.
2. For the M. K. writing , cf. Montet, *Hammamat*, 47, 3; , Weill, *Recueil*, 63, 2.

7. — Very probably *r s3-f* (not *pfy*) *ntr pn mnh* was the reading of G and of the Ms. from which C copied, *pfy* being an individual conjecture on the part of the scribe of C; cf. R 44 = B 68, where *ntr pfy mnh* is apposition to a suffix.

10-11. — I have discussed the word *ri-w3t* in connection with *sm3-t3 n ri-w3t* "a river-bank which served as a way" (*Peasant*, R 49) in my article *Proc. S. B. A.*, 35 (1913), 266, and have there shown that [hieroglyphs] "way" differs from [hieroglyphs] "road" only in having a more relative and less concrete sense. Translate "who stood in my way".

12. — For *msy-t* "evening meal", see Erman, *Lebensmüde*, p. 49-50.

14. — For the rare word [hieroglyphs] OB[1] reads [hieroglyphs]; so too probably C, of which only [hieroglyphs] is left. For *swh*, itself by no means a common word, see Brugsch, *Dict.*, 1177.

From *i(3)kw* "quarry" appears to be derived the title [hieroglyphs], [hieroglyphs] "quarryman", that is common both at Sinai and in the Wady Hammamat. The spelling of these words raises interesting problems: (1) does the "syllabic" writing [hieroglyphs] in [hieroglyphs] indicate the reading *i3kw* (with 3)? (2) whence arises [hieroglyph] in these words? With regard to the latter question, there is no evidence of any word *ik, i3k* meaning "old" whence [hieroglyph] can have been *transferred*; nor again is it likely that [hieroglyph] is a corruption of some sign depicting a quarryman at his work. A third possibility remains, namely that [hieroglyph] has obtained its value *ik, i3k* (cf. [hieroglyphs] *Hammamat*, 108 [Amenemmes I]; [hieroglyphs] *ibid.*, 33 [M. R.]; [hieroglyphs] *ibid.*, 123 [Sesostris I]) through the constant association of *k* with the stem [hieroglyphs] *i3* "old" in the 1st person of the pseudoparticiple; cf. the extension of value of [hieroglyph] in [hieroglyphs] *pds* from [hieroglyphs] (see Dévaud in *Sphinx*, 13, 93); so too [hieroglyph] *d'r* in [hieroglyphs] from [hieroglyphs] and, as I believe, [hieroglyph] *idn* in [hieroglyphs] from [hieroglyphs] "to be deaf"[1].

18-19. — The reading [hieroglyphs] in C is shown by OB[1] to be a real reading, not simply a slip; the absence of the pronoun from B and R shows it to be secondary.

19. — For [hieroglyphs] Dévaud compares [hieroglyphs] Capart, *Une rue de tombeaux*, 77.

21-22. — OB[1] supports the reading of C *hr r ib-t*; although this is certainly a later conjecture it provides some support for the reading of B, which doubtless means "the fall of thirst overtook me".

21. — For *hn-kwi hr* (R), cf. [hieroglyphs] de Morgan, *Cat. des Mon.*, I, 67 (Konosso, stele Tuthmosis IV).

22. — Dévaud points out that the verb *ntb* does exist, *e. g.* "thou art fallen before Osiris" [hieroglyphs] *Pap.*

1. Of course [hieroglyph] is usually supposed to obtain its value *idn* from the Semitic word أذن, און; if however such writings as [hieroglyphs] Blackden-Frazer, *Hatnub*, 7, 4, prove to be invariable in the oldest period then my hypothesis will have to be given the preference.

*Brit. Mus. 10188* (Book of overthrowing Apophis), 24, 11; [hieroglyphs] *ibid.*, 24, 16; possibly the word means "to scorch" or "parch", and B may contain the original reading.—*Nḏ*; also *Rec. de Trav.*, 23, 167 (Dévaud).

23. — OB[4] confirms C in its reading [hieroglyphs], a secondary addition.

25. — OB[3] and OB[4] confirm *gmḥn-wi*, the reading of C, though without lending additional authority to it.

29. — For the land *Ḳdmi* (also below 182, 219) see a geographical list of the reign of Tuthmosis III at Karnak published by Max Müller, *Egyptological Researches*, II, 81; in this list [hieroglyphs] and [hieroglyphs] occur beside one another, obviously reminiscences of the story of Sinuhe and without further historical value. Cf. too [hieroglyphs] *Brit. Mus. 5630* = *Or. Lit.-Zeit.*, 2 (1899), 38.

30. — M. Dévaud has suggested to me that the name of the prince of Retenu (note *Rtn* in OB[3]) should be read [hieroglyphs] "Neshi the son of Amu" on the same principle as [hieroglyphs] in the *Eloquent Peasant* (Sethe, in *Ä. Z.*, 49 [1911], 95). Despite the fact that OB[3] does not support this view, its probability seems to me to amount almost to certainty, for the sign \\ after the biliteral [hieroglyph] would be wholly meaningless[2]. Mr. Battiscombe Gunn points out to me that this hieratic abbreviation of [hieroglyph] has given rise to the hieroglyphic [hieroglyph], an exact analogy to the origin of [hieroglyph] in the hieratic shortening of [hieroglyph]; the earliest hieroglyphic instance of [hieroglyph] seems to be [hieroglyphs] Weill, *Recueil ... de Sinai*, 28, *temp.* Amenemmes III; half-hieratic instances, *Cairo M. K., stele* 200003. M. Dévaud quotes another example in the colophon of the *Shipwrecked Sailor*, 189, where we should read "Ameno, son of Ameny". Of the two names thus obtained [hieroglyphs] is not known to me in this spelling, though a *Nšī* occurs in the *Inscription of Mes*. On the other hand *ʿmw* is a good Egyptian name, cf. [hieroglyphs] on the stele of Sesostris I at Wady Halfa, see *Proc. S. B. A.*, 23 (1901), pl. III, opposite p. 235. Thus the name of the Syrian prince would appear to be Egyptian; similarly in the funerary temple of Sahurē a Libyan prince has the Egyptian name Weni, cf. Borchardt, *Das Grabdenkmal des Königs Sahurē*, II, p. 73.

31. — OB[3] has [hieroglyphs] by which perhaps *nfr ḫrt-k* "happy is thy condition" was intended. The consensus of B and R proves *nfr-tw* to be the original reading.

34-35. — OB[1] and OB[3] confirm the reading of R *ḥr s išst* as against B's apparently inferior text.

36. — OB[1] and OB[3] lend support to my argument that some words for "I spoke" should here be inserted. Whereas R has [hieroglyphs] the later version appears to have been [hieroglyphs].

1. In the footnote (p. 23, footnote 1) I state that the combination of consonants *r*; is not found in any Egyptian word; cf. however the divine name [hieroglyphs], *e. g.* Petrie, *Labyrinth*, 28.

2. In B 142 the shape of the sign favours its identification with [hieroglyph]; in B 30 the sign was added later, an indication that it was regarded as of importance, which would hardly be the case with \\.

R, like OB[3], may possibly have inserted *pw* after *Sḥtpibrꜥ*; this however does not yield a very satisfactory sense. If *wḏꜣ* be regarded as the subject, then we shall have to render, "he who has gone to the horizon is Shetepebrê"; if on the other hand *wḏꜣ* is an attribute of *Sḥtpibrꜥ*, then the correct translation must be "It (the event to which you allude) is Shetepebrê, who has gone to the horizon"[1]. The version of B is superior.

38. — OB[3] confirms the reading *ii-ni* of B; its reading *r tꜣ Tmḥy* is perhaps to be preferred both to *n* in R and to the indeterminate sign in B.

39. — With regard to I am not in the least convinced by Vogelsang's arguments in favour of reading (*op. cit.*, p. 95). Since B 255 omits the determinatives, it is in any case necessary to admit that one of the two spellings is irregular, if not corrupt. Vogelsang has seen that the prefixed substantive in B 255 cannot possibly be joined to the previous sentence, so he simply ignores this later occurrence of the sentence. In the earlier passage he very strangely joins *ḥꜣty* to the previous word *ꜣdw*, though this is fairly obviously a pseudoparticiple; only in this way is he able to make any sense of his version *nn rf m ẖt-i* "There was no .....[2] in my body". It is perfectly clear to me that, however the disputed word be read or interpreted, the whole sentence both in B 39 and B 255 is *ḥꜣty-i n ..... m ẖt-i*.

Vogelsang's suggestion is based however on a perfectly sound observation, namely that the "later absolute pronouns" are not normally used before a prepositional predicate; in other words, that though is regular (see *Anast. IV*, 5, 3) is not. There seemed no way out of this difficulty until I noticed a similar instance in B 185 of which the obvious translation seems to be, "This counsel carried away thy heart, it was not in my heart against thee". Sethe prefers to read here, "there was nothing in my heart against thee", but only because he refuses to admit the possibility of in a prepositional clause; how he would translate B 39, with *ḥꜣty-i* restored to its place at the beginning of the sentence, I do not know. For my own part I have but little doubt that we have here an abnormal and rare use of the pronoun *ntf*.

40. — OB[3] to some extent supports the version of B, though writing *wsfy* for *wfꜣ*[3] and *r-i* for *i*.—In what follows OB[3] has points of contact both with B and R, but it seems impossible to discuss the passage critically.

---

1. Not "It is Shetepebrê who", etc., without comma, for this could only be expressed by means of *in* followed by a participle.

2. Further : even though ⲥⲣϥⲉ = does resemble a causative in Coptic, that is hardly sufficient reason for postulating , no other example of which has been quoted. Vogelsang admits that his supposed *r* is very small, like .

3. I cannot agree with Vogelsang in the sense assigned by him to this word (*op. cit.*, 98); he does not appear to have seen my note.

43-44. — My note needs correction; the text ought to run [hieroglyphs] "without him, (even) that beneficent god". R has in reality *m ḥmt-f* like B, not merely *m ḥmt* as I had imagined.

48. — The word *s;;* "prudent" or "understanding" occurs frequently in M. Golénischeff's new papyri, see *Pap. Petersburg 1116 A*, recto, 33. 54. 111. 115; *111 B*, recto, 6. On the famous stele of Ichernofret at Berlin (Schäfer, *Die Mysterien des Osiris*, p. 13) we should undoubtedly read [hieroglyphs], cf. *Pap. Petersburg 1116 A*, recto, 115-116.

52-53. — For *ḥmʿ* (with the metathesis found in B137), cf. [hieroglyphs] *Urkunden*, IV, 1213 (Dévaud).—For *ri-ḏ;w* Dévaud quotes [hieroglyphs] Möller, *Hatnub*, 26, 6 (also 25, 9); [hieroglyphs] *Ombos*, 652; [hieroglyphs] *Ombos*, 690.

57-58. — Another instance of *s;s;* occurs among the epithets of Nectanebos, [hieroglyphs] "stout-hearted..... not turning himself in the hour of driving back", Naville, *Goshen*, 2, 2. Is *s;s;* possibly the origin of Coptic ⲥⲱⲥ "evertere"?

58-59. — The example *Brit. Mus.*, 334, quoted in my note upon *wmt ib* should be omitted (Dévaud).

65. — For [hieroglyphs], cf. [hieroglyphs] *Siut*, I, 230 (Dévaud).

69. — For an excellent parallel to the reading of R, cf. [hieroglyphs] "coming forth from the womb, his face being directed to kingship", *Urkunden*, IV, 811.

71-73. — *Nk;* can also be construed with *ḥr*, cf. [hieroglyphs] *Pap. Brit. Mus. 10509*, 2, 13 = *Prisse*, 6, 10.

My objection to M. Maspero's translation of [hieroglyphs] "il a été créé" is, as Sethe points out, disposed of by [hieroglyphs] "they (sc. *sïrw* "the officials") were made to contend against evil", *Peasant*, B1, 297. With the present Ms. reading, therefore, M. Maspero's rendering must here be adopted.

81. — For the land [hieroglyphs], see the Additional note on 29.

97-99. — For *štm*, cf. now the epithet(s) [hieroglyphs] *Pap. Petersburg 1116 A*, recto, 147; this I have translated "who was not quarrelsome, the servant of his lord", but it might well be that *štm* is there transitive and governs *b;k* as its object.

As regards the late word [hieroglyphs] "utterances" quoted in my note, Dévaud has proved (*Ä. Z.*, 50 [1912], 129) that this is simply a later variant of [hieroglyphs].

110. — The instance *Anast. I*, 6, 7, must be omitted; see my edition of that text.

115. — For *ʿf;y*, cf. [hieroglyphs] "it (his name [?]) ..... to the vile Khatti on account of their lamentations; they are overthrown, yea their dwellingplaces are (cast) to the ground", Maspero, *Temples submergés*, I, 164 (Ipsamboul, stele of Ramesses II).

115-116. — Sethe suggests, as I now think rightly, that means "it is the case that". This sense suits well in the *Ebers* passage, and here forms a good parallel to the use of below (see note on 162-163); render therefore, "Is it the case that I have opened?" In B 126 is a sentence in itself, lit. "how (is it) that it is?" It is not quite clear whether this is a direct or indirect question, see below on B 126-127.

116-117. — For the preposition *ḥr* followed by the *sḏmf* tense, cf. *Peasant,* B 1, 12.

118. — Dévaud prefers to read which is palæographically equally probable; he quotes the signs above a bull which is being struck by a man, *Beni Hasan,* II, 7, but the division and interpretation of these words are highly problematic.

123. — Dévaud quotes the words as epithet of Rē, MARIETTE, *Dendera,* II, 47.

126-127. — In this very difficult sentence the last words have been explained in the Additional note on 115-116; the earlier part however still presents difficulties. (1) If, as Sethe believes, *nt pw mi mi* is an independent sentence, then it seems necessary to take *rḫ* as the infinitive after *šꜣt-nf* "what he ought to know"; however this construction, though known after the cognate substantive *šꜣw*, does not appear to occur elsewhere after the verb *šꜣ*, except where it means to "command" (cf. B 51). (2) To take *rḫ* as pseudoparticiple, and parallel to *ḫm* ("is God ignorant of what is destined for him, or does he know [it]"?) is impossibly abrupt. (3) Perhaps, after all, *nt pw mi mi* may be the object of *rḫ* ("or does he know how the matter stands"?). Of the three alternatives the last is, I think, on the whole the most likely.

128. — For see the note on 201.

131-132. — Other examples of *mꜣḫ-ib* : *Rec. de Trav.*, 19, 22; 23, 73 (Dévaud).

132. — The translation of as "women" not "women and men" is, as Dévaud has shown me, open to serious objections : (1) if *ḥmt-ṯꜣy* exists at all as a compound expression (see below) it must mean "married woman" not simply "woman", and this meaning is out of place in the present context; (2) in the plural we should expect *ḥmwt-ṯꜣy* and not *ḥmwt-ṯꜣyw*. For these reasons it is preferable to regard *ḥmwt ṯꜣyw* as an unusual, perhaps designedly unusual, variation of the phrase *ṯꜣyw ḥmwt* "men and women".— The question remains as to whether the phrase *ḥmt-ṯꜣy* "married woman" really exists at all. The doubt, as Dévaud points out, is suggested by *Prisse,* 14, 4, which gives some colour to the possibility that *ṯꜣy* is coordinated to *ḥmt* in the two very similar passages *Totb.*, ed. NAV., 125, 19, and PETRIE, *Abydos,* III, 29. Against this view may be urged (1) that *ṯꜣy*, after all, is much less likely in this connection than *ḫrd*, and (2) that if *ṯꜣy* were coordinated here we might expect *ṯꜣy ḥmt*, in this order, rather than *ḥmt-ṯꜣy*. Lastly, in the passage *Prisse,* 10, 3 (to which reference must be made by the reader) *ḥmt-ṯꜣy* seems very probably a phrase for "married woman". For

*ṯ꜡y* in the sense of "husband", see ERMAN, *Lebensmüde*, note on l. 98 (p. 55).

134. — Further variants of the interesting word *minb* (?), cf. [hieroglyphs] *Pap. Petersburg 1116 A*, recto, 95; and [hieroglyphs] quoted by Sethe from unpublished Græco-Roman inscriptions at Karnak. The meaning "axe" is given, I now find, though without proof, already by MAX MÜLLER, *Egyptological Researches*, II, 182. As an analogy for the curious writing [hieroglyphs] Dévaud compares [hieroglyphs] *Mission Arch. franç.*, I, 201 = *mnnfrt*.

136-137. — Sethe, who does not seem to have read my discussion of this difficult passage, proposes (*Ä. Z.*, 50 [1912], 111-112) to divide as follows : *rdi-ni sw꜡ ḥr-i ʿḥ꜡w-f sp* | *n iwt-t wʿ ḥr ḫn m wʿ*. His translation runs "aber nachdem ich seine Waffen hatte herausgehen lassen, seine übrigen Pfeile hatte an mir vorbeigehen lassen, weil einer dem anderen nicht nahe (genug) war, da griff er mich an, da schoss ich ihn"; he thus takes [hieroglyphs] as equivalent to the old expression [hieroglyphs] "because not", for which one might quote [hieroglyphs] in a rather obscure context *Siut*, III, 11 (*ḥr ntt* occurs *ibid.*, III, 14). I must confess myself very sceptical as to Sethe's new version, which (1) ignores the variants [hieroglyphs] in R, (2) isolates *sp* in a very objectionable way, and (3) postulates the possibility of a circumstantial clause after *n iwtt*, though we should certainly expect either a *sḏmf* or a *sḏmnf* tense. For myself I have no new interpretation to advance.

137. — For *ḫmʿ* instead of *ḫʿm*, see the Additional note on 52-53.

140. — Just possibly the word *išnn* may recur in a very obscure phrase from a religious text on the wooden chest of King Dhout, *Berlin 1175* (= *Æg. Inschr.*, I, p. 253), [hieroglyphs].

142. — For *ḥb* in the sense of "triumph", cf. already *Urkunden*, IV, 773 (Sethe); Sethe further suggests that ϩⲏⲃⲉ "luctus" may be derived from *ḥb* in the sense "to mourn".

147-149. — For *ṯs m* Dévaud quotes the following additional instances : [hieroglyphs] *Prisse*, 17, 6-7; [hieroglyphs] (read *srḫ-f*) [hieroglyphs] *Miss. Arch. franç.*, I. 122; "I accompanied him to all the goodly places of his diversion [hieroglyphs] *Brit. Mus.* 614 = *Piers-Breasted stele*, 13.

151. — For *s꜡* Vogelsang prefers to adhere to the old translation "wander" (*Kommentar*, p. 230), but he gives no reasons; to me it seems evident that in *Peasant*, B 2, 127, this meaning is quite unsuitable.

160. — Dévaud quotes the words [hieroglyphs] over a scene of an attendant with flowers in the *Tombeau des Graveurs* (no. 181) = *Miss. Arch. franç.*, V, pl. 4; what the meaning of the phrase there is, is uncertain[1].

166. — Another example of *ḥnwt-t꜡*, *Siut*, IV, 11.

---

1. In my footnote *Rec. de Trav.*, 33, 83 (p. 60 of the offprint) I have made a serious blunder, misunderstanding [hieroglyph] which is really equivalent to the preposition [hieroglyph]; the mistake was pointed out to me by Sethe in a letter, and has been corrected in print by DÉVAUD, *Ä. Z.*, 50 (1912), 129-130.

174. — The construction *wnin* .... *sḏmf* is however also used in simple narrative to express a result; cf. "so then its fringe rested on the water", *Eloquent Peasant*, Bt. 35.

181-185. — Sethe has convinced me that the sentences in 183-184 are to be construed as preterites, and refer simply to Sinuhe's innocence of any misdemeanour prior to his flight. Translate: "What hadst thou done, that one should do aught against thee? Thou didst not revile, so that thy words were reproved; thou didst not speak in the council of the nobles, so that thy utterances were rejected".

183. — Sethe rightly rejects my suggestion that *ir* here stands for *di* "to cause"; in the Pyramidtexts "make nourishment for" is a fixed expression, and *ir* in it is not to be understood as "to cause".

183-184. — For another example of *wꜣꜥ* Dévaud quotes (=?) "I give to thee drunkenness free from fall, and no curse issues from thy mouth", ROCHEMONTEIX, *Edfou*, I, 462. — Dévaud notes that in *Prisse*, 15, 6, the better reading is *btnw*, not *itnw*; the former reading is given by the London fragments.

185. — For , see the Additional note on 39.

190-191. — For , see now ERMAN, *Ä. Z.*, 48 (1910), 52, who decides in favour of *sb-t* and against *s* in this case.

193. — The reference for is wrongly given as C 11; it should be C 15, 8. Dévaud quotes another example from *Florence*, 1640 (*Cat.* SCHIAPARELLI), as follows: (Saite date). — Sethe points out that it is not necessary to supply a suffix after , cf. "[a statue .....] with head of gold", *Urkunden*, IV, 666.

201. — The equation of and as variant writings of one and the same verb *sny* "to pass" seems *a priori* so paradoxical[1] that a reconsideration will not be out of place. Sethe points out that shares many of the meanings belonging in common to and , and that it is not much more difficult to admit the existence of three synonyms (*sny*, *sš* and *swꜣ*) than to admit the existence of two (*sny* and *swꜣ*). Then again it is a serious objection that the determinatives occur only where is written and are there almost invariable, whereas they are never found after .

Let us clear away one preliminary difficulty. The writing in *Anastasi I* and elsewhere seems confined to the meanings "pass", "move"; it is evidently equivalent to the demotic *snyn* "to walk up and down" in *I Kham.*, 4, 38, which Griffith rightly identified with **cnaein**, **cnhini**, a word more or less well authenticated with similar meanings[2]. is therefore a reduplicated form from *snyny* related to in much the same way as to .

1. See Piehl's criticisms of Erman's *Ægyptische Grammatik* in *Sphinx*, 7, 72-73.

2. PEYRON, p. 20ᵛ, and the *Auctarium*, p. 11.

The reasons that make me still adhere to the view that and are variant writings of ⲥⲓⲛⲉ "to pass" are as follows:—(1) It seems impossible not to attach extreme importance to the variant *Pap. Turin*, 114. 115, in a perfectly stereotyped formula in which elsewhere is always found; and the reading with cannot be called in question, as the published facsimile will show. (2) The uncontested variants of the verb "to open" are a sufficient analogy. (3) So far as the determinatives are concerned, these may be borrowed from a real verb *sš*, which would account for their occurring only there where is written; such a verb is probably to "strew", "spread", which as Sethe points out is probably the Coptic ϣⲱϣ "spargere".

202. — For *th* "to lead astray" one or two examples may possibly be quoted, though not with the same literal sense as here, cf. "behold, my heart leads me astray", *Lebensmüde*, 11; "thy sloth will lead thee astray", *Eloquent Peasant*, B2, 40 = B1, 281. The exact nuance of this metaphorical usage is hard to catch, perhaps "lead into difficulties", "betray", "prove a snare to".

For some additional examples may be given, which seem to suggest that the word connotes not only what is "hostile" but what is "foreign" and "strange". In the same adjectival sense as in our tale among epithets of King Apophis, "great of name beyond any king, celebrated (??) in foreign (hostile) lands", *Berlin* 7798 = *Æg. Inschr.*, I, 265. Again in the Saint-Petersburg prophetic text, *Pap. Petersburg 1116 B*, recto, 29. Lastly, Dévaud quotes an instance in a wholly obscure context *Butler*, verso, 19.

208. — Another example of the god *Smsrw* "[seizing] the locks (?) of the chiefs of foreign countries like Semseru", Weill, *Sinai*, 85 (Tuthmosis IV, newly collated).

224. — For *ḳmd* Dévaud quotes Lacau, *Textes religieux*, LXXXVII = *Rec. de Trav.*, 34, p. 178; do the last words in this quotation mean "this god who devised them"?

242. — New evidence for , cf. *Pap. Petersburg 1116 A*, recto, 89.

249. — A good example of *sšp* in the sense of "sphinx" on the Barberini obelisk, "built of good white stone, sphinxes all around it and statues and many columns", quoted Brugsch, *Wörtb.*, 864.—An ingenious suggestion of Mr. Battiscombe Gunn is worth placing on record, though it can, I think, be proved almost with certainty to be wrong; he conjectures that the word Σφιγξ is derived from the epithet *sšp ʿnḫ* illustrated in my note. The objection to this, as Sethe points out to me, is that while the Pharaoh may well be called "the *living* sphinx-shape of Atum" the stone sphinxes themselves could never

have the epithet *'nḫ* applied to them; in other words a sphinx of stone may be termed *sšp*, but never *sšp 'nḫ*.

252. — The new text OP[3] does not favour the suggestion that *nt ḏ'm* in this passage should be omitted.

259. — Vogelsang suggests "Handele nicht weiter so gegen dich, ohne zu reden, wenn dein Name genannt wird", *Kommentar*, p. 102. This is perhaps not quite impossible, though the sense "weiter" for [hieroglyphs] instead of "also" is not properly authenticated.

266. — Vogelsang (*Kommentar*, pp. 69-71) quotes many examples[1] of [hieroglyphs] and adduces important evidence from *Totb.*, ed. Nav., 125, Schlussrede 14, in favour of the reading *dw-yt*.

275-276. — For the sense, cf. [hieroglyphs] "thou hast not given me the reward of these beautiful words", *Eloquent Peasant*, B 1, 318.

278. — Dévaud suggests that [hieroglyphs] might be connected with *ꜣwt* in the sentence [hieroglyphs] *Pyr.*, 924, but this suggestion is difficult since *ꜣyt* can only be a *sḏm-f* form, not a feminine substantive.

282-283. — Kees has produced abundant evidence to show that *pr-dwꜣt* really refers to a toilet-chamber (*Rec. de Trav.*, 36, 1 foll.), but he prefers Erman's translation of *'ḫnwty dwꜣt* in the present passage. I must confess I am unable to agree with this view; it seems obvious to me that Sinuhe is sent off to have a bath, and not to have "his position at Court assigned to him".

301-304. — The infinitive [hieroglyphs] occurs *Pap. Petersburg 1116 A*, recto, 131.

## V

### FURTHER NOTES ON THE COMPARATIVE VALUE OF THE MSS.

The discovery of the new ostraca makes it necessary to re-open some of the questions discussed in the first section. In the first place I wish freely to admit that there is more evidence for an "édition Ramesside" that I was formerly disposed to allow. The ostraca OB[3] and OB[4] possess features in common with C (and possibly with G) which place the entire group in a distinct contrast to R and B. OB[3] has a better text[2] than C, though it shows a few individual mistakes of its own[3]. Its agreements with C are of more consequence :—

R 1 = C 1. — OB[3] agrees with GC against R in the amplification of titles.

R 6 = C 2. — OB[3] first hand agrees with all old texts in giving *sḥr-f*, second hand *s'rw-f* with C.

1. See too Guieysse, *Rec. de Trav.*, 10, 64-66, who offers no certain reading for the sign.
2. A few examples will suffice :—OB[3] omits *m* in C 1 before *smr*; corrects C 1 in its corruption of *bꜣk n(t) ipt nsw-t*; inserts the preposition *m* before *sgr* and *gmw* (C 2); omits *iw grt* in C 2, and rightly gives *sb* for *bs*; etc., etc.
3. E. g. *nfrw-f* for *Nfrw*, l. 4; *itw* for *ist(w)*, l. 9; wrong determinative for *skrt*, l. 10.

R 11 = C 2. — OB$^{3}$ first hand *i*[*m*] as R, second hand *ꜣm* as C.

R 49 = C 8. — OB$^{3}$ has *gmḥ-nwi* with C against *gmḥ-ni* of B and R.

In a similar way OB$^{4}$ agrees with C against the earlier Mss. in several passages[1] : —

R 39 = C 6. — OB$^{4}$ has *swḥ* probably with C against B and R (*swt*).

R 44 = C 7. — OB$^{4}$ has *mꜣꜣ-wi* with C against B and R (*mꜣꜣ*).

R 47 = C 8. — OB$^{4}$ supports *ḫr r* of C as against *ḫr n* of B and R.

R 48 = C 8. — OB$^{4}$ adds *ḥr-st* with C against B and R.

R 49 = C 8. — OB$^{4}$ *gmḥ-nwi* like OB$^{3}$ and C, while B and R have *gmḥ-ni*.

In every case good reasons can be shown for regarding the Ramesside readings here to be secondary and inferior, see the Commentary. It seems however clear that, whether it be through the influence of the schools, or whether it be really due to the influence of one particular manuscript, the Theban text of the Ramesside period is uniform enough to be called a Ramesside "edition" or "recension".

There is no new evidence as to the position of G, but it is still clear that the Ramesside group *plus* G belong together as against R on the one hand and against B on the other, and again that the Ramesside group *plus* G can be legitimately ranged with R against B. Two certain conclusions can be drawn, namely (1) that the consensus of B and R against the later Mss. is conclusive, and (2) that the consensus of B and the later Mss. against R proves the latter to be in error, whether the error be due to carelessness or to conjecture[2].

I am less satisfied than I was that the agreement of RGC (with OB$^{3}$, OB$^{4}$, etc.) is strong evidence against B. It may well be, for example, that the unsupported *ntb-kwi* of B 22 is older than *nḏꜣ-kwi* of the other Mss.; or that the omission of *r ptpt nmiw-šꜥ* in B 17 may possibly be in accordance with the archetype. Here we are on subjective ground, and all that can be said is that R is a good manuscript the readings of which are stronger when they are supported by the Ramesside ostraca than they are without them. Thus the support given by OB$^{1}$ and OB$^{3}$ to *ḥr s išst* in R 58 and to *ꜥḥꜥ-n ḏd-ni* in R 59 is certainly in favour of R, but still is not conclusive in respect of it; the proof in favour of R here, to my mind, lies in the philological and literary arguments that can be adduced on its behalf.

It does not seem to me profitable to go more deeply into these questions. After all, except in the few cases discussed above our decision between two readings will in practice rest on other grounds than the affiliation of the texts. I would only caution the student against too great a contempt of the ostraca containing duplicates of later parts of the text. It seems obvious that OP$^{1}$, OP$^{2}$, OB$^{2}$ and L all belong to that Theban Ramesside recension the existence of which has been vindicated above. This recension, though very corrupt in its worst form (as in C), seems often to have retained readings forgotten by B. In brief, my conclusion is that all variants must be examined and judged on their merits.

1. OB$^{4}$ has several individual mistakes, e. g. *Ptrt* for *Ptny*, l. 5; *ḏd* after *ꜥḥꜥn*, l. 9.
2. As for example in *ii-ni*, B 38 (+ OB$^{3}$) against *i*[*wi*] of R 62.

## VI

### SUNDRY ASPECTS OF THE TALE

§ 1. *The literary aspect.* — The great popularity of the Story of Sinuhe throughout the Theban period is now well established, and if Egyptologists regard it as the classic of classics in their domain they should not be found guilty of a deficient sense of perspective. By the rough and ready test afforded by the number of extant manuscripts our tale is seen to have enjoyed a greater popularity that any other literary Egyptian text except the *Instruction of Amenemhēt I* and the *Satire on the Trades.* Direct allusions to the story are found in the words of the Puntites among the sculptures of Deir el Bahari[1], and in a list of foreign countries of the time of Tuthmosis III at Karnak[2], and probably these allusions escaped no ancient visitor capable of reading the hieroglyphic inscriptions of these temples. To the young scribes of the Eighteenth and Nineteenth Dynasties the adventures of Sinuhe were doubtless as familiar as those of Robinson Crusoe to the English child.

It will not be seriously contended that the story is one of those world-masterpieces of literary skill which stand out for all time as the perfect expression of some side of universal human experience or feeling. None the less I maintain that for us too the Story of Sinuhe is and must remain a classic. It is a classic because it marks a definite stage in the history of the world's literature; and it is a classic because it displays with inimitable directness the mixed naiveté and subtility of the old Egyptian character, its directness of vision, its pomposity, its reverence and its humour. To those students of Ancient Egypt whose culture is not of that narrow type that makes them insensible to what is simple and unsophisticated, the vicissitudes of Sinuhe's wanderings must be full of charm. There is plenty of variety in these three hundred lines; the brief but lofty description of the old King's death; the graphic narrative of Sinuhe's flight; the terrors of the desert and the hospitality of Beduin tribes; the adulatory but not unpoetic encomium of Sesostris I. In the account of the duel with the mighty man of Retenu we breathe the atmosphere of the Old Testament, and the passage describing Sinuhe's longing for Egypt is as perfect a revelation of Egyptian character as may be found anywhere. Then there is Pharaoh's letter of pardon, with its characteristic insistance on the all-absorbing theme of burial rites; and Sinuhe's reply, in which a very lively terror of Pharaoh is blended with a wholly artificial and calculated flattery. There is nothing more vivid in the tale, I might almost say in *any* tale, than the picture of Sinuhe's reception of Court. As by a magic touch we are carried back four thousand years to witness Sinuhe's abject panic as he flings himself on the ground at Pharaoh's feet, and to behold the tolerant *bonhomie* of Pharaoh as he half-ironically introduces the dust-stained wanderer to the Queen; we can almost hear the Queen's incredulous shriek of surprise, almost see the twinkling feet of the little princesses as with dance

1. See note on B 34-35.
2. See Add. note on B 29.

and song they plead that the stranger may be pardoned. The story ends with the conventional description of an old age spent amid luxury and honours, a description that serves to remind us of the strongly materialistic bent of the Egyptians, that love of good cheer and magnificence which is indeed the key-note of the civilization of Ancient Egypt.

The form in which the tale is cast is that of a sepulchral autobiography; and among other peculiarities shared with the inscriptions inscribed upon the walls of tombs[1] it concludes by relating the death of Sinuhe, although it is Sinuhe himself who speaks. So too the famous warrior Amosis of El Kab ends his autobiography with the words "..... and I rest in the tomb which I made for myself[2]". Among Egyptian tales that of Sinuhe stands alone in employing this form; and we cannot positively assert that the choice was dictated solely by literary considerations, for the story might really be based on an actual tomb-inscription, as we shall see.

The diction of the tale is prose, simple and direct (though without baldness) in the narrative portions, but becoming rhetorical and even poetic as occasion demands. The vocabulary employed is large, and if fault can be found with the author's style it is not on the score of clumsy repetitions or a poverty-stricken choice of words. Foreign to our own taste is the use of elaborate metaphor, as when Sinuhe "gives a way to his feet northwards[3]" where we should be content with "I turned northward", or when "the fall of thirst overtook" him[4] where it would suffice to say that he became thirsty. This exaggeration of style is characteristic of the early Middle Kingdom, and is on the whole a healthy symptom, for it indicates an increased attention to delicacies of language. It must be admitted too that some of these affectations, which are not too lavishly strewn, have a certain picturesque humour of their own, as when Sinuhe, ridding himself of the accumulated dirt of years (such appears to be the conceit) is said to give "a load to the desert, and clothes to the Sandfarers[5]".

§ 2. *Geography.* — The topography of Sinuhe's flight is not unattended by difficulties, most of the places-names mentioned being unknown. The discovery of the correct rendering "I crossed (the lake) Mewōti[6]" in B 8 is of some importance. The sheet of water here named cannot be any portion of the Nile, and must therefore, as it appears to me, refer to one of the great lakes in the immediate neighbourhood of the Mediterranean, probably Lake Mareōtis. On this supposition the army of Pharaoh will have been returning from the Libyan campaign against the Temhi and Tehenu along the Mediterranean litoral. Here Sinuhe takes to flight; he turns (B 6) southward before he reaches the lake, and it is probably the southern end of this across which he wades or swims. This brings him to the cultivation, and he spends a whole

1. See the notes on R 1-2, B 179-180, B 309-310.
2. Cf. *Urkunden*, IV, 10.
3. B 15-16.
4. B 21-22.
5. B 291-292.
6. Not, of course, to be confused with the *iw Mꜣ'ty*, sometimes written *š-t Mꜣ'ty*, which Brugsch (*Dict. géogr.*, 248-249) thought to be the name of a sacred lake near Heracleopolis Magna; Grapow has shown (*Götting. Gelehrt. Anz.*, 1913, nr. 12, p. 743) that this is simply the "Island of the Just", a name for Abydos.

day in the open fields near an unknown place called the "Island of Snofru". We are not able to identify the town of Gu which Sinuhe, skirting the edge of the western Delta, reached on the following evening. This must however have lain near the apex of the Delta not far from modern Cairo, for here Sinuhe drifts across the Nile in a barge and quickly comes to the quarries of the Gebel Aḥmar over against Heliopolis (B 15)[1]. At this point he turns definitely northwards, (B 16) and in the course of a few hours reaches the "Wall of the Prince", the well-known wall doubtless near the entrance to the Wady Tumilat which Amenemmes I had built to keep off Beduin encroachments[2]. The rest of the day was spent hiding in a thicket, Sinuhe fearing to be detected by the watchers upon the walls. The fortifications having been passed at dead of night, Sinuhe flees along the depression of the Wady Tumilat, reaching Petny[3] in the early morning. Thence he soon comes to the region of the Salt Lakes, where at the time of the Pyramids there had been a fortified outpost of the name of Kem-wēr[4]. This district is in the story of Sinuhe called the "Island of Kem-wēr", we cannot tell why, and the absence of any mention of a garrison there makes it extremely probable that the old outpost had been abandoned in the period between the Old and Middle Kingdoms. There was evidently no canal in the Wady Tumilat at this period, for Sinuhe finds himself overcome with thirst on arriving at the "Island of Kem-wēr". Here he is fortunate enough to fall in with Beduins, whose treatment of him is so kind that he sojourns with them for a space.

Sinuhe's subsequent itinerary is exceedingly curious. "Land", he says, "handed me on to land; I set forth (?) towards Byblos, and penetrated (?) to Kedme". There he spent half a year, after which the prince of Upper Retenu[5] Enshi son of Amu (?) took him, married him to his daughter, and gave him a tract of land called Yaa rich in fruits of all kinds and growing both wheat and barley, where Sinuhe lived for many years as the prince's general and chief counsellor. In spite of the mention of wheat and barley the life described is more that of a pastoral than that of an agricultural tribe. Herds of cattle and possibly flocks of sheep and goats were the chief possession of these Syrians, who lived not in cities but in encampments[6]. Sinuhe mentions fruit-bearing trees[7] among his belongings, and it is clear that the life of his tribe was not nomadic, though it may well have been of that half-nomadic type usual on the borderland between desert and cultivation[8].

How far can this picture of tribal life be considered a faithful account of conditions in Syria in the twentieth century before Christ? It is impossible to read the

1. See the note on B 14-15.
2. See *Pap. Petersburg 1116 B*, recto, 66.
3. Petny is not mentioned elsewhere; Brugsch's identification with a supposed region called Pat (*Dict. géogr.*, p. 53) is a groundless guess.
4. See Küthmann, *Die Ostgrenze Ägyptens*, p. 33-34, with whose account of the geography of the tale I am in entire agreement.
5. "Upper Retenu" is doubtless here, as later, the name of "das Bergland von Palæstina" (Ed. Meyer, *Geschichte des Altertums*[2], I, § 289); I go no further here into this debated question.
6. The word is *ʿf3y*, on which see Add. note on B 115; Sinuhe speaks of his "tent", B 110.
7. See B 83; B 241.
8. See Ed. Meyer, *Geschichte des Altertums*[2], I, § 333.

story without gaining the impression that the writer describes a kind of life that he has seen and with which he is familiar; but it is also impossible to silence the suspicion that he has transferred to Northern Syria an account of conditions that only holds good for the half-nomadic tribes of Southern Palestine. "Land handed me on to land"—is it not highly suspicious that the writer has no more to tell us of the great tract of country that separates Egypt from Byblos? Even as early as the beginning of the Twelfth Dynasty there were many fortified towns in Palestine of which a few, such as Lachish, Gezer and Megiddo, have been excavated by archæologists; in the tale of Sinuhe not a word is breathed of the existence of towns in Syria. Is it not further highly suspicious that with the exception of the more or less vague word Kedme (*i. e.* "the East") the only place named should be Byblos[1], a place which the Egyptians knew well not from their journeys by land through Syria, but from their constant intercourse with it by sea? Sinuhe thus arrives by the land-route at the one place towards which the Egyptian ships habitually made. The coincidence is remarkable, especially if we remember that Sinuhe was fleeing from Egypt, and will presumably have wished to avoid any place where Egyptians were likely to be found. If the introduction of the name of Byblos be purely and simply a literary artifice, the motive for this is quite explicable : a sense of reality is conveyed by the mention of a genuine Syrian place-name. I am inclined therefore now to take a very sceptical view of the value of our tale as a source of authentic knowledge of conditions in Northern Syria at the beginning of the Twelfth Dynasty[2].

Sinuhe's return journey followed the "way of the land of the Philistines", at a later date the regular military road to and from Syria. He reaches the frontier of Egypt at the garrison-town of Wawet-Hor "The ways of Horus", now known to have been situated near El Kantara on the Pelusiac branch of the Nile[3]. Here he is met by an escort of ships which convey him to the Court at Ethet-toui, the modern Lisht, where the pyramids of Amenemmes I and Sesostris I still stand.

§ 3. *The historical aspect.* — Doubt has been cast in the preceding section on the value of our tale as evidence of the state of culture in Northern Palestine at this period. Hence we are led on to the question whether the tale is to be regarded as pure fiction, or whether and to what extent it contains a historical nucleus. That the author was well-acquainted with the history of the time about which he writes is clear; he knows the names of the pyramids of Amenemmes I and Sesostris I, the length of the former's reign, and the name of the Queen Nofru. The eulogy upon Sesostris is such as would be likely to be composed by a contemporary writer, and indeed there is nothing in the tale which in the least suggests a later date. Further, the manuscript B is evidently some distance removed from the archetype, and yet can itself hardly be placed later than the end of the Twelfth Dynasty. I have stated

---

1. Yaa is very possibly a wholly fictitious name.—That *Kpny* was the reading of the archetype I think to have established by irrefutable evidence, see the note on B 29.

2. In other words I recant the view expressed by me in *Sitzb.*, p. 8-9.

3. See note and Add. note on B 242.

elsewhere my belief that Egyptian literary documents should be assigned to the date to which they purport to belong, unless cogent reasons can be adduced to the contrary[1]. Both on general and particular grounds, therefore, it seems probable that the story of Sinuhe was written in the reign of Sesostris I, and is therefore contemporary with the events that it relates.

The form of the tale so closely resembles other autobiographies that have been found on the walls of tombs that it seems quite likely that its nucleus may be derived from the tomb of a real Sinuhe, who had led a life of adventure in Palestine and was subsequently buried at Lisht[2]. Needless to say we are here on speculative ground, and in such a case no proof or disproof is strictly possible, unless an amazing chance should restore to us the tomb of Sinuhe himself. Even in this case we should doubtless find that literary elaboration had greatly changed the expression and the character of the original narrative, so that in its finished state the story could not claim to be more than "founded on fact".

## VII

### TRANSLATION

The following English version seeks, so far as possible, to preserve the mingled simplicity and artifices of the original, and is based on an eclectic text. Notes of interrogation, comments and alternative renderings have all been omitted, as foreign to the present purpose.

*The hereditary prince and count, governor of the domains of the Sovereign in the lands of the Setiu, true acquaintance of the king, beloved of him, the henchman Sinuhe; he says : —*

*I was a henchman who followed his lord, a servant of the Royal harîm attending*
*on the hereditary princess, the highly-praised Royal Consort of Sesostris in the Pyra-*
R. 5 *mid-town of Khnem-esut, the Royal Daughter of Amenemmes in the Pyramid-town*
*of Ka-nofru, even Nofru, the revered.*

*In year 30, third month of Inundation, day 7, the god attained his horizon, the*
*King of Upper and Lower Egypt Sehetepebrē. He flew to heaven and was united*
*with the sun's disk; the flesh of the god was merged in him who made him. Then*
*was the Residence hushed; hearts were filled with mourning; the Great Portals were*
R.10 *closed; the courtiers crouched head on lap; the people grieved.*

*Now His Majesty had despatched an army to the land of the Temhi, and his*
R.15 *eldest son was the captain thereof, the good god Sesostris. Even now he was return-*
*ing, having carried away captives of the Tehenu and cattle of all kinds beyond*

1. A consideration of *Pap. Petersburg 1116 A*, the *Story of Wenamun*, and the *Proverbs of Ptahhotp* points in this direction; see *Journal of Egyptian Archæology*, I, pp. 35-36.

2. Professor Spiegelberg takes a similar view (*Deutsche Literaturzeitung*, 1912, Nr. 14, p. 861). M. Maspero thinks the composition too artificial to be a real biography (*Les Mémoires de Sinouhit*, p. xxxv). It is clear that the original biography, if such it was, has been greatly modified; but M. Maspero is not justified in arguing from the name of Sinuhe, see the note on R 2.

*number. And the Companions of the Royal Palace sent to the western border to
acquaint the king's son with the matters that had come to pass at the Court. And
R.20 the messengers met him on the road, they reached him at time of night. Not a
moment did he wait; the Falcon flew away with his henchmen, not suffering it to be
known to his army. Howbeit, message had been sent to the Royal Children who
B. 1 were with him in this army, and one of them had been summoned. And lo, I stood
and heard his voice as he was speaking, being a little distance aloof; and my heart
became distraught, my arms spread apart, trembling having fallen on all my limbs.
5 Leaping I betook myself thence to seek me a hiding-place, and placed me between
two brambles so as to sunder the road from its traveller.*

*I set out southward, yet purposed not to approach the Residence; for I thought
there would be strife, and I had no mind to live after him. I crossed the waters of
Mewōti hard by the Sycamore, and arrived in Island-of-Snofru. I tarried there in
10 the open fields, and was afoot early, when it was day. I met a man who rose up in
my path; he showed dismay of me and feared. When the time of supper came, I
drew nigh to the town of Gu.*

*I ferried over in a barge without a rudder, by the help of a western breeze; and
15 passed on by the East of the quarry in the district Mistress-of-the-Red-Mountain.
I gave a road to my feet northward and attained the Wall of the Prince, which
was made to repel the Setiu and to crush the Sandfarers. I bowed me down in a
thicket through fear lest the watcher on the wall for the day might see.*

20 *I went on at time of night, and when it dawned I reached Petni. I halted at the
Island-of-Kemwēr. An attack of thirst overtook me; I was parched, my throat
burned, and I said: This is the taste of death. Then I lifted my heart, and gathered
25 up my body. I heard the sound of the lowing of cattle, and espied men of the Setiu.*

*A sheikh among them, who was aforetime in Egypt, recognized me, and gave
me water; he boiled for me milk. I went with him to his tribe, and they entreated
me kindly.*

30 *Land gave me to land. I set forth to Byblos, I pushed on to Kedme. I spent
half a year there; then Enshi son of Amu, prince of Upper Retenu, took me and said
to me: Thou farest well with me, for thou hearest the tongue of Egypt. This he
said, for that he had become aware of my qualities, he had heard of my wisdom;
Egyptian folk, who were there with him, had testified concerning me. And he
35 said to me: Wherefore art thou come hither? Hath aught befallen at the Residence? And I said to him: Sehetepebrē is departed to the horizon, and none
knoweth what has happened in this matter. And I spoke again dissembling: I came
from the expedition to the land of the Temhi, and report was made to me, and my
40 understanding reeled, my heart was no longer in my body; it carried me away on the
path of the wastes. Yet none had spoken evil of me, none had spat in my face. I
had heard no reviling word, my name had not been heard in the mouth of the herald.
I know not what brought me to this country. It was like the dispensation of God.*

*Then said he to me : How shall yon land fare without him, the beneficent god, the fear of whom was throughout the lands like Sakhmet in a year of plague? Spake I to him and answered him : Of a truth his son has entered the Palace and has taken the inheritance of his father. A god is he without a peer; none other surpasses him. A master of prudence is he, excellent in counsel, efficacious in decrees. Goings and comings are at his command. It is he who subdued the foreign lands while his father was within his Palace, and reported to him what was ordered him to do. Valiant is he, achieving with his strong arm ; active, and none is like to him, when he is seen charging down on Ro-pedtiu, or approaching the mellay. A curber of horns is he, a weakener of hands ; his enemies cannot marshal their ranks. Vengeful is he, a smasher of foreheads ; none can stand in his neighbourhood. Long of stride is he, destroying the fugitive ; there is no ending for any that turns his back to him. Stout of heart is he when he sees a multitude ; he suffers not sloth to encompass his heart. Headlong is he when he falls upon the Easterners ; his joy is to plunder the Ro-pedtiu. He seizes the buckler, he tramples under foot ; he repeats not his blow in order to kill. None can turn his shaft or bend his bow. The Pedtiu flee before him as before the might of the Great Goddess. He fights without end ; he spares not and there is no remnant. He is a master of grace, great in sweetness ; he conquers through love. His city loves him more than itself, it rejoices over him more than over its god. Men and women pass by in exultation concerning him, now that he is king. He conquered while yet in the egg ; his face has been set toward kingship ever since he was born. He is one who multiplies those who were born with him. He is unique, god-given. This land that he rules rejoices. He is one who enlarges his borders. He will conquer the southern lands, but he heeds not the northern lands. He was made to smite the Setiu, and to crush the Sandfarers. Send to him, let him know thy name. Utter no curse against His Majesty. He fails not to do good to the land that is loyal to him.*

*Said he to me : Of a truth Egypt is happy, since it knows that he prospers. But thou, behold, thou art here ; thou shalt dwell with me, and I will entreat thee kindly.*

*And he placed me even before his children, and mated me with his eldest daughter. He caused me to choose for myself of his country, of the best that belonged to him on his border to another country. It was a goodly land called Yaa. Figs were in it and grapes, and its wine was more abundant than its water. Plentiful was its honey, many were its olives ; all manner of fruits were upon its trees. Wheat was in it and spelt, and limitless cattle of all kinds. Great also was that which fell to my portion by reason of the love bestowed on me. He made me ruler of a tribe of the best of his country. Food was provided me for my daily fare, and wine for my daily portion, cooked meat and roast fowl, over and above the animals of the desert ; for men hunted and laid before me in addition to the quarry of my dogs. And there were made for me many dainties, and milk prepared in every way.*

*I spent many years, and my children grew up as mighty men, each one con-*

*trolling his tribe. The messenger who fared north, or south to the Residence, tarried with me, for I caused all men to tarry. I gave water to the thirsty, and set upon the road him who was strayed; I rescued him who was plundered. When the Setiu waxed insolent to oppose the chieftains of the deserts, I counselled their movements; for this prince of Retenu caused me to pass many years as commander of his host. Every country against which I marched, when I made my assault it was driven from its pastures and wells. I spoiled its cattle, I made captive its inhabitants, I took away their food, I slew people in it; by my strong arm, by my bow, by my movements and by my excellent counsels. I found favour in his heart and he loved me, he marked my bravery and placed me even before his children, when he had seen that my hands prevailed.*

*There came a mighty man of Retenu and flaunted me in my tent. He was a champion without a peer, and had subdued the whole of Retenu. He vowed that he would fight with me, he planned to rob me, he plotted to spoil my cattle, by the counsel of his tribesfolk. The prince communed with me and I said: I know him not, forsooth I am no confederate of his, nor one who strode about his encampment. Yet have I ever opened his door, or overthrown his fence? Nay, it is envy because he sees me doing thy behest. Assuredly, I am like a wandering bull in the midst of a strange herd, and the steer of those cattle charges him, a long-horn attacks him. Is there a humble man who is beloved in the condition of a master? There is no Pedti that makes cause with a man of the Delta. What can fasten the papyrus to the rock? Does a bull love combat and shall then a stronger bull wish to sound the retreat through dread lest that one might equal him? If his heart be toward fighting, let him speak his will. Does God ignore what is ordained for him, or knows he how the matter stands?*

*At night-time I strung my bow, and tried my arrows. I drew out my dagger, and polished my weapons. Day dawned and Retenu was already come; it had stirred up its tribes and had assembled the countries of a half of it, it had planned this fight. Forth he came against me where I stood, and I posted myself near him. Every heart burned for me. Women and men jabbered. Every heart was sore for me, saying: Is there another mighty man who can fight against him? Then his shield, his battle-axe and his armful of javelins fell, when I had escaped from his weapons and had caused his arrows to pass by me, uselessly sped; while one approached the other. I shot him, my arrow sticking in his neck. He cried aloud, and fell on his nose. I laid him low with his own battle-axe, and raised my shout of victory over his back. Every 'A'am shrieked. I gave thanks to Montu, but his serfs mourned for him. This prince Enshi, son of Amu, took me to his embrace. Then carried I off his possessions, and spoiled his cattle. What he had devised to do unto me, that did I unto him. I seized what was in his tent, I ransacked his encampment.*

*I became great thereby, I grew large in my riches, I became abundant in my flocks. Thus God hath done, so as to shew mercy to him whom he had condemned, whom he had made wander to another land. For today is his heart satisfied. A fugitive fled in his season; now the report of me is in the Residence. A laggard lagged because of hunger; now give I bread to my neighbour. A man left his country because of nakedness; but I am clad in white raiment and linen. A man sped for lack of one whom he should send; but I am a plenteous owner of slaves. Beautiful is my house, wide my dwelling-place; the remembrance of me is in the Palace.*

*O God, whosoever thou art that didst ordain this flight, show mercy and bring me to the Residence! Peradventure thou wilt grant me to see the place where my heart dwelleth. What matter is greater than that my corpse should be buried in the land wherein I was born? Come to my aid! A happy event has befallen. I have caused God to be merciful. May he do the like again so as to ennoble the end of him whom he had abased, his heart grieving for him whom he had compelled to live abroad. If it so be that today he is merciful, may he hear the prayer of one afar off, may he restore him whom he had stricken to the place whence he took him.*

*O may the King of Egypt show mercy to me, that I may live by his mercy. May I salute the Lady of the Land who is in his Palace. May I hear the behests of her children. O let my flesh grow young again, for old age has befallen, feebleness has overtaken me, mine eyes are heavy, my hands are weak, my legs refuse to follow, my heart is weary, and death approaches me, when they shall bear me to the city of Eternity. Let me serve my Sovereign Lady. O let her discourse to me of her children's beauty. May she spend an eternity over me!*

*Now it was told the King of Upper and Lower Egypt Kheperkerē concerning this pass wherein I was. Thereupon His Majesty sent to me with gifts of the Royal bounty, and gladdened the heart of this his servant, as it had been the prince of any foreign country. And the Royal Children who were within his Palace caused me to hear their behests.*

## *COPY OF THE DECREE WHICH WAS BROUGHT TO THIS HUMBLE SERVANT CONCERNING HIS RETURN TO EGYPT*

*Horus, Life-of-Births; Two Goddesses, Life-of-Births; King of Upper and Lower Egypt, Kheperkerē; Son of Rē, Sesostris, living for ever and ever.*

*A Royal decree unto the henchman Sinuhe. Behold, this decree of the King is brought to thee to instruct thee as following: — Thou hast traversed the foreign lands and art gone forth from Kedme to Retenu; land gave thee to land, self-counselled by thine own heart. What hadst thou done, that aught should be done against thee? Thou hadst not blasphemed, that thy words should be reproved. Thou hadst not spoken in the council of the nobles, that thy utterances should be banned. This deter-*

mination, it seized thine own heart, it was not in my heart against thee. This thy Heaven, who is in the Palace, is established and prospereth daily; she hath her part in the kingship of the land, her children are at the Court.

Mayest thou long enjoy the goodly things that they shall give thee; mayest thou live by their bounty. Come thou to Egypt, that thou mayst see the Residence where thou didst grow, that thou mayst kiss the earth at the Great Portals and have thy lot among the Companions. For today already thou hast begun to be old, thy manhood is spent. Bethink thee of the day of burial, the passing into beatitude : how that the night shall be devoted to thee with ointments, with bandages from the hands of Tayt; and a funeral procession shall be made for thee on the day of joining the earth; the mummy-shell of gold, with head of lazuli; and a heaven above thee; and thou placed upon the hearse, oxen dragging thee, musicians in front of thee; and there shall be performed the dance of the Muu at the door of thy tomb; and the offering-list shall be invoked for thee and slaughterings made beside thy stele; thy columns being shapen of white stone amid the tombs of the Royal Children. Thus shalt thou not die abroad. 'A'amu shall not escort thee. Thou shalt not be placed in a sheep-skin, when thy mound is made. Yea, all these things shall fall to the ground. Wherefore think of thy corpse, and come.

This decree reached me as I stood in the midst of my tribesfolk. It was read aloud to me, and I laid me on my belly and touched the soil, I strewed it on my hair. And I went about my encampment rejoicing, and saying : How should such things be done to a servant whom his heart led astray to barbarous lands? Fair in sooth is the graciousness which delivereth me from death; inasmuch as thy ka will grant me to accomplish the ending of my body at home.

## COPY OF THE ACKNOWLEDGEMENT OF THIS DECREE

The servant of the harîm Sinuhe says : — Fair hail! Discerned is this flight that thy servant made in his witlessness, yea even by thy ka, thou good god, lord of the two lands, whom Rē loves and Montu, lord of Thebes, praises. Amūn lord of Karnak, Sobk, Rē, Horus, Hathor, Atūm with his Ennead, Sopdu, Neferbaiu, Semseru, Horus of the East, the Lady of Imet who rests on thy head, the Conclave upon the waters, Min in the midst of the deserts, Wereret lady of Punt, Har-uer-rē, and all the gods of Ti-muri and of the islands of the sea : they give life and strength to thy nose, they endue thee with their gifts, they give to thee eternity illimitable, time without bourn; the fear of thee is bruited abroad in corn-lands and desert-hills, thou hast subdued all the circuit of the sun.

This thy servant's prayer to his lord to rescue him in the West, the lord of Perception, who perceiveth lowly folk, he perceived it in his noble Palace. Thy servant feared to speak it; now it is like some grave circumstance to repeat it. Thou *great god, peer of Rē in giving discretion to one toiling for himself, this thy servant is in the hand of a good counsellor in his behoof; verily I am placed beneath his guidance. For Thy Majesty is the victorious Horus, thy hands are strong against all lands.*

*Let now Thy Majesty cause to be brought Maki from Kedme, Khentiaush from Khentkesh, Menus from the lands of the Fenkhu. They are renowned princes, who have grown up in love of thee, albeit unremembered. Retenu is thine, like to thy hounds.*

*But as touching this thy servant's flight, I planned it not, it was not in my heart, I conceived it not, I know not what sundered me from my place. It was the manner of a dream, as when a Delta-man sees himself in Elephantine, a man of the marshes in Ta-seti. I had not feared. None had pursued after me. I had heard no reviling word. My name had not been heard in the mouth of the herald. Nay, but my body quivered, my feet began to scurry, my heart directed me, the god who ordained this flight drew me away. Yet am I not stiff-backed, inasmuch as suffering the fear of a man that knows his land. For Rē has set the fear of thee throughout the land, the dread of thee in every foreign country. Whether I be at home or whether I be in this place, it is thou that canst obscure yon horizon. The sun riseth at thy pleasure, the water in the rivers is drunk at thy will, the air in heaven is breathed at thy word. Thy servant will hand over the viziership which thy servant hath held in this place. But let Thy Majesty do as pleaseth thee. Men live by the breath that thou givest. Rē, Horus and Hathor love this thy august nose, which Montu, lord of Thebes, wills shall live eternally.*

*Envoys came to this servant, and I was suffered to spend a day in Yaa to hand over my possessions to my children, my eldest son taking charge of my tribe, all my possessions being in his hand, my serfs and all my cattle, my fruit and every pleasant tree of mine. Then came this humble servant southward and halted at Paths-of-Horus. The commander who was there in charge of the frontier-patrol sent a message to the Residence to bear tidings. And His Majesty sent a trusty head-fowler of the Palace, having with him ships laden with presents of the Royal bounty for the Setiu that were come with me to conduct me to Paths-of-Horus. And I named each several one of them by his name. Brewers kneaded and strained in my presence, and every serving-man made busy with his task.*

*Then I set out and sailed, until I reached the town of Ithtoue. And when the land was lightened and it was morning there came men to summon me, ten coming and ten going to convey me to the Palace. And I pressed my forehead to the ground between the sphinxes, the Royal Children standing in the gateway against my coming. The Companions that had been ushered into the Forecourt showed me the way to the Hall of Audience. And I found His Majesty on a throne in a gateway of gold; and I stretched myself on my belly and my wit forsook me in his presence, albeit this god greeted me joyously. Yea, I was like a man caught in the dusk; my soul fled, my flesh quaked, and my heart was not in my body, that I should know life from death.*

*Thereupon His Majesty said to one of those Companions: Raise him up, let him speak to me. And His Majesty said : Lo, thou art come, thou hast trodden the deserts, thou hast traversed the wastes; eld has prevailed against thee, thou hast reached old age. It is no small matter that thy corpse should be buried without escort of Pedtiu. But do not thus, do not thus, staying ever speechless, when thy name is pronounced.*

*But verily I feared punishment, and answered him with the answer of one afraid : What speaketh my lord to me? Would I might answer it, and may not. Lo, it is the hand of God, yea the dread that is in my body, like that which caused this fateful flight, Behold, I am in thy presence. Thine is life; may Thy Majesty do as pleaseth thee.*

*The Royal Children were caused to be ushered in. Then His Majesty said to the Royal Consort : Behold Sinuhe, who is come as an 'A'am, an offspring of Setiu-folk. She gave a great cry, and the Royal Children shrieked out all together. And they said to His Majesty : It is not really he, O Sovereign, my lord. And His Majesty said : Yea, it is really he.*

*Then brought they their necklaces, their rattles and their sistra, and presented them to His Majesty :—Thy hands be on the Beauteous one, O enduring King, on the ornament of the Lady of Heaven. May Nub give life to thy nose, may the Lady of the Stars join herself to thee. Let the goddess of Upper Egypt fare north, and the goddess of Lower Egypt fare south, united and conjoined in the name of Thy Majesty. May the Uraeus be set upon thy brow. Thou hast delivered thy subjects out of evil. May Rē, lord of the lands, show thee grace. Hail to thee, and also to our Sovereign Lady. The horn of thy bow is slacked, thine arrow loosened. Give breath to one that is stifled, and grant us our goodly guerdon in the person of this sheikh Si-mehyt, the Pedti born in Ti-muri. He fled through fear of thee; he left this land through dread of thee. But as for the face of him who sees Thy Majesty, it blenches not; as for the eye that regardeth thee, it fears not.*

*Then said His Majesty : Nay, but he shall not fear, he shall not dread. For he shall be a Companion among the magistrates, he shall be set in the midst of the nobles. Get you gone to the Chamber of Adornment to wait upon him.*

*So when I was gone forth from the Hall of Audience, the Royal Children giving me their hands, we went together to the Great Portals, and I was placed in the house of a Royal Son. There was noble equipment in it, a bathroom and painted devices of the horizon; costly things of the Treasury were in it. Garments of Royal stuff were in every chamber, unguent and the fine oil of the King and of the courtiers whom he loves; and every serving-man made busy with his task. Years were caused to pass away from my flesh, I was shaved and my hair was combed. A burden was given over to the desert, and clothing to the Sandfarers. And I was clad in soft linen, and anointed with fine oil; by night I lay upon a bed. I gave up the sand to them that dwell therein, and oil of wood to him who smears himself with it. There was given to me the house of a provincial governor, such as a Companion may possess; many artificers built it, and all its woodwork was new appointed. And meals were brought to me from the Palace three times, yea four times, a day, over and above that which the Royal Children gave, without remiss.*

*And there was constructed for me a tomb of stone in the midst of the tombs; the masons that hew tombs marked out its ground-plan; the master-draughtsmen designed in it; the master-sculptors carved in it; and the master-architects who are in the Necropolis bestowed their care upon it. And all the gear that is placed in a tomb-shaft went to its equipment. And* ka*-servants were given to me, and there was made for me a sepulchral garden, in which were fields, in front of my abode, even as is done for a chief Companion. And my statue was overlaid with gold, and its apron was of real gold. It was His Majesty caused it to be made.*

*There is no poor man for whom the like hath been done; and I enjoyed the favours of the Royal bounty until the day of death came.*

*IT IS FINISHED, FROM THE BEGINNING TO THE END, ACCORDING AS IT WAS FOUND IN WRITING.*

---

# POSTSCRIPT

---

Egyptian philology is progressive, fortunately, and my *Additional Notes* (§ IV) themselves already require a few brief additions.

132. — For *ꜥꜥi* "to jabber", "to babble in a foreign tongue", see *Proc. S. B. A.*, 37 (1915), 123.

151. — For a decisive instance of *sꜣ* meaning "to creep", see LACAU, *Textes Religieux*, 51, 27.

285. — In my translation I have ventured to translate *m ḫt*, not temporally "afterwards", but as meaning "together", "in company". The preposition is not rare in this sense, but no similar instance of the adverb is known to me.

306. — Mr. Battiscombe Gunn proposes to understand *dmi* here as a name for the tomb. This makes better sense, and *dmi* appears to be so used in the *Lebensmüde*, see ERMAN's edition, p. 34. — For *ḥrt* see already Piehl in *Ä. Z.*, 23 (1885), 58-59.

Additions to § III, *The Duplicate Texts* (pp. 118-151).

In the excavations carried out by Prof. PETRIE at El-Haragah in the Fayûm a scrap of yellow- brown papyrus (15×8 cm.) was found, bearing the upper portions of four vertical columns in a semi-uncial hieratic hand of the kind familiar from the Kahûn papyri. On examination this proved to contain a duplicate of B 103-109, and I am permitted to publish it here by the kind consent of Professor Petrie. The new fragment, which is probably older than any Ms. of the tale except the Berlin papyrus (B), I have designated by the letter H.

B 103 … 104 …

H … 1 …

B … 105 …

H … 2 …

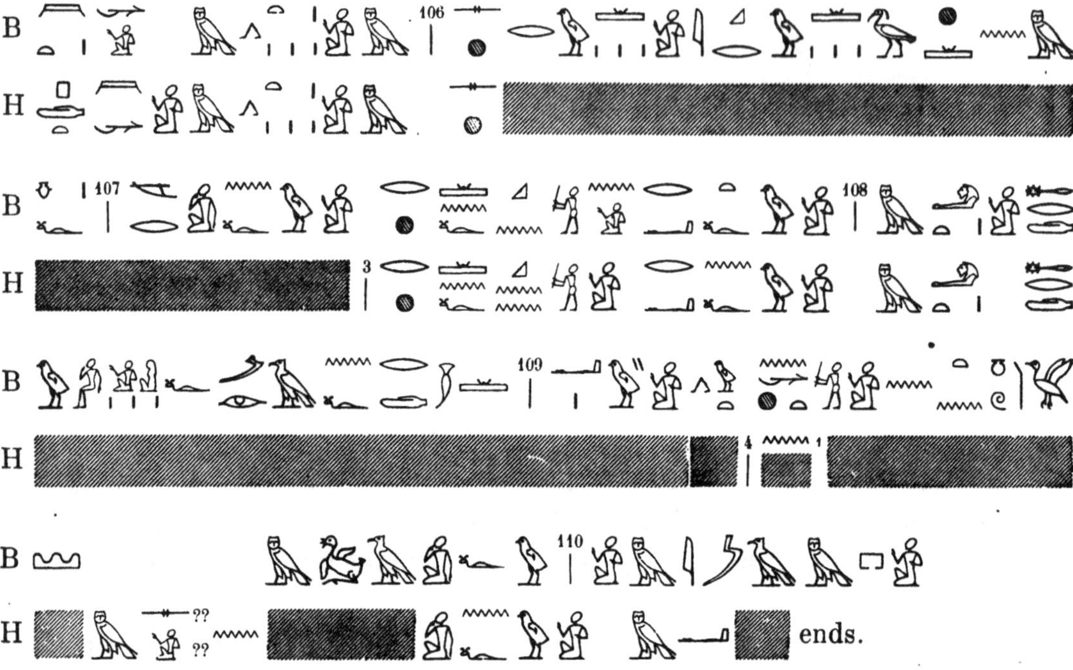


Except in the last line, where it is impossible to reconstitute the readings of H, this Ms. agrees closely with B. It corrects B in its writings of *in-ni*, *ḳnn-i* and *ḥꜣt ẖrdw*. The variants *rdi-nf* for *rdi-ṯf*, and [*mṯꜣ-*]*nf* for *mṯꜣ-f* are quite legitimate; the last word of H was probably *ʿfꜣi-i*, cf. B 115, 201.

A small and fragmentary limestone chip of Ramesside date, inscribed in a hand perhaps identical with OP[2] (see the Plate, p. 119) has recently been identified among the Petrie ostraca now in my hands. Petrie Ostracon 66, here called OP[4], contains fragments of a widely divergent text of B 142-151.

1. It is not certain that this *n* is the first letter of *nḫt*.
2. See Additional Notes on B 30 (p. 155).

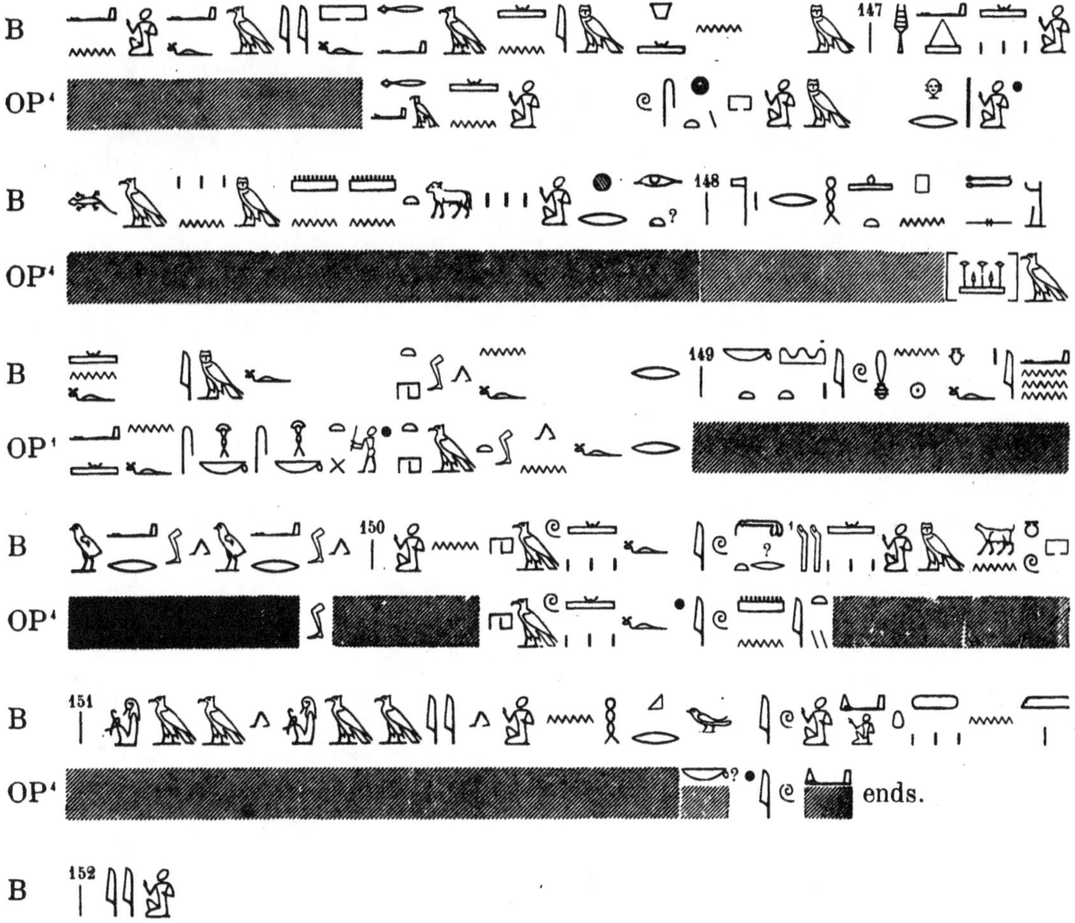

The variations in this short passage are considerable, but owing to the much damaged condition of OP[4] little use can be made of it. In the part corresponding to *ṯs-nf im-f* of B 148 the ostracon gives *š3ʿ-nf sksk* "whom he had begun to destroy", a variation not only in the choice of words but also, apparently, in the sense. The substitution of *mnity* "field-labourer" for *mtr-t* (B 150) is strange and inexplicable.

1. So, or [hieroglyphs], seems more probable than [hieroglyphs], my former reading.

# INDICES

## I. General.

## II. **Egyptian words**.

*in* ( ), convertible with , 11, 153.

*inn* ( ), *ṡḏm-nf* form so written, 23.

*inbw itf-i*, see *inbw ḥḳ3*, 17.

*inbw ḥḳ3* 'the Walls of the Prince', 17, 165-6.

*in ntt* 'is it the case that ...', 60-1.

*ir*, used as auxiliary with *iwt* 'to come' (or perhaps simply as periphrastic imperative), 68.

*ir m ḫpš-f*, as epithet, 33.

*ir* ( ), optatively used, 90.

*irt* ( ), so spelt, infinitive, 108.

*irt*, in sense of 'to create', 157, 39; in sense of 'to traverse' country, 97; perhaps used for *dit* in sense of 'to cause', 65, 160; used as auxiliary with *šmt* 'to go', 154.

*irt m* 'to act according to', 90.

*irt*, in *ḥr irt-f* 'engaged in his duties', 92.

*ihm* 'to linger', 58 (note 1).

*iḫt*, treated as masc. sing., 42.

*is*, enclitic, 'verily', 68.

*is*, particle, never first word in sentence before 18th Dynasty; possible exception, 86.

*ist wrt* 'throne', 96.

*išnn* 'war-cry', 55, 159.

*išst* 'what (?)' (phrase *ḥr išst* = 'why'), 24.

*ik, iky* 'quarryman', 154.

*ikw* (or *i3kw*) 'a stone-quarry', 17, 154.

*ity*, written , 100.

*itmw* 'suffocation' or similar, 106.

*itn*, 1) transitively 'to thwart, reject', 2) with *m* 'to oppose (?)', 66, 160.

*itnw* 'secret', 'mystery', 66.

*itḫ*, early form of *ʿtḫ* 'to strain', 92.

*iṯt* 1) 'to conquer', 'to excel', with object, 37.

*'Iṯ-t3wy*, identified with Lisht, 93.

*itnw* 'foes', 66.

*idw* 'pestilence', 32.

*idnw* ( ), reading *idn* by extension from *id*, 154.

*idḥy* 'a man of the Delta', 87.

*idḥw* 'a man of the Delta (?)', 48.

ʿ, compounded with verbs apparently without affecting their meaning, 61.

ʿ ( ), perhaps corrupt, 108.

*ʿ3b* 'to be pleasant', 75 (note 4).

*ʿiʿi* 'to rejoice' (late), 50.

*ʿʿw* 'to beat', of the heart, 50.

*ʿʿi* 'to shriek', 50; not 'to shriek', but 'to jabber' in a foreign tongue, 177.

*ʿʿb* 'to join', 'to comb (?)', 111-2.

*ʿw3y* 'robber', 18.

*ʿb* 'horn', used for the 'bow', 105.

*ʿbt-ḫ3t* 'burial' (= *sm3-t3*), 59, 98.

*ʿf3y* 'dwelling-place', 'camp', 157, 46.

*ʿmw* ( ), proper name, 155.

*ʿnw*, in sense of 'returning (to the fray ?)', 35.

*ʿr* 1) 'ascend', 2) 'approach', 9, 13.

*ʿrw* 'nearness', 12-13, 35.

*ʿḥ* or *iḥ* (not *ʿḥʿ*) as reading of , 78 (note 1).

*ʿḥʿ-ib* 'persistent', 35.

*ʿḥʿw*, in phrase *irt ʿḥʿw* 'to do service (?)', 110.

*ʿḫ* 'to fly', 'fly away, 11 (note 5).

*ʿḫḫ* (*iḫḫ*) 'twilight', 'dusk', 97.

*ʿḫ* 'to fly', 'fly away', 11 (note 5).

*ʿḫm* 'falcon shape', 'image', 110.

*ʿḫnwty*, the inner private apartments of the Pharaoh, 96.

*ʿḫnwty dw3t*, an apartment of some kind, 108-110.

*ʿš*, in sense of 'to read', 72 (note 1).

*ʿšm*, see *ʿḫm*.

*ʿtḫ* ʿto strain bread-pulpʾ in the making of beer, 92.
*ʿḏ-mr*, a title, 8-9, 152.

*wꜣ*, followed by [hieroglyph], 39.
*wꜣt*, treated as masculine, 15 (note 3).
*wꜣḥ*, intransitively, 'to endure', 'live long', 67; *niswt wꜣḥ* 'long-living King', 104.
*wꜣḥ-ib* 'benevolence', 'goodwill'; also as adjective and as verb, 76.
*wꜣḫ* 'forecourt', 96.
*wi* 'mummy-case', 69, 160.
*wʿ*, in phrases such as *msw niswt m dwt*(?) *wʿt*, 'the Royal Children were in one noise', i. e. 'cried out together', 99.
*wʿꜣ* 'a curse', 'to curse', 66, 160.
*wʿrt* 1) 'district', 2) 'desert-plateau', 30.
*wpw-ḥr* 'but', as conjunction, 87.
*wfꜣ* 'to talk about', 31.
*wmt* 'gateway', 95.
*wmt* 'thick', 95.
*wmt-ib* 'stout-hearted', 35.
*wmtt* 'fortification', 96.
*wn* followed by *śḏm-f*, possible example of, 71.
*wnin* followed by *śḏm-f* form, 1) most ceremonious form for describing actions of the King, 2) expresses result, 63, 160.
*wnmt* 'food', 'fodder', 44.
*wr nf*, in sense of 'he has abundance of ...', 41.
*wrḥ* 'to anoint', constructions of, 112.
*wršy* 'a watcher', 18.
*whm* 'to bruit abroad', 81.
*whm-ʿ* 'to repeat' an action; also in *m whm-ʿ*, 'again', 36.
*whm sꜣ* 'to sound the retreat', 48.
*whmw* 'herald', functions of, 31-2.
*wḥyt* 'tribe', 20.
*wšd* 'to address' a person, 97.
*wgꜣ* 'feebleness', 62.
*wd* (det. [hieroglyph]), 1) 'to send forth', cries, voice (with [hieroglyph] or *ḫrw*), 2) 'to emit' a sound, 55, 99.
*wd* (det. [hieroglyph]), 'to shoot' arrows, 49.
*wd ḥr* 'eager' or 'bold', 35.
*wdb* 'to turn' 61.
*wdpw* 'serving-man', 'butler', 92.
*wḏy* 'stray' (of cattle), 47.
*wḏw* (det. [hieroglyph]) 'cattle allowed to roam freely', 47.
*wḏʿ* 1) 'to sever', 2) 'to divide' true from false, hence 'to judge', 3) 'to assign' to a person that which is his right, 69.

*bꜣꜣwt* 'virile strength', 68.
*bꜣk* (not *bk*), reading of [hieroglyph] in O. K. texts, 64 (note 1).
*bꜣk im*, depreciatory form used by inferior to superior, 64.
*bw*, in phrase *bw ḥwrw*, 'ignominy', 'disgrace', 31.
*bhꜣw* 'fugitive', 34.
*bs* (biliteral, old *ibs*) 'to introduce', 'be introduced into', 71.
*bst* (III. inf.) 'to swell', 'flow forth', 71.
*btꜣ* 'to run', 58.

*pꜣ*, as verb, 'to have done something in the past', 20.
*pw* (pronoun = 'it', 'this') placed at head of clause, 59-60; in verbal form *śḏm pw iry*, 89.
*pr ḫnti* 'harîm', 9.
*pr dwꜣt*, 109-110, 162.
*pr ḏt* 'estate', meaning discussed, 77 (note 2).
*pr-ʿ* 'active', as epithet, 33.
*pry* 'a hero', 'champion'; as adjective, 'famous', 44.

*pry* (det. ), a bull of more than average strength and ferocity, 44, 48.
*prw ḥr* 'more than', 44.
*pḥwy ḥʿw* 'the end of life', 76.
*pẖrt* 'frontier patrol', 91.
*psf*, error for *pfs-f*, 20.
*psḥ* 'to sting', 'bite', 31 (note 3).
*psḫ* 'to be disordered', 14.
*psg* (*pśg* in *Pyr.*) 'to spit', 31.
*pgs* 'to spit', 31.
*pt* 'sky', used metaphorically in *pt-k tn*='this thy mistress', 67; in phrase *pt ḥrk* 'a heaven above thee', probably meaning the lid of the sarcophagus, 69.
*ptr*, interrogative 'what?', derivation of, 48, 59, 60.
*pds*, reading of , by extension from *pd*, 154.
*pḏ*, in *pḏ nmtwt* 'wide of paces', 34.
*pḏtyw* 'foreigners', 'barbarians', 107.

*fꜣ*, written , 95.
*fꜣ ṯꜣw* 'to sail', 93.
*fn* 'to be infirm', 60.
*fnḫw*, 85 and note 1.
*fḫ* 'to depart', 20; in sense of 'to lose', 62, 68.
*ftft* 'to spring', 14.

*m* with infinitive, used as predicate only with verbs of motion, 93.
*m* ( ) 'take', 'receive', 88, note 3.
*mꜣir* 'misery', 35.
*mꜣʿty*, in *iw mꜣʿty* = Abydos, 165.
*Mꜣʿty*, name of a lake or water-way, 16.
*mꜣwt*, phrase *m mꜣwt*, 1) 'anew' of things restored, 2) 'newly', 'expressly', 113.
*mꜣẖ* (with *ib*) 'to be troubled' or 'consumed (with fear)', 50, 158.
*mꜣst*, phrase *tp ḥr mꜣst* 'head on lap', 10.
*mi* (not *mʿ*), reading of  in certain words, 23 (note 1).
*mi* ( ), particle, 23 (note 1); 'behold', 88.
*mi-iḫt*, synonym of  (?), 60.
*min*, phrase *m min* used for simple *min* 'to-day', 67.
*minb* 'battle-axe', 51, 159.
*mint* 'daily fare' or similar, 41.
*mik* (fem. *mit*) = French *voici*, 99.
*miti* 'a copy' (masculine), 63-4.
*mw-w*, dancers of a certain kind, 70.
*mfit*, as writing of *mnfrt*, 159.
*mn*, of a weapon, 'to stick fast in' ( ), 55.
*mnit* 'a bead necklace', not an instrument of music; emblem of Hathor, 100-2.
*mni (mini)* 'to attach to', 'to marry to' (with ), 40, 41.
*mnt*, in phrase *m mnt*, 41 (note 1).
*mr sḫtyw*, a commissariat officer, 91.
*mḥ ḥr* 'to take thought for', 71.
*mḥ-s*, name of crown of Lower Egypt, 104.
*mḫꜣ* 1) 'to match', 'equal', 2) 'to adjust', 3) 'to counterpoise', 4) 'to make level', 5) 'to be like' (followed by ), 49.
*msyt* 'evening meal', 154.
*mstpt* 'portable shrine', 69.
*mšʿ*, verb, 'to make an expedition', 29-30.
*mšʿ* 'expedition', 29.
*mty* 'right', 'exact'; perhaps to be distinguished from *mtr* 'to witness', 85, with note 4.
*mtn* 'to reward' a person with ( ), 106.
*mtn* (det. ) 'sheikh', 20, 107.
*mtt nt ib* 'affection', 'care' (?), 75 (note 3).
*mṯꜣ* 'to flout', 'insult (?)', 44.

*n*, preposition, in temporal sense, 29.

*n*, inserted apparently superfluously between plurals of *śḏmf*-form and their object the old absolute pronoun, 62.
*n* (hieroglyph), pronunciation of, 11; written (hieroglyph), 153.
*n sp* 'not at all', 11.
*nw* (det. hieroglyph) 'weakness' (?), 62.
*nw* (det. hieroglyph) 'weak' like an infant (?), 62.
*Nb* (det. hieroglyph) 'the Golden One', epithet of Hathor, 104.
*Nb-mr*, proper name (?), or corrupt (?), 112.
*nbt 'Imt*, epithet of the goddess Buto, 80.
*nbt idw*, 'Lady of Pestilence', epithet of Sakhmet, 32.
*nbt r ḏr*, epithet of the Queen, 62-3, 105.
*nbt sbꜣw* 'Lady of the Stars (?)', epithet of Hathor, 104.
*nf* 'wrong', 87.
*nfʿ* 'to remove' oneself, 14.
*nfr* 'to be happy', 23, 40.
*nfrw* 'beauty'; 35.
*Nfrw*, name of a Queen, 152.
*nft*, unknown word; read *ntf* (?) 'unloose', 105.
*nftft* 'to leap', 14.
*nmi* 'lowing', 20.
*nmi* 'to cross' water, 16.
*Nmyw-šʿ* 'Sand-farers', epithet of Beduins, 16, 18.
*nm(i)w* 'dwarfs', 70.
*nmty* 'to traverse', 16.
*nmtwt* ('steps'), in sense of 'actions', 44.
*nnyw* 'the weary ones', 'the dead', 70.
*nhw* 'loss', 35.
*nht* 'sycomore' (det. ▭!), 16.
*nḥ* 'prayer' (masculine), 61, 82.
*nḥm* 'to rescue', 42.
*Nḥm-ʿwꜣyt*, a goddess, 42.
*nḥmn*, particle, 32, 46.
*nswt* 'javelins (?)', 'daggers (?)', 52.
*nkꜣ* 'to meditate on', 38-9, 157.
*ngꜣw* 'the long-horned bull', 47.
[*N*]*gꜣw* (?), a town, 17.
*ntb* 'to scorch', 'parch' (?), 19, 154.
*nt pw* 'it is the case that' (?), 46, 158.
*ntf* 'to unfasten', 'unloose', 105.
*ntt*, with personal suffix, 40 (note 1), 60-1; used for *n ntt*, 40, 62.
*nḏ ri*, 'to ask the opinion of', 'consult', 83-4; *nḏ ri ḥr* = 1) 'to talk about', 2) 'to take counsel on behalf of', 83-4.
*nḏꜣ*, 'to be parched', 19, 154.
*nḏnḏ* 1) 'to ask' (about) something, 2) 'to ask' of (hieroglyph) somebody, 'to question' somebody, 3) 'to question' somebody (with direct object of person), 4) 'to confer' with (*ḥnʿ*) somebody; 45.

*r*, in sense of 'away from', 21.
*rꜣḥs*, example of rare combination *r*+ꜣ, 155 (note 1).
*ri* (hieroglyph), used as emphatic particle (later hieroglyph), 32.
(hieroglyph), to be read *ri* not *rꜣ*, 23 (note 2).
*ri*, in sense of 'language', 23.
*ri-wꜣt* 'a way' 'neighbourhood', less concrete than *wꜣt*, 16, 154.
*ri-pḏtyw*, derivative of *pḏtyw*, meaning uncertain, 33.
*ri-sy*, reinforcing *n sp*, 11. See too *rssy*.
*ri-ḏꜣw* 'encounter' (?), 34, 157.
*rwi* 'to make to cease', 'to check', 36; in sense of 'to leave', 107.
*rww* 'to run (?)', 43.
*Rwty*, a lion-god, 95 (note 1).
*rwty wrty* the entrance-gates of the Palace, 109.
*rwḏ (rwd)* 1) 'staircase', 2) 'shaft' of tomb, 116.

*rf*, a postulated verb, probably non-existent, 156.
*rnn* 'to extol', 37.
*rnnwt* 'joy', 'rejoicing', abstract infinitival form, 37-38.
*Rnny*, as personal name, 37.
*rḫyt* 'subjects', 'people', 83.
*rssy*, archaic form of *ri-sy*, 153,
*rḳt-ib* 'ill-will', 'jealousy', 46.

*hꜣ*, transitively 'to charge down upon' a person, 33, 35; confused in hieratic with *hꜣb*, 36, 39.
*hꜣw*, in phrase *m hꜣw-f* 'in his presence', 34.
*hꜣb*, confused in hieratic with *hꜣ*, 36, 39.
*hy* 'hail' to (*n*) a person, 105.
*hwhw* 'to scurry', unknown word, 87.
*hrw nfr* 'holiday', 107 (note 1).
*hd*, with *m*, 'to assail' a person, 97.

*ḥꜥw* 'flesh', not 'limbs', 111.
*ḥwt*, in sense of 'to tread', 97.
*ḥwt tꜣ* 'to banish', 'oppress' (?) (with [hieroglyph] and person), 61; obscure, 71.
*ḥwyt (ḥyt?)* 'trodden', 29 (note 3).
*ḥwiw*, a supposed word for cattle (see *wḏw*), 158.
*ḥwrw*, in phrases *bw ḥwrw* and *ṯs ḥwrw*, 31.
*ḥwtf* (4 rad.) 'to plunder', 'seize as plunder', 44-5.
*ḥb* 'to make festival', whether of joy or grief, 55, 159.
*ḥb* (det. [hieroglyph]) 'to catch fowl or fish', 55.
*ḥbs*, in sense of 'to hide', 'veil', 88.
*ḥpt* 1) 'embrace', 2) 'armful (?)', 52.
*ḥm n stp-sꜣ*, respectful designation of 'the Palace', 83.
*ḥmsw* 'sloth, lassitude', 35.

*ḥmwt ṯꜣyw*, to be translated 'women and men' in *Sinuhe B.*, 132; possibly sometimes means 'married women', 50, 158.
*ḥnwt tꜣ*, 'Mistress of the Land', i. e. 'the Queen'. 62, 159.
*ḥr*, in sense of 'from', 'away from', 43-4.
*Ḥr iꜣbty* 'Horus the Easterner', a god, 80.
*Ḥr*, in *wꜣwt Ḥr* 'Ways-of-Horus', frontier town near El Kantara, 91, 161.
*Ḥr-wr-rꜥ*, a god, 80-1.
*Ḥr ḥry ib ḫꜣswt*, 80.
*ḥr* (det. [hieroglyph]), for *ḥryt*, 88, 107; in phrase *m ḥr(yt) nt* 'for fear of', 'for fear that', 48.
*Ḥryt* 'Lady of Heaven', part of place-name *(Ḥryt nbt ḍw ḏšr)*, 17.
*ḥs* 'to approach' (trans. and intrans.), 23.
*Ḥtimw*, corruption of *Tmḥi ?*, 10-11.
*ḥdb* (det. [hieroglyph]) 'to sit', 'settle down', 'halt', 91.
*ḥdb* (det. [hieroglyph]) 1) 'to overthrow', 2) 'to be prostrate', 91.
*ḥḏ* 'to go forth at dawn' (?), 16.
*ḥḏ ḥbsw* 'white of clothing', 58.

*ḫꜣt* 'illness', 71.
*ḫꜣt* (det. [hieroglyph]), so written for *ḫꜣt* 'corpse', 71, 59.
*ḫꜣt* (det. [hieroglyph]), for *ḫꜣt* 'marsh', 87.
*ḫꜥw* (det. [hieroglyph]) 'gear', used of funeral furniture, 115.
*ḫꜥw* (det. [hieroglyph]) 1) 'weapons', 2) 'tackle' of ship, 3) 'utensils' in general, 115 (note 3).
*ḫꜥm* 'to draw nigh', see *ẖꜥm*, 33, 54, 157.
*ḫbb* 'dance' (substantival infinitive), 70.
*ḫp*, transitively, 'to meet', 16-17.
*ḫpr*, as passive of *irt* (Latin *fieri*), 33.
*ḫft*, preposition, in sense of 'to' after verb of saying, 32.

*ḫft ḥr* (with person), in sense of 'to' after verb of saying, 32.
*ḫm* 'to burn' (of the throat), 19.
*ḫmt* 'to intend', constructions of, 45, 86.
*m ḫmt* preposition, 'without', 32, 37.
*ḫn ḥr* 'to alight on' or 'at', 154.
*ḫnm* 1) 'to gladden', 2) 'to be glad'; *ḫnm* 'to breathe' may be a special case of this, 97.
*ḫnt* 'festival outlay' (?), 106-7.
*ḫnt*, in *m ḫnt r*, compound preposition, 'in front of?', 116.
*ḫntyt;* phrase *m ḫntyt* 'southwards', without reference to the Nile, 91.
*Ḫnt-kš*, place-name (part of Retenu?), 85.
*ḫntš* 'to rejoice', 36.
*ḫr*, in *ꜣwt-ꜥ nt ḫr nìswt*, 'presents of the royal bounty', 63.
*ḫr*, particle, uses of, 53.
*ḫrw nmì* 'the sound of lowing', 20.
*ḫsf*, with det. Λ, intransitive, 'to go upstream', 18.
*ḫsfw* 'proximity', 35; 'the opposite quarter', 13.
*ḫsfw*, in *ìrt ḫsfw* 'to meet', 96.
*ḫtt*, III inf. 'to engrave', 'carve', 114, 162.

*ẖꜣt* 'marshes', 'marshy pools', 87.
*ẖꜥm*, trans., and intrans. with 𓈖, 'to draw nigh', 33, 157, 54.
*ẖmꜥ*, see *ẖꜥm*, 33, 157, 159.
*ẖn* 'to approach', 52.
*ẖnw* 1) 'home' (in *r ẖnw* and *m ẖnw*), 2) 'the royal palace', 59, 76.
*ẖnm* 'to enrich' a person with *(m)* a thing, 81.
*H̱nm ìswt*, name of pyramid, 9.
*ẖnm tp*, of the Uraeus adorning the head of the King, 80.
*ẖr ḥꜣt*, preposition, with person, 'before' in sense of 'superior to', 32.
*ẖrw* 'depth', 35.
*ẖkryt nt nbt pt* 'ornament of the Lady of Heaven', epithet of the *mnìt*, 103-4.

*sꜣ*, earliest use of ⌓ for 𓅭, 155.
*sꜣ*, in phrase *dìt sꜣ n* 'to turn the back to', 34-5.
*sꜣ*, in phrase *mì m sꜣ* 'come to the help of... (?)', 59, 159.
*m sꜣ* 'in charge of', 90; *sꜣ* 'a door', 46.
*sꜣw* 'to keep', possibly 'to spare', 37.
*sꜣt* (III inf.) 'to sate', 33.
*sꜣw* (det. Λ) 'to go slowly', 'linger', 'delay'; its relation to *sꜣw* 'to keep, beware', 37, 58, 159, 177.
*sꜣ ìwt-f* 'cautious in his going', 58.
*sꜣt* 'wisdom' (?), infinitive of a III inf. verb *sꜣy* 'to be wise', 33.
*sꜣꜣ* 'prudent', 33, 157.
*sꜣꜣy* 'a loiterer', 18, 58.
*sꜣì*, for *sìꜣ* 'recognize', 20.
*sꜣb* 'to cause to tarry', 42.
*Sꜣ-mḥyt*, name playfully given to Sinuhe by the queen and princesses, 107.
*Sꜣ-nht*, as a name, 9.
*sꜣsꜣ* 'to drive back', 35 (with note 1), 157.
*sꜣk* 'to gather up', 19-20.
*sìꜣ* 'perception', 83.
*sìn* 'to delay'; with *n* 'to wait for', 11, 153.
*sìhm* 'to cause to linger', 'to hold back', 58 (note 1).
*sꜥr* 'to cause to ascend', 152.
*swꜣ* 'to go by' in sense of 'live and die', 37-8.
*swḥ* 'wind', 154.
*swt* 'wind' (masc.), 17, 154.
*swt*, particle, 25-26.
*swḏꜣ*, in sense of 'death', 62.

*sb*, read *snb* 'to overthrow', 46.

*sbt* (III inf.) : 1) transitive, 'to send', 'conduct', 'pass (time)', 2) intransitive, 'to pass' (into a state), 63, 68, 160.

*sbt* 'burden', metaphorically, 112.

*sbw* 'dirt (?)', 112.

*sp n iwtt* 'in vain (?)', 52, 158-9.

*spr* (reading of B only), 'to cause to go forth', 54.

*sfn* 'to make infirm', 60.

*sfḫ* 'to loosen', 105

*smi*, in sense of 'acknowledgement' of receipt of a Royal decree, 76.

*smwn* 'surely', 'probably', 59.

*smn* 'to fasten' to *(r)*, 48.

*Smsrw*, a god, 79-80, 161.

*sny* ([hieroglyphs], [hieroglyphs]) 1) 'to pass', 2) 'to open', 160, 72-3.

*sny*, in phrase *dit sn(y)* 'to manifest oneself', 'appear', 73.

*sny* '*vomer*' (ⲥⲓⲛⲉ), 50 (note).

*snyn*, demotic, 'to walk up and down', (ⲥⲛⲁⲉⲓⲛ), 160.

*snb* 'to overthrow', 46.

*snny* 'to pass', 'move', 160, 72-3.

*snḏ*, followed by infinitive 'to fear to...', 83.

*srwd* 1) 'to supply', 'establish'; 2) 'to restore' buildings, 113.

*sḥwr* 'to insult', 31.

*sḥr* (det. [hieroglyph]) 'to fly up', 10.

*sḥr* (det. [hieroglyph]) 'to make distant', 'remove', 10, 105, 152.

*sḫꜣw* 'remembrance', 58.

*sḫm*, a kind of *sistrum*, identical with [hieroglyph], 102-3.

*Sḫmt*, goddess Sakhmet, 32.

*sḫr* 'counsel', wide meanings of, 66.

*sḫr*, in *ḫr sḫr* 'under the power (or guidance) of...', 84.

*sḫs* (with *m sꜣ*) 1) 'to pursue', 2) 'to persecute' a person, 87.

*sẖr* 1) 'to sweep' or 'brush over' something; 2) 'to overlay' (with gold), 117.

*sẖkr* 'to decorate', here 'to burnish', 50.

*sš* 'to strew', 'spread', 161, 73.

*sšm*, masc. sing. substantive, 'affair', 'matter' 11, 63.

*sšsꜣ* 'to render wise', 83.

*sššt*, a kind of *sistrum*, 102-3.

*sḳbbw* 'bathroom', 110.

*sk* 'ranks' of an army, 34.

*sgr* 'to be still', 10, 153.

*stt* (III inf.) 1) 'to pierce' (with direct object), 2) 'to shoot at' (with [hieroglyph]), 55.

*stp*, in phrase *m stp n* 'consisting of the best of', 41.

*sd* 'to clothe', 112.

*sḏm* 'to understand' (a language), 23.

*sḏr* 'to spend the night' doing something, 49.

*ši*, not *šꜣ*, value of [hieroglyph], 23, with note 2.

*ši ḥrt* 'tomb-garden', 116.

*šꜣw* 'value', whence perhaps *n šꜣ* with infin. = 'apt to', 'fit for', *n šꜣ n* with noun 'in the capacity of', 47.

*šꜣb* 'meal', 113.

*šwꜣ* 'a poor man', 117.

*šbb* 'to knead' barley-bread and water in the making of beer, 92.

*šbbt*, the kneaded bread-paste used in the making of beer, 92 (note 1).

*šbt*, a drug, distinct from *šbbt*, 92 (note 1).

*špssw* 'splendid things', 'luxuries', 110.

*šmw* 'a goer', 15.

*šmʿ-s*, name of crown of Upper Egypt, 104.

*šms wḏꜣ* 'funeral cortège', 69.

*šnw* 'hair', 58, 72.

*šnw nb n itn* 'the whole circuit of the sun', 81.

*šnby*, read *šnw-i (?)*, 58, 72.
*šnnt itn* 'that which the sun surrounds in his circuit', 81.
*šrm* 'to lay to rest (?)', 105.
*šs*, general word for 'things', 'articles', 111.
*šs nìswt* 'byssus', 'fine linen', 111.
*šsp* 'statue', 'image', derivatively 'sphinx', 94, 161-2.
*štm* 'to oppose' (?), 42, 157.
*šd* (det. [hieroglyph]!) 'to read', 71-2.

*ḳꜣ sꜣ* 'presumptuous', 88.
*ḳꜣw* 'height', 35.
*ḳꜣmdt* 'heroic deeds' (?), 86.
*ḳꜣs* 1) 'to bind', 'tie', 2) 'to string' a bow, 49.
*ḳbḥw* 'cold', 35.
*ḳmꜣ*, as substantive, 'form', 99.
*ḳmꜣ* 'to mourn' (Pyr.), 86.
*ḳmd* 'to devise', 86, 161.
*ḳmd*, later form of *ḳmꜣ* 'to mourn', 86.
*ḳdmi*, the land Kedme, 23, 65, 84.

*kꜣ* 'to intend', 15; 'to think out', 'devise'; not 'to think of', 38-9, 50.
*kꜣ* (det. [hieroglyph]), used in respectful reference to the Pharaoh, 76.
*kꜣ-mr-ꜥḥꜣ* 'bull loving battle', epithet of Rē, 158.
*Kpny*, Byblos, 21-23.
*kf* 1) 'to uncover', 'unclothe'; 2) 'to plunder', 'deprive' a person; 3) 'to despoil', 'strip' a place, 55.
*Kmwr*, an island, 19.
*ksw*, subst., 'a bending (or crouching) posture', 18, 35.

*Gw*, a town, 17, 166.
*gmw* 'mourning', 10, 153.
*gr*, in sense of 'further' (?), 162.
*grg* 'to hunt', 42.
*gs* 'to anoint', constructions of, 112.

*Tꜣ-mry* 'Egypt', 81.
*tꜣw fnḫw* 'the lands of the Fenkhu, 85.
*Tꜣyt*, goddess of weaving, 69.
*tꜣw* 'heat', 35,
*tìsw*, origin of, 153.
*twꜣ* 'man of low station', 'inferior', 47, 105.
*twr* 'to respect', 16.
*tp mꜣꜥ*, compound preposition, 'on the temples of', 'in the presence of', 92.
*tp-ḥꜣt* 'a roof', 18 (note 2).
*tp ḥry* 'a master', 'superior', 47.
*Tnw*, variant (incorrect?) of B for *Rṯnw*, 23, 44, 65.
*tnm* 'to go astray', 42 (note).
*tr* 'to respect', 16.
*tr* 'pray', 'forsooth', 45-6.
*th* 'to err', 'transgress', 'violate', 74; 'to lead astray', 74, 161.
*tšꜣ (tš)* 'to grind', 'smash', 34.
*tšb*, unknown word, 34.

*ṯꜣ* 'to seize' a weapon, 36.
*ṯꜣ* 'to pluck', 'seize', 'shave (?)', 111-2.
*ṯꜣy* 'husband' (see also *ḥmt ṯꜣy*), 50, 158.
*Ṯꜣrw*, the town of Tharu, 91.
*ṯꜣt*, in sense of 'viziership', 89.
*ṯꜣt* (det. [hieroglyph]), corrupt (?), 89.
*ṯmꜣ-ꜥ* 'strong of arm', epithet of Horus, 84.
*Ṯḥnw*, 10-11.
*ṯs*, in phrase *ṯs ḥwrw* 'an insult', 'reproach', 31.
*ṯs*, in phrase *ṯs skw* 'to order the ranks', 34.
*ṯs* (det. [hieroglyph]) *m* 'to feel anger at', 'to bear a grudge against', 57, 159.
*ṯsw*, used of military captains, especially commanders of fortresses, 91.

*dit* 'to cause', followed by object and pseudoparticiple, 60; reflexively 'to place oneself', 'lay oneself' *(hr ht)*, 72.

*dyt* (det. [hieroglyph]), a writing of *dt (?)*, 48.

*dwꜣ sp-sn* 'early', 'very early', 93.

*dwꜣt*, see *pr dwꜣt* and *ʿhnwti dwꜣt*.

*dwi* 'to call out', 99.

*dwt, dyt*, reading of [hieroglyphs], [hieroglyphs] 'noise', 99.

*dbn* 'to go round', a place, 74.

*dbḥt ḥtpw*, the altar decked with the funerary meal, 70.

*dpts*, corrupt (?), 67.

*dm*, 1) *dm rn n* 'to pronounce the name of' a person; 2) *dm... m rnf* 'to mention (a person) by his name', 92, 98.

*dmi*, with accusative, 'to touch'; with *r*, 'to be joined to', 'accrue to', 41.

*dmi*, used of place, 'to reach' 'pass beside', 17.

*dmi sꜣtw* 'to touch earth', i. e. prostrate oneself, 72.

*dhn tꜣ* 'to touch earth with the forehead', 94.

*dkr* 'to press (?)', 60.

*dg* 'to see' (with [hieroglyph]), 107-8.

*ḏꜣ tꜣ r* 1) 'to be occupied about', 2) 'to interfere with', 115.

*ḏꜣis* 'to discuss', 'argue', 42.

*ḏꜣisw* 'utterances' late variant of *ṯsw*, 43, 157.

*ḏꜣisw* 'disputant', 'speaker', 43.

*ḏꜣḏꜣt tpt nwt*, the gods attendant on the god of the waters, 80.

*ḏʿm*, a kind of gold, 117.

*ḏʿr*, reading of [hieroglyph] by extension from *ḏʿ*, 154.

*Ḏw dšr* 'Red Mountain', part of place-name *Ḥryt nbt ḏw ḏšr*, 17.

*ḏr* 'mound' (form obscure), 71.

*ḏrw*, the *'paroi costale'* of the body, 115 (note 2).

*ḏrḏr* 'strange', 'foreign', 'hostile', 74-6, 161.

*ḏrḏri* 'hostility', 74-5.

*ḏt* 'estate', see *pr ḏt*, 77 (note 2).

*ḏt* 'serf', derivation of, 77 (note 2).

*ḏd*, in sense of 'to bid', 89; in sense of 'to consent', 'hope', 15.

*ḏdb*, usually 'to sting'; here 'to spur on', 'incite', 50.

*ḏdf* (?) 'to quiver' (?); of hair 'to stand on end', 87.

[hieroglyph] and [hieroglyph] confused in hieratic, 15 (note 4).

[hieroglyphs] as adjective, 111.

[hieroglyphs] reading of, unknown, 111 (note 2).

[hieroglyphs] 'precious things', 111.

## III. Coptic words.

ⲁϩⲱⲙ 'eagle', 110.

ⲁϭⲱⲙ 'eagle', 110.

ⲙⲟ 'take', 'receive', 88 (note 3).

ⲙⲟⲓ, 23 (note 1).

ⲙ̄ⲛ̄ⲧⲣ̄ⲙ̄ⲛ̄ⲕⲏⲙⲉ, 23.

ⲙ̄ⲛ̄ⲧⲟⲩⲉⲓⲛⲓⲛ, 23.

ⲙⲟⲟϣⲉ, 29.

ⲛ̄ⲧⲟϥ 'however', 25 (note 2).

ⲡⲁϭⲥⲉ 'spittle', 31

ⲥⲉⲓ 'to sate', 33.
ⲥⲓⲃ, '*pediculus*', '*rubigo*', 112.
ⲥⲓⲛⲉ 'to pass', 160, 72.
ⲥⲓⲙⲉ '*vomer*', 50 (note).
ⲥⲛⲁⲉⲓⲛ, S. : ⲥⲛⲏⲓⲛⲓ, B. 'to walk up and down', 160.
ⲥ̄ⲣϥⲉ = [hieroglyphs], 156 (note 1).
ⲥⲱⲥ '*evertere*', 157.
ⲥⲧⲱⲧ '*tremor*', 43 (note 4).
ⲥⲁϩⲣ (ⲥⲉϩⲣ), S. : ⲥⲁⲣϩ, B., '*verrere*', 117.

ⲧⲱϣ 'to smash', 34.

ⲟⲩⲁ '*blasphemia*', 66.
ⲟⲩⲓⲥⲉ 'to swell', 71.
ⲟⲩⲟⲙⲧⲉ '*arces*', '*propugnacula*', 96.
ⲟⲩⲙⲟⲧ 'thick', 95.

ϣⲛ̄ⲥ 'byssus', 111.
ϣⲱϣ '*spargere*', 161.

ϩⲏⲃⲉ, '*luctus*', derived from *ḥb* in the sense of 'to mourn', 159.

ϭⲉⲣⲏϭ 'hunter', 42.
ϭⲱⲣϭ, S. : ϫⲱⲣϫ, B., 'to hunt', 42.

# ERRATA

---

P. 7, l. 9. *For* as *read* us.
P. 8, last line. For *R 2* read *R 1*.
P. 16, footnote 1. *For* ⲣⲁⲧⲡ *read* ⲣⲁⲧⲏ.
P. 30, note on *39*, last line. *For* in *read* is.
P. 30, line 10 from bottom. *For* [hieroglyphs] *read* [hieroglyphs].
P. 35, line 19. *For* see B 17–18, note *read* see B 2, note.
P. 38, line 9 from bottom. *For* Kheperke *read* Kheperkerê.
P. 46, note on *116–117*, first line. *Read* [hieroglyphs].
P. 61, line 15 from bottom. *For* flicted *read* inflicted.
P. 68, note on *190*, first line. *For* [hieroglyphs] *read* [hieroglyphs].
P. 83, line 2 from bottom. *For* tahes *read* takes.
P. 95, line 9 from bottom. *For* [hieroglyphs] *read* [hieroglyphs].
P. 115, line 16. *For* [hieroglyphs] *read* [hieroglyphs].
P. 115, line 21. *For* [hieroglyphs] *read* [hieroglyphs].
P. 117, first line. *For* [hieroglyphs] *read* [hieroglyphs].
P. 117, line 6. *For* eaves *read* lees.
P. 133, line 2, end. *For* \\ *read* [hieroglyphs]; see p. 155.
P. 141. Insert after line 4 the new parallel text published on p. 178.
P. 144, line 6. *For* \\ *read* [hieroglyphs]; see p. 156.
P. 144, line 7. Here add the new parallel text published on p. 177.
P. 155, line 13. *For* Neshi *read* Enshi.
P. 157, last line. For *submergés* read *immergés*.
P. 159, line 7. For *mnnfrt* read *mnfrt*.
P. 160, line 12. For *wꜣʿ* read *wʿꜣ*.

The word for ‘king’, transcribed *śtn*, e. g. p. 9, l. 16, should everywhere be read *nlswt* or *nsw*.

www.ingramcontent.com/pod-product-compliance
Lightning Source LLC
Chambersburg PA
CBHW081129170426
43197CB00017B/2798

* 9 7 8 1 6 6 6 7 4 9 7 9 3 *